Feeling Backward

Feeling Backward

Loss and the Politics of Queer History

Heather Love

HARVARD UNIVERSITY PRESS

Cambridge, Massachusetts

London, England

First Harvard University Press paperback edition, 2009

Library of Congress Cataloging-in-Publication Data

Love, Heather.
　　Feeling backward : loss and the politics of queer history / Heather Love.
　　　　p.　cm.
　　Includes bibliographical references and index.
　　ISBN 978-0-674-02652-0 (cloth : alk. paper)
　　ISBN 978-0-674-03239-2 (pbk.)
　　1. Gays—Social conditions.　2. Gays—History.　3. Gays in literature.
4. Gay culture.　I. Title.
　　HQ76.25.L68 2007
　　306.76'60917521—dc22　　　　2007017269

To D.S.K.

Contents

This homosexual dream of perfect metaphysical union is not so much a reflected heterosexual ideal as it is the compensation for having wept in the darkness.

—Thomas Yingling, *Hart Crane and the Homosexual Text*

Introduction

Who will write the history of tears?

—Roland Barthes, *A Lover's Discourse: Fragments*

A central paradox of any transformative criticism is that its dreams for the future are founded on a history of suffering, stigma, and violence. Oppositional criticism opposes not only existing structures of power but also the very history that gives it meaning. Insofar as the losses of the past motivate us and give meaning to our current experience, we are bound to memorialize them ("We will never forget"). But we are equally bound to overcome the past, to escape its legacy ("We will never go back"). For groups constituted by historical injury, the challenge is to engage with the past without being destroyed by it. Sometimes it seems it would be better to move on—to let, as Marx wrote, the dead bury the dead. But it is the damaging aspects of the past that tend to stay with us, and the desire to forget may itself be a symptom of haunting. The dead can bury the dead all day long and still not be done.

The history of Western representation is littered with the corpses of gender and sexual deviants. Those who are directly identified with same-sex desire most often end up dead; if they manage to survive, it is on such compromised terms that it makes death seem attractive. Looking back at these texts and images can be painful. Many contemporary critics dismiss negative or dark representations entirely, arguing that the depiction of same-sex love as impossible, tragic, and doomed to failure is purely ideological. Recent cultural histories attest to a far wider range of experience across the century. Despite such evidence, however, it has been difficult to dispel the affective power of these representations.

Early work in gay and lesbian studies tended to deny the significance of these depressing accounts. These critics responded to the history of

1

violence and stigmatization by affirming the legitimacy of gay and lesbian existence. More recently, scholars working in the field of queer studies have taken a different approach, attempting to counter stigma by incorporating it. The word "queer," like "fag" or "dyke" but unlike the more positive "gay" or "lesbian," is a slur. When queer was adopted in the late 1980s it was chosen because it evoked a long history of insult and abuse—you could hear the hurt in it. Queer theorists drew on the energies of confrontational, stigma-inflected activism of groups like ACT UP and Queer Nation who had first taken up this "forcibly bittersweet" term.[1] The emphasis on injury in queer studies has made critics in this field more willing to investigate the darker aspects of queer representation and experience and to attend to the social, psychic, and corporeal effects of homophobia.

The turn to the negative in queer studies was also the result of a deep intellectual engagement during this period with the historiography, politics, and philosophy of Michel Foucault. In his account of "reverse" discourse in *The History of Sexuality,* Foucault describes the ways that dominated groups may take advantage of the reversibility of power. He writes that discourse produces power "but also undermines and exposes it"; for those alive to the fragility of power, there are many opportunities to turn situations of domination to advantage. Foucault's paradigmatic example of such a turn is the invention of homosexuality in its modern form out of the sexological, medical, and criminal discourses of the late nineteenth century. Describing the transition from the legal and religious discourses that defined sodomy as a sin to the human sciences that classified homosexuality (or, more properly, inversion) as an illness, Foucault argues that the creation of this new social category enabled the emergence of the first homophile movements: "homosexuality began to speak in its own behalf, to demand that its legitimacy or 'naturality' be acknowledged, often in the same vocabulary, using the same categories by which it was medically disqualified."[2]

Homosexual identity is indelibly marked by the effects of reverse discourse: on the one hand, it continues to be understood as a form of damaged or compromised subjectivity; on the other hand, the characteristic forms of gay freedom are produced in response to this history. Pride and visibility offer antidotes to shame and the legacy of the closet; they are made in the image of specific forms of denigration. Queerness is structured by this central turn; it is both abject and exalted, a "mixture of delicious and freak."[3] This contradiction is lived out on the level of individual subjectivity; homosexuality is experienced as a stigmatizing mark as well as a form of romantic exceptionalism. It also appears at the structural level in the gap between mass-mediated images of attractive, well-to-do gays and lesbians and the reality of ongoing violence and inequality.

The emphasis on damage in queer studies exists in a state of tension with a related and contrary tendency—the need to resist damage and to affirm queer existence. This tension is evident in discussions of the "progress" of gays and lesbians across the twentieth century. Although many queer critics take exception to the idea of a linear, triumphalist view of history, we are in practice deeply committed to the notion of progress; despite our reservations, we just cannot stop dreaming of a better life for queer people.[4] Such utopian desires are at the heart of the collective project of queer studies and integral to the history of gay and lesbian identity. Still, the critical compulsion to fix—at least imaginatively—the problems of queer life has made it difficult to fully engage with such difficulties. Critics find themselves in an odd position: we are not sure if we should explore the link between homosexuality and loss, or set about proving that it does not exist.[5]

This ambivalence is legible in responses to the saddest texts from the queer canon. Radclyffe Hall's 1928 novel *The Well of Loneliness* is a case in point. This melodramatic account of the ill-treatment and suffering of a female invert in the early twentieth century has been the object of re-peated attacks by readers who have found it outdated, homophobic, de-pressing, and manipulative. At the same time, it is one of the most read and discussed of all queer novels. Despite complaints about their toxi-city, such tragic, tear-soaked accounts of same-sex desire compel readers in a way that brighter stories of liberation do not. Although it may be difficult to account for the continuing hold of these texts on us in the present, we have evidence of it in the powerful feelings—both positive and negative—that they inspire.

It is difficult to talk about such effects in critical contexts, where am-bivalence tends to resolve itself into critique and gestures toward politi-cal utility. The premium on strategic response in queer studies has meant that the painful and traumatic dimensions of these texts (and of the experience of reading them) have been minimized or disavowed.[6] In this book I have tried to resist the affirmative turn in queer studies in order to dwell at length on the "dark side" of modern queer representation. It is not clear how such dark representations from the past will lead toward a brighter future for queers. Still, it may be necessary to check the impulse to turn these representations to good use in order to see them at all.

Feeling Backward turns its attention to several late nineteenth- and early twentieth-century literary texts visibly marked by queer suffering. The specific texts I read by Walter Pater, Willa Cather, Radclyffe Hall, and Sylvia Townsend Warner are quite different from each other in terms of political and aesthetic sensibilities; they also offer radically different treatments of the theme of same-sex desire, from the achingly unspecific to the thunderously explicit. These texts form, however, significant points in a tradition of queer experience and representation that I call "feeling backward." These dark, ambivalent texts register these authors' painful negotiation of the coming of modern homosexuality. Such representations constitute a crucial "archive of feeling," an account of the corporeal and psychic costs of homophobia.[7] In their work, I pay particular attention to feelings such as nostalgia, regret, shame, despair, *ressentiment,* passivity, escapism, self-hatred, withdrawal, bitterness, defeatism, and loneliness. These feelings are tied to the experience of social exclusion and to the historical "impossibility" of same-sex desire.

Of course, same-sex desire is not as impossible as it used to be; as a result, the survival of feelings such as shame, isolation, and self-hatred into the post-Stonewall era is often the occasion for further feelings of shame. The embarrassment of owning such feelings, out of place as they are in a movement that takes pride as its watchword, is acute. It is also hard to see how feelings like bitterness or self-hatred might contribute to any recognizable political praxis. Texts that insist on social negativity underline the gap between aspiration and the actual. At odds with the wishful thinking that characterizes political criticism, they are held accountable for the realities that they represent and often end up being branded as internally homophobic, retrograde, or too depressing to be of use. These texts do have a lot to tell us, though: they describe what it is like to bear a "disqualified" identity, which at times can simply mean living with injury—not fixing it.

The Backward Turn

A central myth of queer existence describes the paralyzing effects of loss. The story of the destruction of Sodom and Gomorrah in Genesis 19 is significant not only as an account of the violence perpetrated against those accused of the grave sin of homosexuality; it also describes the consequences of the refusal to forget such losses. Alerted by the visiting angels, Lot and his family are allowed to escape on the condition that they do not look behind them. Although Lot and his daughters obey God's order and go on to produce a new lineage, his wife looks back and thus becomes a pillar of salt. By refusing the destiny that God offers her, Lot's wife is cut off from her family and from the future. In turning back toward this lost world she herself is lost: she becomes a monument to destruction, an emblem of eternal regret.[8]

Feeling Backward is populated by iconic figures that turn backward: Lot's wife turning to look at the destruction of Sodom and Gomorrah; Orpheus turning back toward Eurydice at the gates of the underworld; Odysseus looking back at the Sirens as his boat pulls away; Walter Benjamin's angel of history turning away from the future to face the ruined landscape of the past. My book's central trope of the turn backward might be understood as a figure of figuration itself. The word "trope" derives from "turn"; it indicates a turning of a word away from its literal meaning. In reading figures of backwardness as allegories of queer historical experience, I bring together a range of disparate figures, often pulling them out of their original contexts. My aim is to create an image repertoire of queer modernist melancholia in order to underline both the losses of queer modernity and the deeply ambivalent negotiation of these losses within the literature of the period.

The idea of modernity—with its suggestions of progress, rationality, and technological advance—is intimately bound up with backwardness. The association of progress and regress is a function not only of the failure of so many of modernity's key projects but also of the reliance of the concept of modernity on excluded, denigrated, or superseded others. Dipesh Chakrabarty writes that "if *modernity* is to be a definable, delimited concept, we must identify some people or practices as *non-modern*."[9] If modernization in the late nineteenth and early twentieth century aimed to move humanity forward, it did so in part by perfecting techniques for mapping and disciplining subjects considered to be lagging behind—and so seriously compromised the ability of these others ever to catch up. Not only sexual and gender deviants but also women, colonized people, the nonwhite, the disabled, the poor, and criminals were marked as inferior by means of the allegation of backwardness.

Aesthetic modernism is marked by a similar temporal splitting. While the commitment to novelty is undoubtedly a dominant feature of modernism, no account of the movement is complete without attention to the place of the nonmodern in the movement—whether in primitivism, in the concern with tradition, in widely circulating rhetorics of decadence and decline, or in the melancholia that suffuses so many modernist artworks. Even when modernist authors are making it new, they are inevitably grappling with the old: backwardness is a feature of even the most forward-looking modernist literature. It is generally only when authorial ambivalence toward modernization is unmistakable that an author is named antimodernist. Yet the distinction between modernist and antimodernist seems far too crude to capture the historical ambivalence of most texts in the period.

This historical ambivalence is particularly charged, I want to suggest, in the works of minority or marginal modernists. For those marked as temporally backward, the stakes of being identified as modern or nonmodern were extremely high. Reading for backwardness is a way of calling attention to the temporal splitting at the heart of all modernism; at the same time, I attempt to describe the representational strategies of modern authors who were, in various ways, marked as backward. *Feeling Backward* focuses on queer modernism and on the fate of gender and sexual outsiders more generally. Still, I hope to suggest how attention to backward modernism might be helpful in exploring the aesthetic strategies of modernity's others.[10]

Whether understood as throwbacks to an earlier stage of human development or as children who refuse to grow up, queers have been seen across the twentieth century as a backward race. Perverse, immature, sterile, and melancholic: even when they provoke fears about the future, they somehow also recall the past.[11] They carry with them, as Djuna Barnes writes of her somnambulist heroine Robin Vote in *Nightwood*, "the quality of the 'way back.'"[12] The association of homosexuality with loss, melancholia, and failure runs deep; psychoanalytic accounts of arrested development and representations of the AIDS crisis as a gay death wish represent only a couple of notable variations on this theme. Given that such links are deployed against gays and lesbians so regularly, we have an obligation to counter them, which is not altogether easy. One must insist on the modernity of the queer; like any claim about modernity, though, the argument actually turns on backwardness—a backwardness disavowed or overcome. For queers, having been branded as nonmodern or as a drag on the progress of civilization, the desire to be recognized as part of the modern social order is strong. Narratives of gay and lesbian progress inevitably recall the painful history of the homosexual's birth as one of modernity's backward children.

Arguing against backwardness is further complicated by the often overlooked or unstated difficulty of distinguishing between homophobic discourse and homosexual existence. Accounts of queer life as backward are ideological; however, backwardness has the status of a lived reality in gay and lesbian life. Not only do many queers, as I suggest, feel backward, but backwardness has been taken up as a key feature of queer culture. Camp, for instance, with its tender concern for outmoded elements of popular culture and its refusal to get over childhood pleasures and traumas, is a backward art.[13] Over the last century, queers have embraced backwardness in many forms: in celebrations of perversion, in defiant refusals to grow up, in explorations of haunting and memory, and in stubborn attachments to lost objects.[14]

Feeling Backward groups together a handful of late nineteenth- and early twentieth-century authors under the rubric of backward modernism. Each author's work departs in various ways from classic definitions of modernist literary practice: Walter Pater is generally understood as a late Victorian or aestheticist writer, Willa Cather as an antimodernist, Radclyffe Hall as a popular sentimental novelist, and Sylvia Townsend Warner as a late modernist. These authors are also arrayed across quite a wide political spectrum. While Radclyffe Hall clung to the nationalist agrarian values of her upper-class English background (eventually embracing some forms of fascism), Sylvia Townsend Warner was a committed socialist and anti-imperialist who traveled to Spain during the civil war. These authors also wear their queerness very differently. Walter Pater might be understood as living and writing before the birth of public modern homosexual identity (he died in 1894, one year before Oscar Wilde's obscenity trial). Of the authors I consider, Radclyffe Hall is certainly the figure most readily identified with modern homosexual identity (in the years following the 1928 obscenity trial of *The Well of*

Loneliness, she identified publicly and privately as an invert).[15] Willa Cather, on the other hand, despite some early brushes with a queer identification and her forty-year relationship with Edith Lewis, did not see herself as queer. Although Sylvia Townsend Warner did not resist a queer identification as adamantly as Cather did, she seems to have understood her lesbian relationship with Valentine Ackland as part of a more general identification with social outsiders.

A shared feeling of backwardness in relation to the coming of modern homosexual identity is what draws me to these authors. While contemporary gay, lesbian, and queer critics tend to see queer subjects during this period as isolated and longing for a future community, the texts I consider turn their backs on the future: they choose isolation, turn toward the past, or choose to live in a present disconnected from any larger historical continuum. Some of the texts that I consider do gesture toward a brighter future; at the same time, they often withdraw or cancel this image. In his book *The Renaissance: Studies in Art and Poetry,* for instance, Walter Pater looks breathlessly forward to a reigniting of the buried humanistic warmth of the original Renaissance. At the same time, however, it is understood that the future he desires will be the result of reanimating the dead. To the extent that the future might represent the eruption of the wholly new, it is not something that Pater desires. Such temporal ambivalence is echoed across the texts that I consider. Even in the most patently forward moments—in the longing for a worker's revolution in Sylvia Townsend Warner's *Summer Will Show,* or the call for homosexual acceptance at the end of Radclyffe Hall's *The Well of Loneliness*—these texts engage as deeply with the past as they do with the future.

As I trace a tradition of queer backwardness in this book's central literary texts, I also consider the backward feelings—shame, depression, and regret—that they inspire in contemporary critics. In that these texts do not welcome contemporary critics—instead they turn away from us—they often have proved difficult to integrate into a queer literary genealogy. As queer readers we tend to see ourselves as reaching back toward isolated figures in the queer past in order to rescue or save them. It is hard to know what to do with texts that resist our advances. Texts or figures that refuse to be redeemed disrupt not only the progress narrative of queer history but also our sense of queer identity in the present. We find ourselves deeply unsettled by our identifications with these figures: the history of queer damage retains its capacity to do harm in the present.

Lot's wife clings to the past and is ruined by it. This figure has taken on a new resonance for queers in the decades since Stonewall. While it was once the case that admitting homosexual feelings meant acknowledging one's status as a tragic figure, gay liberation has opened multiple escape routes from those doomed cities of the plain. With increasing legal protection and provisional inclusion in several arenas of civic life, gays and lesbians no longer see themselves as necessarily damned. Although a brighter future for queers is not assured, it is conceivable. However, as in the story of Lot's escape from Sodom, moving into that future is conditional: one must leave the past behind.

Max Horkheimer and Theodor W. Adorno discuss the danger of looking backward in *Dialectic of Enlightenment*. In their retelling of the story of Odysseus and the Sirens, they understand the allure of the Sirens as "that of losing oneself in the past." The Sirens are the repository of historical memory, but to answer their call is to be destroyed: "if the Sirens know everything that has happened, they demand the future as its price." This story, for Horkheimer and Adorno, offers an allegory of the modern relationship to history: in a society that is based on use and appropriation, the relation to the past can only be instrumental. The creation of a "fixed order of time" serves to "liberate the present moment from the power of the past by banishing the latter beyond the absolute boundary of the irrecoverable and placing it, as usable knowledge, in the service of the present." Such a relation to the past does not seek to rescue it as "something living" but rather to transform it into "the material of progress."[16]

By being bound to the mast, Odysseus survives his encounter with the Sirens: though he can hear them singing, he cannot do anything about it. What saves him is that even as he looks backward he keeps moving forward. One might argue that Odysseus offers an ideal model of the relation to the historical past: listen to it, but do not allow yourself to be destroyed by it. Certainly for queer subjects "on the move," the notion of losing oneself in the past is not appealing. Yet the emphasis on progress in contemporary gay and lesbian politics has meant that today we must, like Odysseus, steel ourselves against close encounters with the queer past. This refusal to be held back or turned around has made it difficult to approach the past as something living—as something dissonant, beyond our control, and capable of touching us in the present. Clearly annihilation is not a goal for the movement, but an absolute refusal to linger in the past may entail other kinds of losses. Are we sure we are right to resist the siren song of the past?

"Advances" such as gay marriage and the increasing media visibility of well-heeled gays and lesbians threaten to obscure the continuing denigration and dismissal of queer existence. One may enter the mainstream on the condition that one breaks ties with all those who cannot make it—the nonwhite and the nonmonogamous, the poor and the genderdeviant, the fat, the disabled, the unemployed, the infected, and a host of unmentionable others. Social negativity clings not only to these figures but also to those who lived before the common era of gay liberation—the abject multitude against whose experience we define our own liberation. Given the new opportunities available to *some* gays and lesbians, the temptation to forget—to forget the outrages and humiliations of gay and lesbian history and to ignore the ongoing suffering of those not borne up by the rising tide of gay normalization—is stronger than ever.

The Politics of Affect

My attention to feeling in *Feeling Backward* has been influenced by the work of many critics who have sought to think systematically about the relation between emotion and politics. In works on racial melancholy, gay shame, and historical trauma, critics have struggled to bring together traditionally polarized terms such as the psychic and the social, subject and structure, politics and loss, affect and law, and love and history. You can see this yoking together of heterogeneous things in several recent titles: *Loss: The Politics of Mourning*; "Feeling Brown"; *The Melancholy of Race*; *Racial Castration*; *Melancholia and Moralism*; *The Psychic Life of Power*. A question hangs over this new body of work: what if psychic life and social life were simply too different to be usefully articulated together?

Several critics interested in or even invested in the conjunction of the psychic and the social have expressed concern about the dangers of forgetting the differences between them. Lauren Berlant in "The Subject of True Feeling" considers the conflicts in scale and political goals between psychic life (and particularly the putative authenticity of pain and trauma) and structural social transformation. Specifically, she questions the aptness of feeling as a ground for thinking the social, both because of feeling's weird phenomenology and because of chronic twentieth-century overinvestment in the authenticity of its being:

> What does it mean for the struggle to shape collective life when a politics of true feeling organizes analysis, discussion, fantasy, and policy? When feeling, the most subjective thing, the thing that makes persons public and marks their location, takes the temperature of power; mediates personhood, experience, and history; takes over the space of ethics and truth? When the shock of pain is said only to produce clarity when shock can as powerfully be said to produce panic, misrecognition, the shakiness of perception's ground?[17]

Politics and feelings are very different kinds of things: the public sphere is big, feelings are small; social life happens out there, psychic life, somewhere inside; public time is collective time, measured by the clock, whereas in psychic life the trains hardly ever run on time. Such problems of scale, location, and temporality simply serve to remind us that the public sphere and affect are different kinds of objects; as such, they have different histories and critical frameworks, and they call for different kinds of responses.

Like many other recent critics, I have been deeply influenced by Raymond Williams's concept of "structures of feeling" in *Marxism and Literature*. Williams offers a crucial link between cognition and affect and, in doing so, advances an argument against what Rei Terada has called the "expressive hypothesis"—the idea that feeling flows naturally from the subject and expresses the truth of that subject.[18] Williams defines a structure of feeling as follows:

> We are talking about characteristic elements of impulse, restraint and tone; specifically affective elements of consciousness and relationships: not feeling against thought, but thought as felt and feeling as thought: practical consciousness of a present kind, in a living and interrelating continuity. We are then defining these elements as a "structure": as a set, with specific internal relations, at once interlocking and in tension. Yet we are also defining a social experience which is still in process, often indeed not yet recognized as social but taken to be private, idiosyncratic, and even isolating, but which in analysis (though rarely otherwise) has its emergent, connecting, and dominant characteristics, indeed its specific hierarchies.[19]

Williams proposes that the term "structure of feeling" might have special relevance to literature in that literature accounts for experience at the juncture of the psychic and the social. The term has also been crucial to queer studies, where the analysis of uncodified subjective experiences is an important supplement to the study of the history of formal laws, practices, and ideologies. The saturation of experience with ideology is particularly important to queer critics because homophobia and heterosexism inflect everyday life in ways that can be difficult to name.

For Williams, the primary value of feeling in this essay is diagnostic. In paying attention to things like tone, dress, and habit, one may discover "social experiences in solution." It is possible to detect impulses that are not yet organized as movements; we can understand and respond to a historical moment that is not yet fully articulated in institutions as the dominant mode of existence. Williams considers the diagnostic usefulness of affect in relation to social groups (the generation is a significant grouping for him) and to aesthetic texts, but I think we might also consider the diagnostic usefulness of affect in relation to individual subjects. Particularly in thinking about the psychic damage of social exclusion, it seems useful to consider a range of negative affects as indexes of social trauma. Antihomophobic inquiry depends on sustained attention to the intimate effects of homophobia. In *Feeling Backward,* personal encounters and the feelings that they elicit stand in for theories of history and of the social.[20]

In addition to the diagnostic understanding of affect's usefulness, critics have also recently explored affect as a motivational system and as the grounds for forging new collectivities. This understanding of affect is important today because of a crisis of political motivation on the Left (what Wendy Brown, returning to an essay by Walter Benjamin, has identified as a condition of "Left Melancholy"). This crisis of motivation helps explain a certain paradox: critics who are interested in the politics of affect often tend to be interested in bad affects—and by that I do not mean simply ones that make you feel bad but also those that seem especially bad for politics. The most widely discussed bad feelings are shame and melancholia—feelings associated more closely with blushing and crying than with traditional political activities like grassroots organizing and demonstrating.

Sianne Ngai combines a diagnostic approach to affect with attention to the problem of action in *Ugly Feelings*. Ngai takes on affects that seem especially unsuited to politics (things like envy, irritation, paranoia, anxiety). These "minor and generally unprestigious feelings" are not even cathartic—they are sustained and distracting in a way that tends to block action. Ngai distinguishes these "intentionally weak and therefore often politically ambiguous" feelings both from "grander passions like anger and fear" (partly understood as grand because they can motivate people to do things, even grand things) and bad feelings like shame and melancholia and sympathy that are associated with (or can be linked to) notions of virtue.[21]

Ngai's account of affect's usefulness is primarily diagnostic. The ugly feelings she surveys are useful insofar as they help critics to understand the contours of the contemporary political situation, but they are not likely to ignite revolutionary action or even mass resistance. I do not think it would be right to read this interest in intentionally weak feelings or this refusal to directly link affect and action as a disinterest in action. Rather, I would venture that this persistent attention to "useless" feelings is all about action: about how and why it is blocked, and about how to locate motives for political action when none is visible. Ngai only indicates such a potential link between affect and action negatively, for instance when she suggests that the diagnostic power of particular affects is in inverse relation to their inability to make things happen: "the unsuitability of these weakly intentional feelings for forceful or unambiguous action is what amplifies their power to diagnose situations, and situations marked by blocked or thwarted action in particular" (27). The most significant of these "situations marked by blocked or thwarted action" will be for many of us, of course, simply our own historical situation. The utopian image of feelings actually making something happen is banned here, I would suggest, in the same way that the image of the future is banned in the messianic last moment of Benjamin's "Theses on the Philosophy of History."

Many queer critical and activist projects are more sanguine about the possibilities of feeling as a basis for political action. The feeling of shame—once understood as a poison that must be purged from the queer community—has proven to be particularly attractive as a basis for alternative models of politics. Eve Kosofsky Sedgwick has written at length on the contagiousness and volatility of shame and has made the concept central to her understanding of performativity.[22] In *The Trouble with Normal,* Michael Warner considers shame as the basis for a "special kind of sociability" in queer culture: "a relation to others" in queer circles "begins in an acknowledgement of all that is most abject and least reputable in oneself." This understanding of a shared abjection cuts through hierarchies. "Queer scenes," Warner writes, "are the true *salons des refusés,* where the most heterogeneous people are brought into great intimacy by their common experience of being despised and rejected in a world of norms that they now recognize as false morality."[23] Drawing on work by Sedgwick and Warner, Douglas Crimp considers the potential of shame to articulate "collectivities of the shamed."[24]

If shame will bring us together, it is also the case that it can, will, and does tear us apart. Although producing positive affects and identifications as a basis for collective action is certainly a significant part of the politics of feeling, I argue that we need to pursue a fuller engagement with negative affects and with the intransigent difficulties of making feeling the basis for politics. Such an approach means engaging with affects that have not traditionally been thought of as political and also dealing with the disjunction between affective and the social. Anne Anlin Cheng addresses these difficulties in *The Melancholy of Race: Psychoanalysis, Assimilation, and Hidden Grief.* In considering the gap between social grief and social grievance, she asks whether grievance would ever be capable of responding to the psychic wounds of social inequality. For Cheng, a central problem is that the effects of grief might unfit us for the redress of grievance: there are ways of feeling bad that do not make us feel like fighting back. That does not mean we should not fight back; it only means that we need to think harder about how to bring that aspiration in line with the actual experience of being under attack.

Feeling Better?

The 1995 documentary film *The Celluloid Closet,* directed by Rob Epstein and Jeffrey Friedman, offers an interesting site for thinking about the importance of damage in the history of queer representation. Like the Vito Russo book on which it is based, the film provides a history of images of gays and lesbians in Hollywood over the course of the twentieth century. The directors intersperse film clips with interviews with actors, directors, and critics, many of whom not only comment on the films themselves but also recount their own experiences of seeing them. By using multiple voices, the film offers a history of gay and lesbian reception over the last several decades. At the same time, *The Celluloid Closet* creates a new context for the reception of these clips using voice-over and montage. While many of the people interviewed in the film attest to what we might call a trauma of queer spectatorship—most often articulated as an isolated and uninformed viewing of negative images of homosexuality—the film counteracts this experience by placing these images in layered historical and personal contexts. The use of interviews creates the atmosphere of a group screening, in which knowing subjects speak over and against the images we see on the screen and so drain them of their pathologizing force. Through these techniques and through the construction of a narrative of progress across the century, *The Celluloid Closet* seeks to contain many of the negative images it includes.

An interesting moment of reception is staged in response to a clip from William Wyler's 1961 film *The Children's Hour*. In this scene, Martha Dobie (Shirley MacLaine) declares her love to Karen Wright (Audrey Hepburn) by telling her, "I feel so damned sick and dirty, I can't stand it."[25] When Karen attempts to comfort her, Martha cries, "Don't touch me," and buries her face in the sofa. A signal moment in the history of American cinema and in the history of lesbian representation, this scene between Martha and Karen was produced at the end of a thirty-year prohibition against depictions of "perverse sexuality" in Hollywood films. The film itself was instrumental in allowing the introduction of "tasteful" representations of same-sex relations in mainstream cinema. As Patricia White argues in her 1999 book *unInvited*, however, the introduction of more explicit representations of lesbianism was hardly an unambiguous victory. If female same-sex desire becomes more visible in the 1960s, it is only as a lamentable perversion, inextricably linked with images of loneliness, shame, and failure. Even in a "sympathetic" production like *The Children's Hour*, visible lesbians do not fare well. White remarks that Martha's "coming-out" scene in this film is immediately followed by her " 'tasteful' suicide by hanging."[26]

The scene of Martha's confession is literally "contained" within a section of *The Celluloid Closet* entitled "Shame" that features several disturbing images of homosexual abjection. This section is introduced by an inter-title that features the word "Shame" in bold black type as well as a graphic representation of prison bars closing over a white background. At the same time that this graphic serves to represent the repression suffered by gays and lesbians, it also effectively locks away these images, as if to prevent them from contaminating the rest of the film. But if the film seeks to neutralize these representations, the individual voices it includes often work against the general ethos of containment. The filmmakers include two very different responses to the scene of Martha's confession. The first of these is by Shirley MacLaine, who discusses her participation in the making of the film. In her commentary, MacLaine reflects on the strangeness of making the film in the 1960s, when there was so little public discourse about homosexuality. She mentions how odd it was that no one on the set ever talked about the issues of homosexual representation raised insistently by the screenplay. While MacLaine appears mildly amused by their "innocence," her tone darkens as she considers the results of their efforts. She bemoans the film's representation of Martha's tragic fate, and expresses her regret that they did not "do the movie right."[27] These comments accord with the progressivist ethos of *The Celluloid Closet*, which presents stereotypical images as errors on the way to a more accurate and positive reflection of gay and lesbian existence. In this scene, the directors replace the abject image of Martha writhing on the sofa with an older MacLaine who, miked and smiling, assures the viewer that the earlier representation was a mistake.

MacLaine's appearance is followed by a brief commentary from the writer and sex-activist Susie Bright, who discusses the film in terms of her own queer identification. Like MacLaine, Bright expresses sadness over this image, but she refuses to situate this representation in the past. Describing the scene and her response to it, she says:

> The loathing she feels, how sick she is with herself . . . it still makes me cry when I see that. And I think, you know, "Why am I crying? Why does this still get to me? This is just an old, silly movie, you know, and people don't feel this way anymore." But I don't think that's true. I think people do feel that way today still. And there's part of me despite all of my little signs, you know, like, "Happy!" "Proud!" "Well-adjusted!" "Bisexual!" "Queer!" "Kinky!"—you know, no matter how many posters I hold up saying, "I'm a big pervert and I'm so happy about it"—there's this part of me that's like, "How could I be this way?"

Bright discusses her familiarity with the shame and self-loathing depicted in the movie; she contrasts her reaction to the film with the discourse of gay liberation that she knows to be the antidote to such feelings. She describes her own efforts to believe the narrative of progress that for MacLaine is simply the truth of gay history ("That wouldn't happen anymore"). But in discussing her powerful identification with the film, Bright reflects on the unexpected continuities between the queer past and the queer present. Although Bright embraces the contemporary culture of pride marches, sex radicalism, and queer activism, she recognizes its inadequacy in countering a long history of shame and social exclusion.[28] In giving voice to the question, "How could I be this way?" Bright avows her susceptibility or openness to two stigmatizing frameworks: on the one hand, the moral framework that brands her as "dirty" and demands, "How *could* you?"; on the other hand, the medical framework that brands her as "sick," and raises, more dispassionately, the question of etiology: "How did you get to be this way?"

MacLaine's comments about *The Children's Hour* help us understand the conditions of production for the film, and in particular the culture of homophobia in the United States in the 1960s. They help us understand it—but they do not help us feel it. By historicizing the film, MacLaine seals it off from the present, burying it in a superseded realm of ignorance, shame, and suffering. Not only does she assure us that the cast and crew did the film wrong, she also tells us that the conditions of queer representation and queer existence have since been utterly transformed. Describing Martha's renunciation and suicide, MacLaine asserts, "That's not what she would do today. She would fight for her budding preference."[29] In her response to the film, Bright collapses past and present, partly effacing the specificity of that earlier moment and opening up the film as a resource for contemporary queer viewers who may have unexplained or excessive identifications with such texts.

Although critics have been attentive, especially in the last couple of decades, to the importance of shame, violence, and stigma in the historical record, certain forms of experience still remain off limits for most. These are representations that offer too stark an image of the losses of queer history. What has resulted is a disavowal of crucial aspects of this history and of the conditions of queer existence in the present.

Still Hurting

The classic statement on the importance of stigma in queer studies appears in Judith Butler's article "Critically Queer." Butler lauds *queer*'s ability to recall the long history of homophobic violence, but wonders whether the term can "overcome its constitutive history of injury."[30] She argues that in order to use the word productively, we need to recognize its difficult history and at the same time rework it for current political uses: "if the term queer is to be a site of collective contestation, the point of departure for a set of historical reflections and futural imaginings, it will have to remain that which is, in the present, never fully owned, but always and only redeployed, twisted, queered from a prior usage and in the direction of urgent and expanding political purposes" (228).

Butler's attention to the implication of "queer" in personal and collective injury is crucial in recalling the "mixed history" of queer subjectivity, and this essay has largely set the terms for the "turn to stigma" in queer studies. Those terms are laid out clearly here: stigma is crucial, but its acceptance is conditional on its ability to be "turned" to good use in an antihomophobic political project. As in Foucault's discussion of the "invention of homosexuality," the invention of queer studies depends on the strategy of reverse discourse. Butler's emphasis on the need for constant turning and constant reclamation is striking. Those who would risk taking on the name queer are subject to a double imperative: they must face backward toward a difficult past, and simultaneously forward, toward "urgent and expanding political purposes." According to this vision, the work of "queering" is never done. If, in embracing "queer," we have shown our willingness to engage with a "history of injury," Butler makes it clear that we must not linger there but must constantly work to turn this term away from the past and toward the future.

While the field of queer studies has emphasized the limitations of reverse discourse, its methodology remains deeply bound to this strategy; it retains a faith in the possibility of transforming the base materials of social abjection into the gold of political agency. In this sense, the historical moment of the turn to "queer" is not very different from the moment of the invention of homosexuality or the moment of gay liberation. Early gay and lesbian criticism tended to ignore the difficulties of the past in order construct a positive history; queer criticism by contrast has focused on negative aspects of the past in order to use them for positive political purposes. Given that issues like gay shame and self-hatred are charged with the weight of difficult personal and collective histories, it is understandable that critics are eager to turn them to good use. But I am concerned that queer studies, in its haste to refunction such experiences, may not be adequately reckoning with their powerful legacies. Turning away from past degradation to a present or future affirmation means ignoring the past as past; it also makes it harder to see the persistence of the past in the present.

In his book on the Broadway musical *Place for Us,* D. A. Miller suggests a way to think about the relationship between the queer past and the queer present in terms of continuity rather than opposition or departure. Considering the ambivalent status of the musical in "the psyche of post-Stonewall man," Miller suggests that the affective lives of queer subjects continue to be structured in much the same way they were before gay liberation:

> "Broadway" denominates those early pre-sexual realities of gay experience to which, in numerous lives, it became forever bound: not just the solitude, shame, secretiveness by which the impossibility of social integration was first internalized; or the excessive sentimentality that was the necessary condition of sentiments allowed no real object; but also the intense, senseless joy that, while not identical to these destitutions, is neither extricable from them. Precisely against such realities, however, is post-Stonewall gay identity defined: a declarable, dignified thing, rooted in a community, and taking manifestly sexual pleasures on this affirmative basis. No gay man could possibly regret the trade, could do anything but be grateful for it—if, that is, it were actually a trade, and his old embarrassments (including that of whatever gratification he was able to find through them) had not been retained, well after the moment of coming out, in the complex, incorrigible, rightly called fatal form of character.[31]

Reflecting on his resistance to the call of gay pride, Miller tracks the surprising persistence of pre-Stonewall feelings in the wake of liberation. Although he acknowledges the important social and cognitive changes that have occurred in the wake of gay liberation, Miller points to the continuity between individual experience "before" and "after" such transformations. This image of character as stamped or branded by its early experience of shame captures a sense of the indelible nature of ideology's effects. Contemporary gay identity is produced out of the twentieth-century history of queer abjection: gay pride is a reverse or mirror image of gay shame, produced precisely against the realities it means to remedy. In the darkroom of liberation, the "negative" of the closet case or the isolated protogay child is developed into a photograph of an out, proud gay man. But the trace of those forgotten is visible right on the surface of this image, a ghostly sign of the reversibility of reverse discourse.

Miller describes the persistence of adolescent feelings in the adult man; the early destitutions and joys visit him with their original force, though in an entirely changed context. There is something uncanny, of course, about the appearance of such feelings after the fact and out of context, but such temporal and spatial warpings are not unusual: more often than not these are the conditions that prevail in the adult human consciousness. The appearance of such feelings outside of their proper historical context, in subjects whose only experience of gay identity is of the post-Stonewall variety, is still more disturbing. The circulation of pre-Stonewall forms of life and structures of feeling throughout the post-Stonewall world suggests a historical continuity even more complex, incorrigible, and fatal than that of individual character. The evidence is written in the subjectivities of queer men and women who grew up after Stonewall and who are as intimately familiar with the structures of feeling Miller describes as with the rhetoric of pride that was meant to displace it. Such continuities suggest that direct experience of the pre-Stonewall moment is not solely responsible for a range of feelings that we today designate as pre-Stonewall, feelings that are all the more shameful given the "tolerance" of the contemporary moment.

Miller's work suggests that we may not be able to confine these feelings to the past; an important connection exists between queer experience and the feelings of shame and secrecy that have long been associated with it. This is not to suggest an essential or "natural" connection between homosexuality and melancholia. Queer critics have argued against naturalizing this link, and it is certainly important to understand it as neither essential nor inevitable. But critiquing such a link ought to be distinguished from denying its existence; registering our protest against social exclusion should not keep us from thinking through its effects. Although there are crucial differences between life before gay liberation and life after, feelings of shame, secrecy, and self-hatred are still with us. Rather than disavowing such feelings as the sign of some personal failing, we need to understand them as indications of material and structural continuities between these two eras. As resignifying or refunctioning stigma has become synonymous with the political in queer criticism, stigma itself has fallen by the wayside. I do not want to discount the importance of the queer politics of the future; I want to suggest, however, that we cannot do justice to the difficulties of queer experience unless we develop a politics of the past.

The Art of Losing

The effort to recapture the past is doomed from the start. To reconstruct the past, we build on ruins; to bring it to life, we chase after the fugitive dead. Bad enough if you want to tell the story of a conquering race, but to remember history's losers is worse, for the loss that swallows the dead absorbs these others into an even more profound obscurity. The difficulty of reaching the dead will not keep us from trying. Virginia Woolf invokes the pathos of this failure in Lily Briscoe's address to the dead Mrs. Ramsay in *To the Lighthouse:* "'Mrs. Ramsay! Mrs. Ramsay!' she cried, feeling the old horror come back—to want and want and not to have. Could she inflict that still?"[32] Mrs. Ramsay is inaccessible not only because she is dead but also because, it is implied, the desires of a "skimpy old maid" (269) like Lily are not the kind that can ever be satisfied. "Could she inflict that *still?*" While contact with the dead is impossible, queer history is marked by a double impossibility: we will never possess the dead; our longing for them is also marked by the historical impossibility of same-sex desire.

Jacques Lacan tells us—if anyone needs reminding—that love is an exercise in failure. His famous assertion that "there is no sexual relation" may stand in for the central psychoanalytic insight that sexuality is constituted by failure and impossibility rather than complementarity and fulfillment. Although such an assertion is true for everyone, some loves are more failed than others. Same-sex desire is marked by a long history of association with failure, impossibility, and loss. I do not mean by this that homosexual love is in its essence failed or impossible, any more than regular love is. The association between love's failures and homosexuality is, however, a historical reality, one that has profound effects for contemporary queer subjects. In a Freudian psychoanalytic framework, homosexuality is often seen as a result of a failure of maturation or a failure to overcome primary cathexes, and it has been associated with narcissism and infantilism as well as with incomplete or failed gendering. At the same time, homosexual relations are often seen as marked by immaturity and selfishness, by the refusal to compromise (to "settle" for marriage or monogamy) or to give back to society (to raise children). For these reasons and many others, gay and lesbian relationships are seen as short-lived, fleeting, and doomed.

In such damning and dismissive accounts of homosexuality, one sees the way that homosexuality and homosexuals serve as scapegoats for the failures and impossibilities of desire itself. This insight is at the center of Lee Edelman's 2004 book, *No Future,* the most important recent response to the affirmative turn in gay, lesbian, and queer criticism and to gay normalization as a social phenomenon. In a discussion of Hitchcock's *The Birds,* Edelman discusses the "antisocial bent of sexuality"—its resistance to normative social forms—and points out that it is "acknowledged, and then only as pathology, only in those who are bent themselves."[33] Edelman argues that rather than trying to deny their associations with the antisocial (or the death drive), queers should take up "the figural burden of queerness" (27)—the burden of representing the dissolution of the social—and not shuffle it off to someone else. Instead of insisting, in other words, that we are "good gays," as capable of monogamy and childrearing as everyone else, Edelman recommends that queers embrace their association with the antisocial, while still pointing to the antisocial energies that run through all sexuality. He argues that "queerness attains its ethical value precisely insofar as it accedes to [the place of the social order's death drive], accepting its figural status as resistance to the viability of the social while insisting on the inextricability of that resistance from every social structure" (3).[34]

Feeling Backward owes a debt to a long tradition of work on queer negativity—to Edelman's *No Future,* and to the work of Leo Bersani, Tim Dean, and Christopher Lane.[35] I am especially compelled by Edelman's complete refusal of the affirmative turn in gay, lesbian, and queer contexts. My own emphases in this book, however, are rather different. I am ultimately less interested in accounts of same-sex desire as antisocial or asocial than I am in instances of ruined or failed sociality. Although I share a deep skepticism with Edelman about political appeals to the future, I do not follow him in calling for the voiding of the future. Several of the texts that I consider evince ambivalence toward the future, but very few are marked by the blank refusals Edelman describes. I am more interested in the turn to the past than I am in the refusal of the future itself, and this concern puts me in a closer dialogue with critics working on shame, melancholia, depression, and pathos—the experience of failure rather than negativity itself.

Although this book is centrally concerned with psychic experience, I engage psychoanalysis only sporadically. My resistance is to psychoanalysis as a diagnostic reading practice—to reading through experience for structure. This resistance also informs a move away from the central methodology of cultural criticism: ideology critique, or lifting the veil of mystification to reveal the truth of social processes. Many critics in recent years have sought to articulate alternatives to this interpretive practice. Notable among these is Eve Kosofsky Sedgwick's call for a swerve away from "paranoid" toward "reparative" reading in her 2003 book *Touching Feeling*. Following on Sedgwick's suggestion for a turn away from exposure as a reading protocol, my account of the history of queer feeling tends toward the descriptive rather than the critical. I have tried throughout to avoid the exposure of queer historical figures as "internally homophobic." This charge could certainly be levied against the authors (and a few of the critics) in my study; however, I tend to think with them rather than against them, identifying with rather than critiquing their refusals and their backwardness.

The danger of such an approach, of course, is that it is insufficiently distant from the kinds of thinking and feeling that are inimical to queer ways of life. One can be too close to one's subject and simply repeat his or her mistakes. If I take this risk in *Feeling Backward*, it is because I do not think it is clear, even by the light of the post-Stonewall day, what would constitute a "mistaken" way of being or feeling queer. It is never easy to tell the difference between ideology and real life, and for a social identity like homosexuality, so saturated with negative ideology, tearing away the veil may leave us with very little. Sidestepping critique, my aim in *Feeling Backward* is to suggest the value of some aspects of historical gay identity—deeply ideological though they may be—that have been diminished or dismissed with successive waves of liberation. Central among these is the association between homosexual love and loss—a link that, historically, has given queers special insight into love's failures and impossibilities (as well as, of course, wild hopes for its future).

Claiming such an association rather than disavowing it, I see the art of losing as a particularly queer art.

Impossible Love

Each chapter in this book considers a moment of failed or interrupted connection. Broken intimacies characterize the texts under consideration; they also might be said to define the relation between contemporary critics and the texts I consider. In making such failures central, I follow Leo Bersani's call in *Homos* for queer critics to confront the impossibility at the heart of desire. He writes of the need for a "theory of love based not on our assertions of how different and how much better we are than those who would do away with us (because we are neither that different nor that much better), but one that would instead be grounded in the very contradictions, impossibilities, and antagonisms brought to light by any serious genealogy of desire."[36] Although this book does not propose a "theory of love," it does take impossible love as a model for queer historiography.

Feeling Backward begins with a reconsideration of queer historiography by focusing on Michel Foucault's experience in the archive. Foucault's legacy to queer studies is most closely allied with his critique of identity and his development of the method of genealogy. Recently, Carolyn Dinshaw has explored his ambivalent investment in the queer past in her book *Getting Medieval*. Following on her work, I consider Foucault's method of genealogy in relation to his comment in a late interview about homosexual love: the best moment of an encounter is when you are putting the boy in the taxi. I take this moment of impossible connection as an emblem of Foucault's desire for a historical "real" that is always receding, always already lost.

One figure who has proved especially difficult to reach is Walter Pater, the late nineteenth-century novelist and essayist. Pater's position in a genealogy of queer authorship is awkward, mostly because he is understood to have lived "before" the invention of modern homosexuality; he participated in male homosocial and homoerotic circles that are not entirely legible under the rubric of twentieth-century homosexual community. Through his essays and novels devoted to homoerotic classical and early Christian relations, Pater's work offers a rich archive of queer historical structures of feeling. His attachment to the past makes him a key figure for *Feeling Backward.* I also mean to focus on the reticence that characterizes his aesthetics. Pater imagines a form of social rebellion that is sedate, retiring, shy—what he calls "the revolutionism of one who has slept a hundred years."[37] Although such revolutionism does not count as revolutionism at all in contemporary understandings of the political, I argue that Pater offers a way to imagine a form of queer politics informed by the experience of homophobic exclusion. I trace the characteristic gesture of refusal or shrinking in his work to his resistance to newly public and explicit forms of homosexual identity and consider the problem of reaching out to queer historical figures who may be turning their backs on us.

Pater's shy refusals give way to the antimodernism and the explicit homophobia and misogyny of Willa Cather. The debates around Cather's lesbianism—Is she one? Does it matter?—have been acrimonious. In Joan Acocella's book *Willa Cather and the Politics of Criticism*, she derides feminist and queer scholars for reading Cather against her own explicit resistance to identification with women and with a newly public culture of homosexuality.[38] I am also concerned with these aspects of Cather's writing; however, I argue that it is her resistance that makes a queer reading of her work unavoidable. Cather's queerness is bound up with her powerful disidentifications, her ambivalence, and her refusal of community. She is "one of ours" but she is not our own. This chapter reflects on the ethics of approaching Cather in light of that resistance. I consider Cather's approach to her precursor Sarah Orne Jewett as recorded in her essay "148 Charles Street." I understand this essay as Cather's reflection on the death of female romantic friendship as an affective and social mode; the regret and melancholy that suffuse the essay are bound up not only with the failing health of Jewett and her companion Annie Fields but also with Cather's own identification with a way of life that is passing from the world. I read Cather's desire to identify across an impossible historical divide in relation to contemporary critics' approach to Cather and consider the possibilities and shortcomings of friendship as a model for queer relations across time.

The next chapter, "Spoiled Identity," considers critical discomfort with *The Well of Loneliness.* Critics and readers over the past several decades have found this novel horribly depressing and have tended to dismiss this representation of the tragedy of the mannish woman as merely ideological, the product of Radclyffe Hall's self-hatred.[39] I argue that this portrait of Stephen Gordon's loneliness offers a crucial account of what it felt like to bear a newly public and newly stigmatized identity in the 1920s. In particular, Hall depicts the congenital invert as constituted by social rejection or refusal—in her words, as the bearer of "unwanted being." This stark description of personhood made in the image of the other's hatred has survived attempts to reread the novel as a narrative of heroic resistance; it constitutes an ongoing provocation to (and a drag on) contemporary utopian accounts of lesbian, butch, and transgender existence.

The final chapter considers the work of British novelist Sylvia Townsend Warner. I am particularly interested in Warner's 1936 novel *Summer Will Show*, in which she imagines an improbable lesbian love affair against the backdrop of the failed 1848 revolution in Paris. The novel links the "impossibility" of lesbian love to the impossible object of revolutionary transformation. The novel ends as its heroine sits down to read *The Communist Manifesto* after the failure of the coup and the death of her lover. I argue that Warner describes a form of hope inseparable from despair, a structure of feeling that might serve as a model for political life in the present.

In the epilogue, I consider the importance of feeling backward in contemporary queer cultural production. I try to imagine how this approach to the past might constitute an alternative form of politics in the present. As the revolutionary hope of earlier political generations has been exhausted, many on the Left have been searching for modes of resistance and coalition that respond to contemporary conditions. In response to the call to "Keep Hope Alive," some have asked, "How might we make change even if we can't muster hope?" I am particularly interested in the historical antecedents and political possibilities of projects like the Chicago-based feeltank. This group has attempted to mobilize negative feelings such as paranoia and despair in order to make social change; they have attempted to publicize events like the yearly depression march, where marchers wear bathrobes and slippers, pass out prescriptions for Prozac, and carry placards that say things like "Depressed? It might be political."

Though bad feelings have been central to the history of queer experience and queer feeling, there is little room for them in the contemporary climate. Some new work in queer and cultural studies has taken up the politics of negative affect. I have been particularly influenced by work on gay shame (Eve Kosofsky Sedgwick, D. A. Miller, Douglas Crimp, Michael Warner); disidentification (José Esteban Muñoz); melancholia (David Eng); ugly feelings (Sianne Ngai); and trauma (Ann Cvetkovich). Such feelings resist the kind of idealist affirmation that is so attractive to a marginalized and despised social group. Perhaps closest to my own emphasis in this book is Anne Anlin Cheng's work in *The Melancholy of Race*. Cheng explores a range of negative feelings produced by the experience of social exclusion, but her claims about the efficacy of these feelings are strikingly austere: sometimes damage is just damage. Queers are hated; we wish we were not; but wishing does not make it so.[40]

While I do not argue for the political efficacy of any particular bad feeling in this book, I do argue for the importance of such feelings in general. Backward feelings serve as an index to the ruined state of the social world; they indicate continuities between the bad gay past and the present; and they show up the inadequacy of queer narratives of progress. Most important, they teach us that we do not know what is good for politics. It is true that the small repertoire of feelings that count as political—hope, anger, solidarity—have done a lot. But in this case a lot is not nearly enough.

Mixed Feelings

Queers face a strange choice: is it better to move on toward a brighter future or to hang back and cling to the past? Such divided allegiances result in contradictory feelings: pride and shame, anticipation and regret, hope and despair. Contemporary queers find ourselves in the odd situation of "looking forward" while we are "feeling backward."

A particularly jarring version of this disjunction appears in *Without You I'm Nothing,* John Boskovich's 1989 film of Sandra Bernhard's one-woman show. In one sequence, Bernhard takes on the persona of a homophobic straight man whose friend takes him to a gay bar. The scene is the 1970s, the height of both sexual liberation and the gay liberation movement. Bernhard's character begins his monologue looking forward to a night on the town with his best bud and hoping to meet some Playboy bunnies; soon after climbing into his friend's Camaro, he ends up in an unfamiliar part of town, following his friend into a bar with no girls—or not "his kind of girls" anyway.[41] He notes a "couple dancing

together in the corner with flannel shirts and jeans, with big fat asses."
Initially frightened and disgusted by this scene, Bernhard's character
warms up quickly; within a few moments he is doing poppers and
mixing with the locals. The story takes a sudden turn as Bernhard begins to play the tambourine, and three black leathermen magically appear at her side, back-up singers for her rendition of the Sylvester an-
them "You Make Me Feel (Mighty Real)." The conversion is complete a
few moments later: Bernhard's character gives himself sexually to a drag
queen and likes it. In this absurdly sped-up sequence, racial fantasies of
overpowering desire and authentic being effect a turn from hatred and
shame to joy and self-revelation. The sad and lonely patrons of a backstreet bar are transformed into luminous creatures "here to take you
higher!"

This moment is absurd, and yet what is absurd about it is not its content but its pacing. The story is, after all, a familiar one: the movement
from abjection to glorious community is the underlying structure of the
story of coming out of the closet, and it informs both personal and collective histories of liberation. The origin story of gay liberation describes
how on one particular night an underground bar turned into the front
line of a struggle for freedom and civil rights. Early work in lesbian and
gay studies was marked by the legacy of Stonewall and by the sudden
turn of this moment of reverse discourse; the emergent field's powerful
utopianism, affirmation of gay identity, and hope for the future resonated
with the seemingly magical power of this new movement to transmute
shame into pride, secrecy into visibility, social exclusion into outsider
glamour.

I do not think we can or should forego the strategy of reverse discourse, and I would not deny the power of queer alchemy. Our very dependence on this strategy demands, however, that we recognize how
tenuous it is. We can turn shame into pride, but we cannot do so once
and for all: shame lives on in pride, and pride can easily turn back into
shame. We need to take as our starting point the reversibility of reverse
discourse and to keep our gaze directed toward the past, toward the bad
old days before Stonewall.

Although we cannot do away with the notion of progress, I want to
attend more closely to what remains unthought in the turn toward the
future. The commitment to affirmation should not shut down the possibility of the kind of radical intellectual experiments that gave birth to

queer theory in the first place: Foucault's challenge to the ideology of liberation; Cherríe Moraga's attention to betrayal and sexual exposure in *Loving in the War Years;* Leo Bersani's critique of the "culture of redemption"; Judith Butler's gender trouble, which I take to mean not only acting up but also feeling bad.

These interventions are, I would argue, what has made queer studies "queer," but the vibrations they set off are what is hardest to keep alive in queer studies as it ages. In 1993 Judith Butler wondered if the term "queer" would ever "overcome its constitutive history of injury." It has not entirely, although its regular appearances in both college classrooms and on popular television shows suggest that it is moving in that direction. This book focuses on that history of injury. The links between the texts I consider and "urgent and expanding political purposes" tend to be oblique rather than direct. What counts as political in the contemporary context is, however, out of touch with the longer history of queer experience. Rather than disavowing the history of marginalization and abjection, I suggest that we embrace it, exploring the ways it continues to structure queer experience in the present. Modern homosexual identity is formed out of and in relation to the experience of social damage. Paying attention to what was difficult in the past may tell us how far we have come, but that is not all it will tell us; it also makes visible the damage that we live with in the present.

Criticism serves two important functions: it lays bare the conditions of exclusion and inequality and it gestures toward alternative trajectories for the future. Both aspects are important; however, to the extent that the imaginative function of criticism is severed from its critical function—to the extent that it becomes mere optimism—it loses its purchase on the past. It is crucial to find ways of creating and sustaining political hope. But hope that is achieved at the expense of the past cannot serve the future. The politics of optimism diminishes the suffering of queer historical subjects; at the same time, it blinds us to the continuities between past and present. As long as homophobia continues to centrally structure queer life, we cannot afford to turn away from the past; instead, we have to risk the turn backward, even if it means opening ourselves to social and psychic realities we would rather forget.

In her essay "Packing History, Count(er)ing Generations," Elizabeth Freeman considers the importance of melancholic identifications with

earlier moments of queer history, suggesting that the present is constituted through such identifications: "If identity is always in temporal
drag, constituted and haunted by the failed love-project that precedes it,
perhaps the shared culture-making projects we call 'movements' might
do well to feel the tug backwards as a potentially transformative part of
movement itself."[42] This book feels that way. I am particularly attuned to
the queer historical experience of failed or impossible love and have tried
to make this feeling the basis for my own approach to the past. It is this
disposition toward the past—embracing loss, risking abjection—that I
mean to evoke with the phrase "feeling backward."

Such an emphasis is particularly important now, when the burdens of
social exclusion are being significantly reduced. While it would be neither possible nor desirable to go back to an earlier moment in the history of gay and lesbian life, earlier forms of feeling, imagination, and

community may offer crucial resources in the present. Attending to the
specific histories of homophobic exclusion and violence—as well as
their effects—can help us see structures of inequality in the present. It is
also a way of claiming homosexual identity in the face of a call to
abandon it. The invitation to join the mainstream is an invitation to jet-
tison gay identity and its accreted historical meanings. Insofar as that
identity is produced out of shame and stigma, it might seem like a good
idea to leave it behind. It may in fact seem shaming to hold onto an
identity that cannot be uncoupled from violence, suffering, and loss. I
insist on the importance of clinging to ruined identities and to histories
of injury. Resisting the call of gay normalization means refusing to write
off the most vulnerable, the least presentable, and all the dead.

Emotional Rescue

The Demands of Queer History

Take history at night; have you ever thought of that, now? Was it at night that Sodom became Gomorrah? It was at night, I swear! A city given over to the shades, and that's why it has never been countenanced or understood to this day.

—Djuna Barnes, *Nightwood*

Recently, long-standing debates about gay and lesbian history have shifted from discussions of the stability of sexual categories over time to explorations of the relation between queer historians and the subjects they study. The turn from a focus on "effective history" to a focus on "affective history" has meant that critics have stopped asking, "Were there gay people in the past?" but rather have focused on questions such as: "Why do we care so much if there were gay people in the past?" or even, perhaps, "What relation with these figures do we hope to cultivate?" Critics such as Christopher Nealon, Carolyn Dinshaw, Ann Cvetkovich, David Halperin, Carla Freccero, Scott Bravmann, Elizabeth Freeman, L. O. A. Fradenburg, and Valerie Traub have shifted the focus away from epistemological questions in the approach to the queer past; rather, they make central "the desires that propel such engagements, the affects that drive relationality even across time."[1] Exploring the vagaries of cross-historical desire and the queer impulse to forge communities between the living and the dead, this work has made explicit the affective stakes of debates on method and knowledge. Mixing psychoanalytic approaches with more wide-ranging treatments of affect, they have traced the identifications, the desires, the longings, and the love that structure the encounter with the queer past.[2]

My approach to queer history is profoundly indebted to this new field of inquiry. I focus on the negative affects—the need, the aversion, and the longing—that characterize the relation between past and present. This decision to look on the dark side comes out of my sense that contemporary critics tend to describe the encounter with the past in idealizing terms. In particular, the models that these critics have used to describe queer cross-historical relations—friendship, love, desire, and community—seem strangely free of the wounds, the switchbacks, and the false starts that give these structures their specific appeal, their binding power. Friendship and love have served as the most significant models for thinking about how contemporary critics reach out to the ones they study. I would like to suggest that more capacious and de-idealized accounts of love and friendship would serve to account for the ambivalence and violence of the relation to the past—to what is most queer in that relation.

Today, many critics attest that since Stonewall the worst difficulties of queer life are behind us. Yet the discomfort that contemporary queer subjects continue to feel in response to the most harrowing representations from the past attests to their continuing relevance. The experience of queer historical subjects is not at a safe distance from contemporary experience; rather, their social marginality and abjection mirror our own. The relation to the queer past is suffused not only by feelings of regret, despair, and loss but also by the shame of identification. In attempting to construct a positive genealogy of gay identity, queer critics and historians have often found themselves at a loss about what to do with the sad old queens and long-suffering dykes who haunt the historical record. They have disavowed the difficulties of the queer past, arguing that our true history has not been written. If critics do admit the difficulties of the queer past, it is most often in order to redeem them. By including queer figures from the past in a positive genealogy of gay identity, we make good on their suffering, transforming their shame into pride after the fact. I understand this impulse not only as a widespread but as a structural feature of the field, a way of counteracting the shame of having a dark past.[3]

Someone Will Remember Us

In *A Lover's Discourse,* Roland Barthes writes that "the discourse of Absence is a text with two ideograms: there are the raised arms of Desire, and there are the wide-open arms of Need. I oscillate, I vacillate between the phallic image of the raised arms, and the babyish image of the wide-open arms."[4] Barthes construes the relation between desire and need as consecutive: the lover vacillates between two different responses to absence. It is striking to note, however, how often these images converge. Desire in its most infantile, its most reduced state is difficult to distinguish from need; need in its most tyrannical form nearly approaches the phallic image of desire. Barthes offers an image of such convergence in the photograph of himself as a boy in his mother's arms reproduced at the beginning of *Roland Barthes by Roland Barthes*. The caption reads, "The demand for love."[5] For Barthes, the notion of "demand" captures the close link between need and desire.[6] In this photograph, the young Barthes offers an image of the demanding child, that slumped, pathetic figure who nonetheless manages to press his needs home with real force.[7]

If this photograph reveals the adult force of childish need, we can call to mind many examples that reveal the babyish element in adult desire. Think, for instance, of the sneering, sulking pout of that consummate erotic bully, Mick Jagger. In almost any song by the Rolling Stones, the call to "just come upstairs" gets its heat not only from the authority of the desiring father but also from the hunger of the prodigal son. In "Emotional Rescue," for instance, macho posturing shades into schoolboy whining as Jagger intersperses deep-voiced promises to be your "knight in shining armor," to "come to your emotional rescue," with half-mumbled assertions that last night he was "crying like a child, like a child." In the chorus, Jagger gives us the cry itself: "You will be mine, mine, mine, mine, mine, all mine / You could be mine, could be mine, / Be mine, all mine." In the infantile repetition of the possessive, one hears the pathetic cry of the child who is not in a position to own anything.[8]

You will be mine; you could be mine—but you probably won't be mine. This combination of demand and desperation characterizes the relation to the gay past. But queer critics tend to disavow their need for the past by focusing on the heroic aspect of their work of historical recovery. Like many demanding lovers, queer critics promise to rescue the past when in fact they dream of being rescued themselves.

In imagining historical rescue as a one-way street, we fail to acknowledge the dependence of the present on the past. Contemporary critics tend to frame the past as the unique site of need, as if the practice of history were not motivated by a sense of lack in the present. We might conceive of the work of historical affirmation not, as it is often presented, as a lifeline thrown to those figures drowning in the bad gay past, but rather as a means of securing a more stable and positive identity in the present.[9] At the same time, such acts of resolve allow us to ignore the resistance of queer historical figures to our advances toward them.

In order to better describe how this fantasy works, I consider an exchange between the Greek poet Sappho and one of her most rapt modern readers. Anne Carson offers the following version of one of Sappho's lyrics: "Someone will remember us / I say / even in another time."[10] Sappho's poem offers to its audience what sounds like foreknowledge: "Someone will remember us." The prediction seems to have the simple status of truth, but the "I say" at the center of this lyric attests to the longing and uncertainty that is the poem's motive and its subject. In making the prediction more emphatic, "I say" tips the hand of the speaker, shows this prophecy to be a matter of wishful thinking. The speaker protects her audience from the unpredictability of the future by means of a personal guarantee; the "I" of the poem offers its auditors a shelter from oblivion. (One of the uncanny aspects of the poem is its ability to offer this consolation—in person, as it were—not only to its immediate audience but also to its future readers.)

The sheer density of longing in this short poem is striking. Crack the shell of its confident assertion of immortality and questions emerge: "Can one be remembered in one's absence?" "When I leave the room, will you still think about me?" "Will we be remembered after death?" The poem answers "yes": "Someone will remember us / I say / even in another time." The speaker promises her audience that they will be thought of not only tomorrow, or the day after, but "in another time," and by strangers. Sappho's lyric promises memory across death: once we and everyone we know and everyone who knows us is dead, someone is still going to think about us. We will be in history.

This fragment offers a nearly irresistible version of what queer subjects want to hear from their imagined ancestors. It is what Christopher Nealon refers to in *Foundlings* as the "message in the bottle" dispatched from the queer past—sent seeking a "particular historical kind of afterlife," "some historical 'other' place" where "the unspeakability" of same-sex love "can gain audition" (182). For the early twentieth-century lesbian poet Renée Vivien, Sappho's poetry was just such a message in a bottle. In order to read it, she learned Greek and began obsessively translating and expanding Sappho's fragments and even traveled to the island of Lesbos with her lover Natalie Clifford Barney to recreate the legendary school for girls. In her 1903 volume *Sapho*, Vivien offers translations and expansions of Sappho's fragmentary lyrics that take up themes of tormented desire, isolation, and lost love in the originals and amplify the historical resonances in them.

Vivien's attention to the vulnerability of cross-historical contacts is legible in her version of "Someone will remember us."

> Quelqu'un, je crois, se souviendra dans
> l'avenir de nous.
>
> Dans les lendemains que le sort file et tresse,
> Les êtres futurs ne nous oublieront pas . . .
> Nous ne craignons point, Atthis, ô ma Maîtresse!
> L'ombre du trépas.
>
> Car ceux qui naîtront après nous dans ce monde
> Où râlent les chants jetteront leur soupir
> Vers moi, qui t'aimais d'une angoisse profonde,
> Vers toi, mon Désir.
>
> Les jours ondoyants que la clarté nuance,
> Les nuits de parfums viendront éterniser
> Nos frémissements, notre ardente souffrance
> Et notre baiser.
>
> [Someone, I believe, will remember us
> in the future.
>
> In the tomorrows that fate spins and weaves,
> Those who come after us will not forget us . . .
> We have no fear, O, Atthis my Mistress!
> Of the shadow of death.
>
> Because those who are born after us in this world
> Filled with death-cries will cast their sighs
> Toward me, who loved you with deep anguish,
> Toward you, my Desire.
>
> The wavering days that the clear light limns
> And the perfumed night will render eternal
> Our tremblings, our ardent suffering,
> And our kiss.][11]

Although "making the moment last" is a commonplace of the Western lyric tradition, this trope takes on tremendous weight in Vivien's rewritings of Sappho's lyrics. The promise of immortality that is associated with the aesthetic is put to work here as a bulwark against historical isolation and social exclusion. How can connections across time be forged out of fear and erotic torments? Vivien compares the transformation of fleeting moments into tradition to the way that "les jours ondoyants" make up an eternity even though they are made of nothing more substantial than light and shade. In this comparison, a love that is fleeting and filled with anguish becomes eternal simply by aging—by being continually exposed to the light of day and the perfumed shades of night.[12] Vivien also invokes a specifically erotic mystery: how the experience of shared erotic suffering, obsession, and anxiety can add up to eternal devotion.

Of course, it is not assured that such torments do lead to eternal devotion (just as it is not assured that the messages cast out in bottles ever get read). The fantasy of permanence is, however, the central conceit of the poem and it represents the deepest wish of Sappho's lonely historical correspondent. Vivien makes true love the model for cross-historical fidelity, and, speaking in Sappho's voice, promises recognition. Taking up the role of adoring lover, Vivien answers Sappho's call, leaving no doubt that someone in another time would in fact think of her. Through such a response, Vivien seems to rescue Sappho—to repair the torn fragments of her text, and to stitch up the gap in the temporal fabric that her lyric address opens. But it is clear that by translating Sappho Vivien was working against the profound sense of alienation and historical isolation that she felt at the turn of the twentieth century. By coming to Sappho's rescue, Vivien manages to rescue herself. She enters history by becoming Sappho's imagined and desired "someone."[13]

Although many cast queer historical subjects in the role of Sappho—as lonely, isolated subjects in search of communion with future readers—I want to suggest that it makes sense to see ourselves in the role of Vivien. That is to say, contemporary queer subjects are also isolated, lonely subjects looking for other lonely people, just like them. Vivien finds in Sappho an almost perfect interlocutor; the echo chamber in which she replayed Sappho's fragments afforded profound satisfactions. But few encounters with the queer past run so smoothly. These texts rarely express such a perfect longing for rescue and are often characterized by a resistance to future readers and to the very idea of community. We do encounter some texts that say, "Someone will remember us / I say / even in another time." But some of these lost figures do not want to be found. What then?

Noli Me Tangere

Carolyn Dinshaw's book, *Getting Medieval,* investigates the affective dynamics of queer history. Dinshaw focuses on the metaphorics of touch in the relation of contemporary critics to the medieval past; she explores the "strange fellowships" and the "partial connections" that link queer subjects across time. Through such connections, queer subjects build an imagined community of the marginal and the excluded. By trying to create relations across time, Dinshaw follows what she calls "a queer historical impulse, an impulse toward making connections across time between, on the one hand, lives, texts, and other cultural phenomena left out of sexual categories back then and, on the other hand, those left out of current sexual categories now. Such an impulse extends the resources for self- and community building into even the distant past" (1). Rather than seeing herself as the heroic savior of the past, Dinshaw puts herself into relation with it, describing her own desires for "partial, affective connection, for community, for even a touch across time" (21).

The longing for community across time is a crucial feature of queer historical experience, one produced by the historical isolation of individual queers as well as by the damaged quality of the historical archive. Like Dinshaw, Christopher Nealon surveys these desires for connection across time in *Foundlings* through his accounts of the "affect-genealogies" and "hopeful analogies" to other historical forms of community in twentieth-century queer (or "foundling") texts. It makes sense to consider these works in affective historiography within the context of larger efforts in queer studies to describe or invent new models of queer community and coalitional politics: nonbiological inheritance, new forms of kinship, "the friendship ethic," queer families, stigma- or shame-based alliances, and so on.[14] This work on new forms of queer community has been generative. At the same time, others working in queer studies have been critical of the concept of community. In *Against the Romance of Community,*

Miranda Joseph wonders about the "relentless return" of a "celebratory discourse of community" in queer and feminist criticism despite long-standing critiques of the exclusionary force of the term.[15] In *Queer Fictions of the Past*, Scott Bravmann points to the way that current debates over historical meaning "indicate a lack of consensus on who or what gay and lesbian people are and even highlight the anti-community aspects of the differences between and among queer historical subjects."[16]

Dinshaw is certainly alive to the force of these critiques, and she notes that she uses the term community in a way that does not "imply unity or homogeneity" (22).[17] Dinshaw is at pains to emphasize the way that desires for queer community are in a state of tension with queer isolation and resistance to community.[18] In several passages, she explores the paradox of shared isolation and she argues that the connections she describes are partial and incomplete. Dinshaw specifically contrasts this fellowship of the "isolated, the abject, [and] the shamed" with a more idealized version of community. In a forum about *Getting Medieval*, she writes, "I want to stress that the community across time formed of such vibrations, such touches, is not necessarily a feel-good collectivity of happy homos."[19]

Despite Dinshaw's critical take on community and her interest in exploring shared isolation, the emphasis in *Getting Medieval* sometimes falls on community at the expense of isolation. A crucial example in the book is the work of Roland Barthes, an exemplary figure owing to his dual interest in isolation and community. Yet there are forms of resistance to community in Barthes's work that seem particularly difficult to accept, at least in part because they threaten to remove him from the affective circuit of Dinshaw's study. Dinshaw cites Barthes from *Writer Sollers*: " 'We allow people to be different (that is our master stroke), but not unusual. We accept types, but not individuals . . . But what about the person who is absolutely alone? Who isn't a Breton, a Corsican, a woman, a homosexual, a madman, an Arab, etc.? Somebody who doesn't even belong to a minority? Literature is his voice' " (cited in Dinshaw, *Getting Medieval*, 45). Reading this passage, Dinshaw remarks that the "prospect of community is very unclear," but goes on to argue that "despite the emphasis on the 'absolutely alone,' relations between lives, between entirely contingent and profoundly singular lives, were indeed a concern throughout the long and otherwise uneven span of Barthes's texts" (45). Not only does this passage from Barthes present the ongoing question of whether or in what way it makes sense to consider him a "gay author," it also raises the specter of the person who is "absolutely alone."[20] If literature is "his voice," does it then follow that by reading those works we undo the absoluteness of that solitude? And is counteracting solitude or singularity something that we, as contemporary readers, should even aim to do?

Dinshaw is interested in the presence of the body in Barthes's ruminations on reading and collectivity; she is particularly interested in his work on Michelet as an example of an embodied, loving historical practice. She cites Barthes on Michelet: "For Michelet the historical mass is not a puzzle to reconstitute, it is a body to embrace. The historian exists only to recognize a warmth."[21] Barthes lovingly describes such relations throughout his work, and his identification with Michelet is undoubtedly grounded in his tendency to form similar attachments. But he also considers Michelet's physical repulsions at length. In another passage cited by Dinshaw, Barthes writes that "fits of nausea, dizziness, oppression do not come only from the seasons, from the weather; it is the very horror of narrated history which provokes them: Michelet has 'historical' migraines." (cited in Dinshaw, *Getting Medieval,* 47). Barthes's relation to Michelet is forwarded here as a model of the "tenderness" that is possible between contemporary queer critics and the subjects they study. Dinshaw writes that Barthes "created his own queer relation to Michelet by 'living with' him" (48). Do we need to be reminded that such an arrangement tends to be a source of pain as well as pleasure? That the darkened bedroom is a site not only of caresses but also of migraines?

Dinshaw focuses on the queer impulse to "touch the past" through a meditation on Christ's words to Mary Magdalene after his resurrection: *Noli me tangere* (Don't touch me). Dinshaw's chapter on Margery Kempe's "too heavy, queer touch" begins with an epigraph from Leslie Feinberg's work *Stone Butch Blues:* "Touch is something I could never take for granted" (cited in Dinshaw, *Getting Medieval,* 143). By attending to the history of queer abjection, Dinshaw constructs a genealogy of untouched and untouchable figures, subjects constituted through refusal. These subjects are portrayed, however, as yielding to, even warming to the touch of the queer historian. It is striking that in her extended meditation on the phrase *Noli me tangere,* Dinshaw does not consider the potential resistance of such figures to the touch of contemporary queer historians. At stake in this omission may be not only the desire of the queer historian for a response from the past but also a tendency to read the queerness of queer desire as excess rather than lack. Queer desire is often figured as "loving too much," as in Dinshaw's reading of Margery Kempe's excessive, dissonant desire. But it would also make sense to understand queerness as an absence of or aversion to sex.[22]

Untouchability runs deep in queer experience. Here is Willa Cather on the subject, thinking about the "sweetness and anguish" that characterize family life in Katherine Mansfield's stories: "One realizes that human relations are the tragic necessity of human life; that they can never be wholly satisfactory, that every ego is half the time greedily seeking them, and half the time pulling away from them."[23] Or Cherríe Moraga: "My recurring sense of myself outside the normal life and touch of human beings was again, in part, a kind of revelation."[24] *Noli me tangere* is, in this sense, an apt motto for queer historical experience, but its effects are unpredictable. Although it serves as protection against the blows of normal life, the family, and homophobic violence, it also works against other forms of community and affiliation, including, of course, queer community.

Contemporary critics approach these figures from the past with a sense of the inevitability of their progress toward us—of their place in the history of modern homosexuality. Their relation to this future remains utterly tenuous, however. If their trajectory to a queer future seems inevitable, this appearance is perhaps best explained by the fact that *we are that future*. Our existence in the present depends on being able to imagine these figures reaching out to us. One is reminded constantly of the fragility of these connections in Dinshaw's text. Still, it remains difficult to hear these subjects when they say to us, "Don't touch me."

Against Identification

In *The Renaissance of Lesbianism in Early Modern England*, Valerie Traub takes a step backward from the intimacies that Dinshaw explores. More circumspect in its attachments than *Getting Medieval*, Traub's book offers a reflection on the ascendancy of the identificatory impulse in lesbian and gay historiography. Explicitly comparing her own project to

Dinshaw's, Traub offers her own analysis: "Whereas Dinshaw's impulse is to foster queer community by 'touching' the medieval past, to make 'new relations, new identifications, new communities with past figures' . . . my impulse is to analyze the desires that propel such identifications."[25] Rather than making alliances with the dead through taking up and extending such impulses, Traub offers a genealogy of identification, considering why it is that "looking at ourselves in the mirror" has become the dominant methodology in gay and especially in lesbian studies.

Dinshaw figures pleasure as a resource for queer studies; in *The Renaissance of Lesbianism,* pleasure—insofar as it is bound up with identification—is a problem. Though Traub suggests that it would be impossible to completely rid historical or political practice of the impulse to identification, she links the pleasures of identification to cognitive failure. In the final passages of her book, Traub effects a turn away from identification and toward desire, suggesting that we might approach the figures from the past "not as subject *to* our identifications, but as objects *of* our desire" (354). In this way, Traub hopes to borrow some of the pleasure of psychic and historical identification and reinvest it in desire, which she understands as an authentic encounter with another who is different from and external to the self.

Eroticizing historical alterity is only part of the story, though. Traub's more pressing concern is with the melancholic nature of lesbian studies. She argues that the "discovery" of early modern lesbianism is a way of "compensating for the fact that, despite the categories we inhabit, our knowledge of ourselves as individuals as well as within group identities is vexed, uncertain, in continual and oft-times painful negotiation. Quite simply, we do not know who and what 'we' are, or how we might go about defining ourselves beyond the reaction formations conceived under the influence of heterosexism and homophobia" (352). According to Traub, lesbian critics have not come to terms with the pain of historical isolation and instead reenact that trauma through repeated searches for other lesbians "just like them" in the past: "The effort to identify early modern *lesbians* is not so much a case of individual misrecognition as a collective melancholic response to the trauma of historical elision. Despite the common invocation of how homosexuals have been 'hidden from history,' there has been little investigation into the effects on the collective *lesbian* psyche of the systematic denial of historicity" (350).[26]

Traub's attention to the pain that is at the heart of lesbian and gay historiography is welcome, as is her call for an investigation of the psychic costs of repeated encounters with the "empty archive." One may certainly see both pain and the disavowal of pain in Renée Vivien's textual approaches to Sappho. Traub's solution to this problem is to move lesbian historiography beyond the impasse of melancholic disavowal by mourning those losses and by giving up on the dream of identification. She draws a distinction between personal and collective responses to loss, suggesting that "the desire to view oneself in the mirror, however enabling personally, need not be the procedural ground of lesbian history" (334). Traub continues: "Rather than mourning our disconnection from women of the past and allowing them to exist autonomously through their textual traces, we have disavowed our mourning and encrypted the pain of that disavowal within our own critical procedures . . . Such a response is understandable and, at the level of the individual psyche, potentially productive. On a cultural and methodological level, however, it ensures a continued melancholic identification with, and dependence upon, the terms of erotic similitude, in a paralyzing enactment of queer trauma" (350).

Drawing on Wendy Brown's concept of "wounded attachments" as the basis of identity politics as well as works on mourning and melancholy by Judith Butler and Nicolas Abraham and Maria Torok, Traub suggests that contemporary critics work through psychic impasses in order to get over paralyzing and debilitating engagements with the historical past. What is troubling about such a suggestion is the fact that some aspects of lesbian history only live on in the present through such wounded attachments and that severing them will mean putting important—albeit traumatic—parts of the past to rest. Queer history is, in a sense, nothing but wounded attachments: a "debilitating engagement with the past" (351) might just be another name for the practice of history. Confronted with the unresolved grief of lesbian historical feeling, Traub suggests cutting the knot in an act of methodological triage. While there are aspects of the past we may be unable to see because of unresolved grief, the key to making historical losses present is not necessarily to mourn them: mourning can be another name for forgetting.

Henry Abelove gestures toward another relation to the queer past in his recent book *Deep Gossip* with a citation from Allen Ginsberg's elegy for Frank O'Hara, "City Midnight Junk Strains." Ginsberg describes O'Hara as a "curator of funny emotions." Abelove argues that Ginsberg refers not only to O'Hara's job at the Museum of Modern Art but also to his exemplary relation to an imagined queer community. For Abelove, curating contrasts sharply with curing: "Curating, taking care of, isn't curing—or wanting to cure—or supposing or imagining that a cure is needed."[27] We might take this distinction to suggest that the work of the historian is a kind of "interminable analysis." Taking care of the past without attempting to fix it means living with bad attachments, identifying through loss, allowing ourselves to be haunted.

Carla Freccero suggests something very similar in *Queer/Early/Modern* when she proposes "an approach to history—and to justice—that would neither 'forget the dead' nor 'successfully' mourn them" (78). Freccero's final chapter, "Queer Spectrality," focuses on the murder of Brandon Teena and its subsequent replaying in popular media, film, and academic criticism. Freccero's insistence on Brandon's afterlife in the present offers an example of a queer ethics of historical practice, a willingness to live with ghosts and to remember the most painful, the most impossible stories. Still, it is not clear what would constitute proper care for ghosts like these (with their funny emotions). Turning back toward them seems essential, but it also demands something that is, in the end, more difficult: allowing them to turn their backs on us.

Against Consolation

The historiographic method of Michel Foucault is regularly invoked in contemporary queer contexts as exemplary in its resistance to the temptations of identification and mirroring. In his work on genealogy, Foucault argues for the need to develop a historical method that does not rely on the past to secure the stability of the present. In his much-cited essay, "Nietzsche, Genealogy, History," he writes:

> "Effective" history differs from the history of historians in being without constants. Nothing in man—not even his body—is sufficiently stable to serve as the basis for self-recognition or for understanding other men. The traditional devices for constructing a comprehensive view of history and for retracing the past as a patient and continuous development must be systematically dismantled. Necessarily, we must dismiss those tenden-

cies which encourage the consoling play of recognitions. Knowledge [*savoir*], even under the banner of history, does not depend on "rediscovery," and it emphatically excludes the "rediscovery of ourselves." History becomes "effective" to the degree that it introduces discontinuity into our very being—as it divides our emotions, dramatizes our instincts, multiplies our body and sets it against itself.[28]

Rather than moving forward from a determinate origin and proceeding according to a smooth logic of progression, history through the lens of genealogy begins accidentally and proceeds by fits and starts. Such a history, while useless for the "consoling play of recognitions" that is the favored mode of history by historians, serves to disrupt the seeming inevitability of the present. Divisive and incendiary, genealogy points out the otherness of the past, and shows us our own image in the present as multiple, subject to an internal alienation.

Elsewhere in this essay, Foucault writes that "the purpose of history, guided by genealogy, is not to discover the roots of our identity, but to commit itself to its dissipation. It does not seek to define our unique threshold of emergence, the homeland to which metaphysicians promise a return; it seeks to make visible all those discontinuities that cross us" (386–387). In his descriptions of the unpredictable and accidental nature of events, Foucault argues against the idea that history's movement is continuous or marked by progress. As a result, he suggests that we can find no solid epistemological basis in the present for identifications in the past. Resemblances across time are not dependable since over time the very terms of inquiry shift.

Queer critics have generally understood the concept of identity to be both politically and philosophically bankrupt. Although such critiques of identity have made for important changes in gay and lesbian politics and theory, it seems that the queer stance against identity has short-circuited important critical work on the history of identity. Identity is, as many of these critics have attested, a deeply problematic and contradictory concept; nonetheless, it remains a powerful organizing concept in contemporary experience. We need an account of identity that allows us to think through its contradictions and to trace its effects. Such a history can offer a critique of identity without dispensing with it as a category of historical experience.

The commitment to the "dissipation of identity" among queer critics has often blinded them to the tenacity of this concept both in history

and in individual subjectivity. Identity accounts not only for the shape
of the past but also for the feelings that we continue to have about that
past. It is in large part because we recognize figures, emotions, and images from the past as like ourselves that we feel their effects so powerfully. Rather than attempt to "overcome" identity, I want to suggest a
mode of historiography that recognizes the inevitability of a "play of
recognitions," but that also sees these recognitions not as consoling but
as shattering. What has been most problematic about gay and lesbian
historiography to date is not, I want to argue, its attachment to identity
but rather its consistently affirmative bias. Critics imagine that no one
would search out the roots of his or her identity if that history were not
positive. But we are condemned to the search for roots and for resemblances; we cannot help searching the past for images of ourselves. In
their introduction to *Premodern Sexualities,* Louise Fradenburg and
Carla Freccero suggest the inevitability of historical identification: "History is riddled by the paradoxes of identification: by the impossible pleasures and obligations of imitating the past" (xvi).

Fradenburg and Freccero go on to argue that the pleasure of forging
historical identifications is not a bad thing: "one of the central challenges queer perspectives offer to historicist practice is their insistence
that the purpose of recognizing pleasure's role in the production of historical discourse is not necessarily to launch yet another renunciation of
such pleasure" (xvii–xviii). Still, such identifications are not pleasurable
in any simple or straightforward way. Fradenburg and Freccero suggest
that a closer look at the processes of historical identification might actually serve to undermine rather than to stabilize identity. Considering
the importance of writing "long histories," they wonder "how would we
write the history of the ways in which the past is *in* us, our identities
being perhaps as temporally unstable as they are in other ways?" (xix).
Fradenburg and Freccero illuminate the way that identifications across
time do not serve merely to consolidate identities in the present; instead, such identifications can illuminate the uncanny life of the past inside our present. I would add that negative or ambivalent identifications
with the past can serve to disrupt the present. Making connections with
historical losses or with images of ruined or spoiled identity in the past
can set into motion a gutting "play of recognitions," another form of effective history.

At Night

In *Getting Medieval,* Dinshaw argues that "pleasure may be afforded by a break with the past, a rupture of historical identity . . . ; the loss of the past might carry an erotic charge" (36). Foucault's work on the archive and his reflections on historiographical method offer an example of the manifold pleasures afforded by "the loss of the past." The following passage from "Nietzsche, Genealogy, History" begins coolly enough with methodological injunctions and slowly builds toward a fantasy of historical encounter:

> A genealogy of values, morality, asceticism, and knowledge will never confuse itself with a quest for their "origins," will never neglect as inaccessible all the episodes of history. On the contrary, it will cultivate the details and accidents that accompany every beginning; it will be scrupulously attentive to their petty malice; it will await their emergence, once unmasked, as the face of the other. (373)

The genealogist appears here as an inexhaustible lover, attentive to every detail, waiting for the other's appearance as for the break of day. Foucault's approach to history is indelibly though often invisibly marked by desire, and, I would suggest, by specifically queer experiences, rhetorics, and longings. Foucault's own account of his famously ascetic historical practice appears to be anything but devoid of desire. Rather, it is grounded in an anxious, restless desire—a desire for a recognition that could hardly be called consoling.

In an essay that Dinshaw reads at length, "The Lives of Infamous Men," Foucault describes his own experience in the prison archives of the *Hôpital general* and of the Bastille. Foucault attends to the difficulties of studying the lives of obscure men whose only trace is a criminal record and who reach contemporary readers through improbable and unnecessary paths:

> Having been nothing in history, having played no appreciable role in events or among important people, having left no identifiable trace around them, they don't have and never will have any existence outside the precarious domicile of these words . . . This purely verbal existence, which makes these forlorn or villainous individuals into quasi-fictional beings, is due to their nearly complete disappearance, and to that luck or mischance which resulted in the survival, through

the peradventure of rediscovered documents, of a scarce few words that speak of them or that are pronounced by them. A dark but, above all, a dry legend . . . By nature, it is bereft of any tradition; discontinuities, effacement, oblivion, convergences, reappearances: this is the only way it can reach us. Chance carries it from the beginning . . . So that between these people of no importance and us who have no more importance than they, there is no necessary connection. Nothing made it likely for them to emerge from the shadows, they instead of others, with their lives and their sorrows.[29]

Foucault's wan description of the belated emergence from the archive of these obscure figures is at some distance from heroic plots of historical discovery. Underlining the chance nature of the encounter between historians and the subjects they study, Foucault attempts to drain away the affect that surrounds the historical encounter: the legend of Foucault's "infamous men" is dark but, "above all, dry."

Foucault's de-cathexis of the historical encounter is also linked to a critique of the specular logic of historical discovery. Between these figures and "us" there is "no necessary connection": there is no reason that their traces should have reached us and furthermore no reason why they should resemble us. Yet it is at the moment that Foucault emphasizes the purely contingent and unmotivated relation between these infamous men and contemporary readers that he draws an explicit comparison between us and them: "so that between these people of no importance and us who have no more importance than they, there is no necessary connection." Although there may not be a necessary connection here, there is in fact a sufficient connection: what we share with these figures is a lack of importance. We might say that this lack of importance is the only important thing about us.

In a moment that is crucial to Dinshaw's theory of queer touches across time, Foucault describes being "physically affected" in the archive: he feels a vibration "still today" from these texts. He avows his affective investment in these stories, describing the book to follow as "a mood-based and purely subjective book," a "little obsession that found its system." The community of "abject others" that Dinshaw locates in Foucault's essay is grounded in a logic of the improbable, the contingent, and the insignificant. The world of the shadows that Foucault traces in this passage looks, on the one hand, like the dustheap from which all historical figures must be rescued; on the other hand, it looks like a kind of demimonde or queer underworld where men of no importance can meet for chance encounters.[30]

Foucault's attachment to these figures resonates perhaps most strongly in his descriptions of their encounters with power. Foucault suggests that these subjects reach us only because of the violence that touched them:

> What snatched them from the darkness in which they could, perhaps should, have remained was the encounter with power; without that collision, it's very unlikely that any word would be there to recall their fleeting trajectory. The power that watched these lives, that pursued them, that lent its attention, if only for a moment, to their complaints and their little racket, and marked them with its claw was what gave rise to the few words about them that remain for us. ("The Lives of Infamous Men," 161)

Defending his methodology, and answering an imaginary critic who would argue that he imagines historical subjects not in themselves ("from below") but only in relation to power, Foucault responds with a question: "would anything at all remain of what [these figures] were in their violence or in their singular misfortune had they not, at a given moment, met up with power and provoked its forces?" (161). The catch in his voice is audible as he describes the obscurity and violence that marked these lives—had they not met up with power, would anything at all remain? A bit later in the essay, Foucault amplifies this point, arguing that these figures are *constituted* by the violence that they experienced. They are "infamous in the strict sense: they no longer exist except through the terrible words that were destined to render them forever unworthy of the memory of men . . . Useless to look for another face for them, or to suspect a different greatness in them; they are no longer anything but that which was meant to crush them—no more nor less" (164). Hunted down by power, here figured as a lion rampant (or is it a clumsy bear?), these figures are legible only in their misery: it is in the cut, as it were, that we can locate Foucault's attachment. In this sense, we might say that his investment is not so much in these infamous men themselves but rather "in the darkness in which they could, perhaps should, have remained."

In drawing attention to this moment in the essay, I want to suggest that the sensation—the cross-historical touch—that Foucault feels in the archive may be as much a mauling as a caress. He quickens not only to the caress of a queer or marginal figure in the past but also to the more brutal touch of the law. What happens in the archive is an encounter with historical violence, which includes both physical injury and the violence of obscurity, or annihilation from memory. Is it possible that Foucault wants his historical encounter that way?

Consider a related moment in a 1967 interview when, discussing his methodology, Foucault narrates a bad dream:

> A nightmare has haunted me since my childhood: I am looking at a text that I can't read, or only a tiny part of it is decipherable. I pretend to read it, aware that I'm inventing; then suddenly the text is completely scrambled, I can no longer read anything or even invent it, my throat tightens up and I wake up.
>
> I'm not blind to the personal investment there may be in this obsession with language that exists everywhere and escapes us in its very survival. It survives by turning its looks away from us, its face inclined toward a darkness we know nothing about.[31]

Here it appears that the "personal investment" that drives Foucault's approach to history is not an attachment to precursors but rather an "obsession with language . . . that escapes us in its very survival." The tightening of the throat that he feels in the dream seems to be a response to historical loss and to ignorance and to an expression of shame about pretending to read what he cannot. Despite the trauma of this loss, however, Foucault does not end by expressing a desire for the intact document. He does not, it seems, want to look history in the face; rather, the fascination here is with the face that turns away, and, even more, perhaps, with the darkness toward which it turns.

This moment recalls Foucault's discussion of "Eurydice and the Sirens" in his 1966 essay on Maurice Blanchot, "The Thought of the Outside." Foucault compares the heroic narrative of Ulysses' encounter with the Sirens with the story of Orpheus's failed journey to bring back Eurydice from the underworld, suggesting that there is not much to distinguish the triumphant narrative from the tragic one:

> Each of their voices is then freed: Ulysses' with his salvation and the possibility of telling the tale of his marvelous adventure; Orpheus's with his absolute loss and never-ending lament. But it is possible that behind Ulysses' triumphant narrative there prevails the inaudible

lament of not having listened better and longer, of not having ventured as close as possible to the wondrous voice that might have finished the song. And that behind Orpheus's lament shines the glory of having seen, however fleetingly, the unattainable face at the very instant it turned away and returned to darkness—a nameless, placeless hymn to light.[32]

Although Foucault does not read these figures explicitly in relation to the work of the historian, they are legible in terms of a contrast between history as a tale of heroic rescue and "marvelous adventure" and history as a narrative that breaks off midway and that fails to bring the beloved back from the underworld. Clearly, Foucault throws in his lot in with Orpheus, who offers an apt emblem of the practice of queer history. The failed attempt to rescue Eurydice is a sign of the impossibility of the historical project per se: the dead do not come back from beyond the grave, and this fact constitutes the pathos of the historical project. But we might also read the Orphic lament as an effect of the particular losses suffered by queer historical subjects. We can trace the aftereffects of that history in the characteristically minor key in which Foucault's desire for the past is played.

To explain what I mean, I want to turn to Blanchot's staging of this moment in the "The Gaze of Orpheus," the essay that Foucault discusses. Describing the way that the work of art must be wrested from the "heart of night," Blanchot writes that

> by turning toward Eurydice, Orpheus ruins the work, which is immediately undone, and Eurydice returns among the shades. When he looks back, the essence of night is revealed as the inessential. Thus he betrays the work, and Eurydice, and the night. But not to turn toward Eurydice would be no less untrue. Not to look would be infidelity to the measureless, imprudent force of his movement, which does not want Eurydice in her daytime truth and in her everyday appeal, but wants her in her nocturnal obscurity, in her distance, with her closed body and sealed face—wants to see her not when she is visible, but when she is invisible, and not as the intimacy of familiar life, but as the foreignness of what excludes all intimacy, and wants, not to make her live, but to have living in her the plenitude of death.[33]

Blanchot casts Orpheus's relation to Eurydice as an impossible relation: by turning back he betrays her, losing her forever in the lower depths; but the refusal to turn back would count as a betrayal as well.

Such is the relation of the queer historian to the past: we cannot help wanting to save the figures from the past, but this mission is doomed to fail. In part, this is because the dead are gone for good; in part, because the queer past is even more remote, more deeply marked by power's claw; and in part because this rescue is an emotional rescue, and in that sense, we are sure to botch it. But, according to Blanchot, not to botch it would be a betrayal. Such a rescue effort can only take place under the shadow of loss and in the name of loss; success would constitute its failure.

Blanchot's reflections on Orpheus and Eurydice recall the moment when, in a 1983 interview, Foucault speculated that the "best moment" in the life of the homosexual is "likely to be when the lover leaves in the taxi."[34] Foucault links this feeling to the availability of homosexual contacts; he suggests that because there is no contest to get someone into bed that the erotic is more bound up with retrospect than anticipation. But as he invokes this explanation, Foucault also gestures toward a history of queer feeling grounded in the social impossibility of homosexual love. Foucault's desire for the boy has a queer specificity; he would not easily give up the dreamy and rueful retrospect he inspires. He wants the love of "that boy," already receding into the distance—not the daytime love, the easy intimacies, of a domestic partner. He wants him in the taxi, just as Orpheus wants Eurydice in the night, in the underworld.

This structure of feeling is not a pathology, nor does it describe the essential nature of the homosexual. I would not call it, either, an effect of the "dark pulsions" of the unconscious, though I suppose they play their part in this scene. Anyone, I want to insist, might be seduced by the figure of Eurydice: she is radiant in her withdrawal. But her specific attraction for queer subjects is an effect, I want to argue, of a historical experience of love as bound up with loss. To recognize Eurydice as desirable in her turn away is a way of identifying through that loss. Such an approach would be consistent with an important aspect of contemporary queer politics, which has tended to define community not as constituted by a shared set of identity traits, but rather as emerging from a shared experience of social violence. In this sense, following the trace of violence and marginalization—studying not only obscure men, but obscurity itself—would allow us to deflect questions of identity and to acknowledge the losses of both the past and the present.

I hear the trace of such losses in my own fantasized relation to Foucault. I do dream about being with Foucault, but I imagine joining him in the underworld, after the moment he has turned away. I want him in that darkness—bearing the marks of power's claw. How to explain such perverse, such intransigent desires? Queer history has been an education in absence: the experience of social refusal and of the denigration of homosexual love has taught us the lessons of solitude and heartbreak. What I want to suggest, though, is that it has also, in its way, taught us "how to do the history of homosexuality"—because, in the words of Neil Bartlett, "history can be a dark night too."[35]

2

Forced Exile

Walter Pater's Backward Modernism

Abraham's grief will pass, because Abraham himself will pass, because he is
condemned to be nothing but the origin of a glorious collective identity.

—Leo Bersani, *The Culture of Redemption*

In his book on the modernist work of art, *Untwisting the Serpent,* Daniel
Albright characterizes modernism as an art of extremity. He writes,
"Much of the strangeness, the stridency, the exhilaration of Modernist
art can be explained by [its] strong thrust toward the verges of aesthetic
experience: after certain nineteenth-century artists had established a
remarkably safe, intimate center where the artist and audience could
dwell, the twentieth century reaches out to the freakish circumference of
art."[1] Albright describes the extremist impulse in modernism as a desire
to cross boundaries, to set off from the center of culture toward its
"freakish circumference." What is crucial in such a definition, however,
is the different valence of exile for those escaping from the center of
culture and for those who find themselves already positioned on the
"freakish circumference." The meaning of modernist transgression—of
crossing the line—depends to a great extent on which way you are
headed: it is one thing to light out for the Territory and quite another
thing to live there.

Recently, critics have begun to rethink this image of modernism as
a "drive to the margins" by situating aesthetic modernism within a
broader geographical and cultural framework. The ascendancy of American and European high modernism has been challenged by work that
explores black and white modernism, nonelite cultural production in
the period, the gender of modernism, and the global dimensions of

modernity. Although it is possible to understand the transgressive aspect of modernism as an escape from the crumbling center of culture (the white flight model), it was also an era of new social possibilities for a range of marginal or dominated subjects. If the prevailing image of modernism remains the drive to the margins, it is in part because modernism itself is still defined from the center; recent work on alternative cultures of modernity has not been integrated into an understanding of the early twentieth century as a period marked by traffic between the center and the margins. The exemplary modernist gesture of self-exile is at some distance from the experience of forced exile—whether through migration or marginalization—which is one of the most widespread and characteristic effects of modernization. If one has not departed consciously and under one's own steam, being on the margins looks less like heroic sacrifice and more like *amor fati*. Such a modernism cannot easily be celebrated: in recording the experience of forced exile, it undermines the heroism of modernist transgression, revealing the uneven terrain of twentieth-century modernity.

As important as it is to be aware of the real differences between "dominant" and "marginal" modernisms, it is also important to remember how difficult it can be, in any given case, to tell the difference. Consider the example of James Joyce, who is in one sense a perfect representative of dominant modernism. Joyce's position is significantly complicated by his status as a subject of British colonial rule. In the case of Joyce's decision to leave Ireland, it would be difficult to say whether this exile was forced or chosen. Stephen Dedalus's embrace of Lucifer as his role model in *A Portrait of the Artist as a Young Man* is perhaps the most iconic gesture of modernist transgression. Stephen is modernism's proudest exile: he takes the rebel angel's motto—*non serviam*: "I will not serve"—as the cornerstone of his aesthetic and moral program. "I will not serve that in which I no longer believe, whether it call itself my home, my fatherland, or my church: and I will try to express myself in some mode of life or art as freely as I can and as wholly as I can, using for my defense the only arms I allow myself to use, silence, exile, and cunning."[2] In the conventional account of divine history, voiced by the pastor at the school retreat, exile is figured as the punishment for Lucifer's rebellion; by contrast, Stephen embraces exile as the very means of his rebellion. Stephen's decision to betray the sacred trinity of family, God, and nation is one of the defining moments of modernism. In this by-now familiar narrative, the proud exiles of Joyce's generation abandoned the bankrupt certainty of the world of their fathers in order to construct new modes of "life or art": they betrayed the old world in order to forge a new one.

While modernism may have destroyed the old world, it is not clear that it successfully created a new one. In this sense, Lucifer is an apt emblem of high modernism: his stand against God is both courageous and doomed from the start. Milton offers the paradigmatic account of the tragic rebellion of the most beautiful of angels. He draws attention to the intimate link between defiance and abjection at the beginning of *Paradise Lost,* when we find Satan "vanquish'd, rolling in the fiery gulf" (52). In these opening lines, Milton constantly juxtaposes Satan's continued defiance with his utter misery, as he describes him "prone on the flood" (195), raising his head above the waves to speechify against God. The cumulative effect of these descriptions of the contrast between Satan's condition and his rhetoric is to emphasize the continuity between them: Milton suggests that it is because Satan is feeling so bad that he is talking so big.

We hear a similar quaver in Stephen's voice when he tells his friend Cranly that he is willing to bear damnation. The irony of Stephen's pledging himself to eternal solitude as he "thrills" to Cranly's touch is not lost on the reader (269), who hears the imminent disappointment in this oath of defiance. Stephen's namesake Daedalus captures the ambivalence of modernist transgression: he is at once heroic artificer—the architect of the labyrinth—and a failed creator and an involuntary exile. I think we can trace the underside of modern Satanism in the word apostasy, derived from the Greek *apostasia:* "to stand off, withdraw" (OED). Given God's absolute power, the angels can do nothing but "stand back" from Him. As a form of aesthetic and moral apostasy, modernism joins the image of revolt to the image of abject failure. While Stephen claims to fly in the face of God, his act of apostasy is an act of refusal, a step backward rather than a lurch forward.

In his article "'Salt Peanuts,'" Clyde Taylor offers a version of modernism that resonates with this Satanic version of rebellion. In a consideration of the relation between black and white modernism, Taylor suggests that we think of all modernism as a response to the experience of alienation and exclusion:

All people in extreme situations are either experimenters or passive
victims . . . The displaced Africans shared the same motivations for ex-
perimentation and for indifference to faithful representation of the
world ordered by Western rationalist intelligence as those which drove
Picasso, Stravinksy, and Ezra Pound. In both the African American oral
tradition and the [European] art movements we find a driving search
for forms of spiritual and human expression that could withstand the
alienation of modern industrial culture and its inclination to transform
human relations into commodity relations.[3]

Taylor traces modernist innovation as a response to victimization, and
sees continuity between the kinds of experiments undertaken in both
dominant and vernacular cultures. The only difference, he notes, is
that "African experimenters in America" have less choice than "the experimenters of Western creativity [about] whether or not to try something new" (3). Given the specific exclusions faced by black Americans in the early twentieth century, it is necessary to qualify Taylor's
far-reaching claim. While we might understand modernization and its
effects as a generalized form of forced exile, there are important differences between structural forms of domination and a generalized alienation. In this sense, Taylor's suggestion that black Americans had "less
choice" in forging a new aesthetics is asked to bear a great deal of historical and conceptual weight.[4] Taylor offers a compelling framework
for thinking about all modernism as a reaction to the experience of marginalization: setting the heroics of modernist innovation side by side with
the experience of victimization, Taylor draws out the strain of failure that
runs through all modernism. Such a framework offers a richer account
of "dominant" modernism, of "marginal" modernism, and of the many
modernisms ranged along this spectrum. It also demands, however,
attention to the specific forms of exclusion faced by these early twentieth-
century subjects. We need to rethink the image of modernist rebellion
as heroic resistance and to bring out the strain of failure in all modernism.

In this chapter, I consider the modernism of the late nineteenth-
century critic and novelist Walter Pater, drawing a link between his aesthetics of failure and his experience of bearing a marginalized sexual
identity. Classified alternately as a late Victorian, a decadent aesthete,
and an early modernist, Pater is difficult to situate within traditional literary periods. *Studies in the History of the Renaissance* (1873), his most

significant work, looks backward to exemplary moments in the history of Western culture, celebrating the coming together of the Greek and the Christian spirit in the Renaissance. Pater's turn toward the past aims to transform the present and the future; he explored such moments in an effort to ignite a cultural revolution in the present. He drew on the past in part to break with it; his thoroughgoing critique of religious, moral, and social tradition is legible as modernist. Pater's social position is equally difficult to classify. In one sense, we can see him as situated within the inner sanctum of traditional English culture, especially if we understand Oxford's Brasenose College (where he was employed as a don) as answering to that description. He was also positioned, however, at the "freakish circumference" of culture. Pater's distance from norms of gender and sexual behavior meant for him a kind of internal exile; his position of educational and national privilege could be maintained only by fending off the constant threat of exposure. While Pater avoided the fate of the most famous martyr to homosexual persecution Oscar Wilde, his position at Oxford was seriously undermined after rumors spread of his affair with an undergraduate, William Money Hardinge.[5]

A "queer" Pater has emerged in recent criticism, as several critics have explored the relation between his status as a sexual outsider and his aesthetics. Although these critics have attended most fully to the effects of secrecy and concealment in Pater's work, I am particularly interested in drawing out his investment in failure and in victimization. We might read all of Pater's writings as dedicated to the figure of the victim: in this sense, he cultivates a modernist aesthetic based not on violent transgression but rather on refusal and passivity. Such a form of shrinking resistance is at odds with the protocols of modernist rebellion, and it has often been read as a sign of Pater's aestheticist withdrawal from the field of the social. I suggest recasting his aesthetics of failure as a complex response to a particular historical experience of exclusion. His own situation was paradoxical; he participated in older, private forms of homosexual subcultural life at the same time that he witnessed the birth of homosexuality as a modern category of identity. In this sense, I think it is possible to understand Pater as doubly displaced, inhabiting a threatened position as someone with secrets to keep and as someone whose particular form of secrecy was fast becoming superannuated. Living through this moment of profound historical transformation, he imagined a world in which time was suspended.

Pater's break with the future and with the hard revolutionism of the modernists has made him the cause of some embarrassment. He has been closely linked to the ills of aestheticism: political quietism, withdrawal from the world, hermeticism, nostalgia, a slack relativism, and the elevation of beauty above justice. I want to suggest that what has been seen as a lack of political commitment might be better understood as Pater's failure to approximate the norms of modernist political subjectivity. I read withdrawal in his work not as a refusal of politics but rather as a politics of refusal and see in this shrinking politics a specifically queer response to the experience of social exclusion. The key practices of such a politics—secrecy, ascesis, the vaporization of the self, and temporal delay—depart significantly from the modernist protocols of political intervention. Nonetheless, I argue that we should understand his backwardness as an alternative form of politics—one that is consonant with the experience of marginalized subjects.

Delicious Recoil

Pater begins the famous conclusion to *The Renaissance* with an epigraph from Heraclitus ("All things are in motion and nothing at rest") and a gloss on this citation: "To regard all things and principles of things as inconstant modes of fashion has more and more become the tendency of modern thought. Let us begin with that which is without—our physical life. Fix upon it in one of its more exquisite intervals, the moment, for instance, of delicious recoil from the flood of water in summer heat."[6] The profound anonymity of Pater's writing is in evidence here as he moves from an infinitive construction ("To regard") to a generalizing use of the first person plural ("Let us begin") to a moment of narration that is introduced by an invocation to the reader ("Fix upon") and then to a complete vaporization of the subject.

The agentless action that Pater describes ("the moment of delicious recoil from the flood of water in summer heat") recalls the dynamic that Eve Kosofsky Sedgwick identifies in her work on Henry James as "queer performativity." For Sedgwick, this term describes a combination of reticence and virtuosic stylistic performance; she traces this dynamic to the experience of queer childhood, with its combination of alienation, extreme self-consciousness, and lots of time for reading. Sedgwick draws on Silvan Tomkins's description of shame as "interrupted interest" in order to describe queer performativity as a gesture of approach followed by a blushing withdrawal. This dual movement of solicitation and self-effacement occurs throughout Pater's writing. In his approach to the reader, Pater somehow manages to be both forward and shrinking, both suggestive and withdrawn. What is striking in this passage in particular is the way that Pater identifies the movement of recoil as the most delicious moment: this investment in recoil is matched rhetorically by the delicious secreting of the subject in the text.

Throughout his writing, Pater evinces a fascination with the disappearing subject. In his first published essay "Diaphaneitè," delivered as a lecture to the Old Mortality Society at Oxford in July 1864, Pater offers a breathtakingly abstract account of a particular "type of character," a type that "crosses rather than follows the main current of the world's life" (154):

> There are some unworldly types of character which the world is able to estimate. It recognizes certain moral types, or categories, and regards whatever falls within them as having a right to exist. The saint, the artist, even the speculative thinker, out of the world's order as they are, yet work, so far as they work at all, in and by means of the main current of the world's energy. Often it gives them late, or scanty, or mistaken acknowledgement; still it has room for them in its scheme of life, a place made ready for them in its affections . . . There is another type of character, which is not broad and general, precious above all to the artist . . . It crosses rather than follows the main current of the world's life. The world has no sense fine enough for those evanescent shades, which fill up the blanks between contrasted types of character . . . For this nature there is no place ready in its affections. This colourless, unclassified purity of life it can neither use for its service, nor contemplate as an ideal. (154)

In his description of this crystal character, Pater describes a figure even less welcome in the world than unworldly, yet recognizable, historical actors like the saint, the artist, and the speculative thinker. Pater sketches a character without characteristics; nothing positive attaches to this figure, defined solely by his imperceptibility and by his state of permanent exile. This figure occupies the blanks between recognizable social forms and between other people. This colorless character is not solid enough to be the object of antipathy or aggression; so complete is the world's refusal of him that his only response is to evanesce, to become transparent.

Such diaphanous types appear throughout Pater's work. They populate in particular the world of *The Renaissance*. Pater imagines the Renaissance through a series of extended reveries on the lives of historical and fictional characters. The book describes an enchanted realm that extends from the twelfth to the eighteenth century and includes nearly all major movements in Western aesthetics and philosophy. This world is populated by characters or types who are indecisive, shrinking, transparent.[7] The beautiful passivity of these figures is enabled by the quality of suspended animation that pervades this realm. As Pater describes it, the Renaissance is a realm free from surveillance and from the necessity of taking sides: "within the enchanted region of the Renaissance, one need not be forever on one's guard. Here there are no fixed parties, no exclusions" (17). In a world without warfare, warriors are not needed: one is freed up to imagine a domain populated exclusively by crystal characters. In *The Renaissance,* Pater creates a world that appears more and more as the "counterimage" of the paranoid world of the late nineteenth century. Many of the central descriptions of this world are taken from a lexicon of homosexual secrecy: this language of suggestion indexes the diffuseness and suggestibility of male homoerotic subcultures on the eve of the invention of the modern homosexual.

In his article "Pater's Sadness," Jacques Khalip suggests that transparency in Pater is "allied . . . to a need for defensiveness" (5), and he explicitly links Pater's embrace of anonymity to his experience bearing a marginalized sexual subjectivity. In a discussion of ascesis in Pater's work, Khalip writes, "We suffer because of our lack of knowing, but for Pater, the willful suffering that accompanies ascesis, or his kind of renunciation, is a far better gesture than the arrogant effort to extend and insinuate oneself over other persons and things."[8] Khalip understands Pater's withdrawal as a way of diminishing his epistemological hold over the world, a renunciation of dominance. In Pater's case, such a willed act of self-overcoming can often have the air of a forced march. Khalip continues, "That sadness characterizes and vivifies a sense of absence is made clear in the way that certain habitual failures to attend both in and to the social world register the effect of various coercive routines of concealment" (147). Out of this experience of marginalization, Pater imagines an ideal type or character "whose first act of descent is a death, a self depleted by the simultaneous disappearance of the fields of sociality which are available for its self-realization" (141). In this sense, we may understand Pater's moment of ascesis not only as a withdrawal of the subject from the world but also as a withdrawal of the world from the subject.

In her account of Pater's historical romance, *Marius the Epicurean,* Maureen Moran writes that Pater draws attention to "the value of the excluded and the victimized."[9] This emphasis on the "heroic importance of the marginalized" is legible not only as a strategy for redefining Victorian manliness but also as a way of registering a particular experience of exclusion. In "Diaphaneitè," Pater describes the redemptive significance of his "basement type": "Over and over again the world has been surprised by the heroism, the insight, the passion, of this clear crystal nature. Poetry and poetical history have dreamed of a crisis, where it must needs be that some human victim be sent down into the grave. These are they whom in its profound emotion humanity might choose to send" (157–158). Pater's crystal character is defined not only by his transparency but also by his status as victim. Heroism, insight, and passion are here all bound up in an experience of martyrdom, even scapegoating, as this figure is sent to the grave by all of humanity.

Pater offers a specific image of the victim as hero in a story borrowed from Heine's *Gods in Exile,* reproduced in a chapter on Pico della Mirandola in *The Renaissance.* Heine's tale recounts the twilight existence of the Greek gods after the triumph of Christianity: rather than disappearing with the coming of Christianity, the pagan gods go into hiding and live their lives out in disguise, drinking beer instead of nectar. Pater cites Heine: "Let me briefly remind the reader . . . how the gods of the older world, at the time of the definite triumph of Christianity, that is, in the third century, fell into painful embarrassments, which greatly resembled certain tragical situations in their earlier life. They now found themselves beset by the same troublesome necessities to which they had once before been exposed during the primitive ages . . . Unfortunate gods! They had then to take flight ignominiously, and hide themselves among us here on earth, under all sorts of disguises" (21).

Pater is particularly concerned with the fate of Apollo, the god of light, who fell under suspicion "on account of his beautiful singing." A spiritual tribunal ensues, during which Apollo confesses his true identity "on the rack." Condemned to death, Apollo makes a last request: "Before his execution he begged that he might be suffered to play once more upon the lyre, and to sing a song. And he played so touchingly, and sang with such magic, and was withal so beautiful in form and feature, that all the women wept and many of them were so deeply impressed that they shortly afterwards fell sick" (21).

In part, this is a story of the triumph of the villagers, who force Apollo's confession before executing him: they not only discover him but also torture and bury him.[10] Still, the villagers are not content to let him lie in the grave, but dig him up to make sure that he is dead. The narrative continues: "some time afterwards the people wished to drag him from the grave again, that a stake might be driven through his body, in the belief that he had been a vampire, and that the sick women would by this means recover. But they found the grave empty" (21).

Heine's story demonstrates the strategic value of disappearance under a regime in which vigilance takes the form of identification and surveillance. The gods in Heine's story are already in disguise, but such a strategy of camouflage (or "fitting in") does not prove to be adequate. Apollo's most effective form of resistance is through sacrifice—his death at the hands of his torturers. It is only when he is dead that he is finally able to disappear completely, absenting himself from the grave they have sunk him in. In the final turn of this story, Apollo abandons the strategy of disappearance, revealing his identity in a performance that infects the locals with its beauty. We might understand Pater's own aestheticist practice in a similar vein; like Apollo, he "kills us softly" with his gorgeous prose.

In his conclusion to *The Renaissance,* Pater cites Victor Hugo: "Well! we are all condamnés, as Victor Hugo says: we are all under sentence of death, but with a sort of indefinite reprieve" (153). In this vision of a universal death sentence, we can read an allegory of Pater's historical position. His experience of displacement leads him not only to a politics of camouflage and disappearance but also to a politics of deferral. His investment in this story of the gods lingering on after they have been dispossessed is legible in terms of the lingering on of queer figures as the new era of homosexual identity approached. According to Khalip, Pater's crystal figures indicate the possibility of a transformed future without ever moving toward that future: "The crystal character is imbued with a type of visionary beauty specific to his (or its) diaphanous description, but this transparent, recuperative alien, most himself when he is not himself, can only remind us of the process of liberation he is meant to perform, without ever actually accomplishing it" (148).

The power of this figure for Pater is represented in terms of latency, potential, and delay: "Those who prosecute revolution have to violate again and again the instinct of reverence. That is inevitable, since after all progress is a kind of violence. But in this nature revolutionism is softened, harmonized, subdued as by a distance. It is the revolutionism of one who has slept a hundred years" (158). In such passages, Pater gestures toward an underworld politics that draws on the potential that gathers beneath and behind the visible social world. Rather than violate revolution, Pater recommends sleep. Rather than rise up against the onset of modernity, Pater responds to it with a weak refusal: he quails at its approach.

Intolerable Honor

In his chapter on Botticelli in *The Renaissance,* Pater traces a "middle world" in which "men take no side in great conflicts, and decide no great conflicts, and make great refusals." Pater specifically contrasts Botticelli's attitude toward these melancholy figures to Dante's: "what Dante scorns alike of heaven and hell, Botticelli accepts" (36). The explicit reference here, as Paul Tucker notes, is to Dante's consigning of "the neutral angels, together with the historical figures guilty of futility and indecision," to the vestibule of hell.[11] These indecisive, neutral angels are the subject of Pater's luminous essay on Botticelli. Taking his cue from a poem by Matteo Palmieri, Pater describes a "fantasy" that "represented the human race as an incarnation of those angels who, in the revolt of Lucifer, were neither for Jehovah nor for His enemies" (35). In this alternative genealogy, Pater suggests that humanity itself is the residue or trace of a failed or weak apostasy. Like their heavenly forebears, these human figures "take no side in great conflicts, and decide no great causes, and make great refusals" (36). Their gesture of apostasy is not an act of heroic revolution; rather, they take an almost imperceptible step back from God. They are marked by loss of an indeterminate nature, a sweet melancholy that infuses each gesture and look. This melancholy is intimately tied to their refusal to act, and, as Pater writes, these figures are "saddened perpetually by the great things from which they shrink" (36).

Pater never names the "great things" from which Botticelli's sad angels shrink, but we might read his description of the world they inhabit
as an allegory for spaces of male-male intimacy before the advent of
"homosexuality" as such. The queerness of Botticelli's figures is suggested by several of the traits that Pater ascribes to them—wistfulness, a
peculiar beauty, the air of victimization and underground existence that
marks them—but also by the particular quality of their exile, which is
described here as both a spatial and a temporal displacement. In tracing
the celestial genealogy of these figures, he writes:

> True or false, the story interprets much of the peculiar sentiment
> with which he infuses his profane and sacred subjects, comely, and
> in a certain sense like angels, but with a sense of displacement or
> loss about them—the wistfulness of exiles, conscious of a passion
> and energy greater than any known issue of them explains, which
> runs through all his varied work with a sentiment of ineffable melan-
> choly. (36)

The sense of loss about these figures seems to be a result of their alienation from dominant social structures: with only vaporous, insubstantial
parents and no known issue, these figures fall outside structures of kinship. Their place is not in the home, but they do not seem to belong in
the closet either. Rather, Pater seems to propose here an epistemology of
the vestibule, as he imagines a community of subjects defined through
indecision and delay. This liminal, semipublic space allows for a beautiful deferral and, one assumes, for the emergence of alternative forms
of sociability. As attractive as this world is, the air of melancholy that infuses it serves as a reminder of the fact that it is not a dwelling-place that
is freely chosen. One ends up there not by choice but rather by refusing
to choose.

The spatial displacement of these figures is matched by a temporal
displacement: they fall outside the home but also outside of the linear
narratives and ordered temporalities of blood kinship. These figures are
outside time, suspended in an endless present of indecision. While we
might think of the strange beauty of these figures as an effect of their resistance to age, they are also beautiful because they are "out of it," at a
distance from the pulsions of anticipation. Pater explicitly describes the
refusal of the future as beautiful in a passage on Greek sculpture in his
essay on Winckelmann. He writes:

In the best Greek sculpture, the archaic immobility has been stirred, its forms are in motion; but it is a motion ever kept in reserve, and very seldom committed to any definite action. Endless are the attitudes of Greek sculpture, exquisite as is the intervention of the Greeks in this direction, the actions or situations it permits are simple and few. There is no Greek Madonna; the goddesses are always childless. The actions selected are those which would be without significance, except in a divine person—binding on a sandal, or preparing for the bath. When a more complex and significant action is permitted, it is most often represented as just finished, so that eager expectancy is excluded. (139)

The beauty of these figures is specifically tied for Pater to their lack of expectancy and to their timeless embodiment of "motion in repose." The minute gestures of the statues invoke a timeless present, imaging forth a heaven in which nothing—or nothing of significance—ever happens. To be beautiful in Pater's view is to expect nothing, least of all a child. It is significant that reproduction itself is signaled as the culprit for linear temporality itself: the birth of a child is defined as the "great event" that demands the breaking up of immobility into a grasping expectancy.[12]

Despite Pater's equation of beauty with childlessness, he focuses on a mother in his chapter on Botticelli: the essay centers on that shy and shrinking figure, the Madonna of the Magnificat. For Pater, however, this figure is compelling precisely for the "great refusals" of which she is capable. Not only does this peevish mother seem to be the victim of an unwanted pregnancy, she also refuses the historical facts of the coming of Christ and of her own deification. Through her impassivity and melancholy, Botticelli's Madonna signals her weak protest; in the end, however, like Apollo, she is subject to a forced confession. Pater writes:

For Botticelli she too, though she holds in her hands the "Desire of all nations," is one of those who are neither for Jehovah nor for his enemies; and her choice is on her face. The white light on it is cast up hard and cheerless from below, as when snow lies upon the ground, and the children look up with surprise at the caress of the mysterious child, whose gaze is always far from her, and who has already that sweet look of devotion which men have never been able altogether to love, and which still makes the born saint an object almost of suspicion to his earthly brethren. Once, indeed, he guides her hand to transcribe in a book the words of her exaltation, the *Ave*, and the *Magnificat*, and the *Gaude Maria*, and the young angels, glad to rouse her for a moment from her dejection, are eager to hold the inkhorn and to support the book. But the pen almost drops from her hand, and the high cold words have no meaning for her, and her true children are those others, among whom, in her rude home, the intolerable honor came to her. (37)

The great event that Pater describes in his account of this painting is the birth of Christ, whose divinity casts a shadow over those who receive him. I understand this passage as a melancholic meditation on the inevitability of historical change. Pater's Madonna seems burdened by her knowledge of the profound difference that Christ's birth will make. Pater suggests that Mary is saddened in particular by the inevitability of her own deification as a result of having borne the Son of God. As he describes the infant Christ guiding his mother's hand to trace out the words of the Marian Liturgy, Pater suggests that the Virgin was exalted against her will.

I want to suggest that we might read this passage as an allegory of Pater's resistance to his future exaltation. The "intolerable honor" that came to him was the onset of late nineteenth-century modernity—and with it the birth of homosexuality as a newly public and newly recognizable social identity. Pater was situated on the verge of a new era of possibility for queer subjects, and his ambivalence about this historical development is palpable: his choice is on his face. In this image of the Madonna, Pater produces another image of forced confession, reminiscent of Apollo's singing before his execution. As in Heine's account of Apollo's final moments, being identified or named is tragic, and at the same time a moment of glorification.

What is lost in such transformations is suggested by the opening words of the *Magnificat*, one of the prayers Pater's Madonna is forced to copy out. The words of the prayer record Mary's response to her cousin Elizabeth's praise ("Blest are you among women and blest is the fruit of your womb") after her own unborn child leaps when she hears Mary's voice. The passage from Luke begins: "And Mary said: My soul proclaims the greatness of the Lord, and my spirit rejoices in God my Savior; because He has looked upon the humiliation of His servant. Yes, from now onwards, all generations will call me blessed." What is compelling to Pater about the figure of Mary is the contradiction she embodies: she is both God's humble servant and the Blessed Virgin, a kind of deity in her own right. What is depressing to Pater, it seems to me, about the moment of her glorification is that it entails the forgetting of her life of obscurity and servitude. Once God looks on her humiliation, it is transformed into glory: as if magically, her shame is transmuted into pride. Pater suggests that if such a deification means erasing the record of one's life on earth, it might be better to resist it. This shrinking, melancholic Madonna serves as a reminder of all those lost subjects. As unsettling as it is, this passage resonates in surprising ways for those future generations, contemporary queer subjects forced to copy out the *Ave* and the *Magnificat* of modern gay and lesbian identity.

The Great Refusal

Critics continue to disagree about the specific meaning of the great refusal in Dante's *Inferno,* arguing about whether this unnamed figure in the vestibule of hell is Celestine V, Boniface XIII, or Pontius Pilate. At the same time, the notion of the great refusal has been linked to a queer tradition of the refusal of reproduction and of the future-oriented temporality of the family. We might think, for instance, of the reworking of this passage from Dante in *Che fece . . . il gran refuto,* by the Greek modernist poet C. P. Cavafy:

> For some people the day comes
> when they have to declare the great Yes
> or the great No. It's clear at once who has the Yes
> ready within him, and saying it,
> he goes from honor to honor, strong in his conviction.
> He who refuses does not repent. Asked again,
> he'd still say no. Yet that no—the right no—
> drags him down all his life.[13]

Cavafy's poem adumbrates a model of queer subjectivity based on the experience of refusal, and on the failure to find the "great Yes" within. Cavafy suggests that this affirmation might be replaced by "the great No"—a form of refusal that, while linked to degradation, is nonetheless "right." Eve Kosofsky Sedgwick alludes to this poem of Cavafy's in the introduction to *Performance and Performativity,* when she argues that performatives can work negatively as well as positively.[14] Recent work on queer performativity has focused on the importance in J. L. Austin's work of positive performatives; Sedgwick and Judith Butler have both drawn attention to the importance for Austin of the example of "I do," the "great Yes" of the wedding ceremony. In this context, we might understand Cavafy's refusal, his "great No," as the inverse of "I do," a queer performative that is articulated in resistance to the heterosexual order.

Herbert Marcuse also takes up the idea of the great refusal in *Eros and Civilization* when he contrasts the rational, reproductive order of sexuality (identified here with the figure of Prometheus) with an alternative tradition of sexuality as pleasure and affirmation. Marcuse identifies this alternative tradition with two figures long associated with perverse desire, Orpheus and Narcissus. Prometheus, for Marcuse, defines the dominant image of the "culture-hero": "the trickster and (suffering) rebel against the gods, who creates culture at the price of perpetual pain. He symbolizes productiveness, the unceasing effort to master life; but, in his productivity, blessing and curse, progress and toil are inextricably intertwined."[15] The culture-making revolt of Prometheus is contrasted with the Orphic-Narcissistic revolt "against culture based on toil, domination, and renunciation" (164). While Prometheus is marked by suffering, his suffering is in the service of a higher aim: out of his rebellion and his work, he makes the future. Against the background of these dialectical struggles and reversals, Marcuse describes the powers of Orpheus and Narcissus as "the redemption of pleasure, the halt of time, the absorption of death; silence, sleep, night, paradise—the Nirvana pleasure not as death but as life" (164).

While Marcuse sees a great potential for liberation in the figures of Orpheus and Narcissus, he also describes the difficulty in translating these figures out of art and into politics. Describing the "order of gratification"—both aesthetic and sensual—that defines the Orphic-Narcissistic realm, he writes: "Static triumphs over dynamic; but it is a static that moves in its own fullness—a productivity that is sensuousness, play, and song. Any attempt to elaborate the images thus conveyed must be self-defeating, because outside the language of art they change their meaning and merge with the connotations they received under the repressive reality principle" (165). In Marcuse's description of a dynamic stillness and a static productivity realized in song, we hear echoes of Pater's aesthetic ideal. But as in the case of Pater's basement types, his drowsy revolutionaries, one gets the feeling that Orpheus and

Narcissus do not travel well. These are figures that are at home in the realm of art, but their interventions remain "isolated" and "unique" (209).

In describing the contrast between the Promethean world and the Orphic-Narcissistic world, Marcuse recapitulates the contrast between a heroic and a failed modernism. He writes:

> In contrast to the images of the Promethean culture-heroes, those of the Orphic and Narcissistic world are essentially unreal and unrealistic. They designate an "impossible" attitude and existence. The deeds of the culture-heroes also are "impossible," in that they are miraculous, incredible, superhuman. However, their objective and their "meaning" are not alien to the reality, on the contrary, they are useful. They promote and strengthen this reality; they do not explode it. But the Orphic-Narcissistic images do explode it; they do not convey a "mode of living"; they are committed to the underworld and to death. At best, they are poetic, something for the soul and the heart. But they do not teach any "message"—except perhaps the negative one that one cannot defeat death. (165)

In contrast to the heroic, active rebellion of Prometheus, Orpheus and Narcissus are defined by their withdrawal from the world of the real. These queer figures protest "against the repressive order of procreative sexuality. The Orphic and Narcissistic Eros," writes Marcuse, "is to the end the negation of this order—the Great Refusal" (171). The problem according to Marcuse, is how to make refusal count as anything more than refusal; the question is how to make a revolt against productivity productive rather than simply negative. Like Pater's victim-heroes, Orpheus and Narcissus are pledged to the underworld: whatever their designs on the world, they do not see the light of day.

Pater himself has been understood entirely through the terms of the Orphic-Narcissistic tradition: his drowsy, shrinking form of revolution has been understood as perfect for the aesthetic sphere, a mere impossibility in terms of politics. It is almost as if Cavafy were telling Pater's fortune in *Che fece . . . il gran refuto*: Pater found his no—the right no, the most beautiful no—and it dragged him down all his life. In rethinking this legacy, however, I want to suggest that we might understand the Orphic-Narcissistic world not only as an aesthetic mode but also as a "mode of living"—as an alternative form of political subjectivity.

In his essay "The Commitment to Theory," Homi Bhabha writes:

> The language of critique is effective not because it forever keeps sepa-
> rate the terms of the master and the slave, the mercantilist and the
> Marxist, but to the extent to which it overcomes the given grounds of
> opposition and opens up a space of translation: a place of hybridity,
> figuratively speaking, where the construction of a political object that
> is new, neither the one nor the other, properly alienates our political
> expectations, and changes, as it must, the very forms of our recogni-
> tion of the moment of politics.[16]

 If we are to discover new political objects, we need to rethink the structures and affects of political subjectivity and political expectation. We
want our politics to respond to inequalities of power, but we construct a
model of politics that has nothing in common with the experience of the
powerless. The modernist conception of political agency guards itself
against the traces of such a history. The fear, of course, is that the political consciousness that incorporates the "damage done" by social violence will be ineffectual, isolating, weak. I would suggest, however, the
streamlining of the political—of "proper" political subjectivities and
affects—excludes potential political subjects, in particular, those "unrecognizable" types who "cross rather than follow the main currents of
the world's life."

We might think of Foucault's *History of Sexuality* as another queer
site for the articulation of a politics of refusal. In this project, Foucault
aims to recast power as something other than a stark confrontation between the powerful and the powerless. Foucault's reframing of power is
legible as an attempt to rethink strategies of resistance in response to
shifting modes of domination. At the same time, we might understand
Foucault's rethinking of power as clearing the way for alternative forms
of political subjectivity. He writes, "Where there is power, there is resistance . . . These points of resistance are present everywhere in the
power network. Hence there is no single locus of great Refusal, no soul
of revolt, source of all rebellions, or pure law of the revolutionary"
(95–96). Foucault denies the concept that there is one great refusal,
suggesting instead that resistance is made up of an endless number of
refusals, a "plurality of resistances, each of them a special case" (96).
Given the history of queer refusal, we might read Foucault's theory
of power as an attempt to make room for "special cases"—to create a

politics for subjects who do not credibly embody the "pure law of the revolutionary."

The historical experience of shame and secrecy has left its imprint on queer subjectivity. The effects of this history are often understood simply as historical waste products, visible traces of homophobia considered shaming in themselves. Rather than denying or trying to "get over" this past, however, queer subjects might begin to forge a politics that keeps faith with those who drew back and those whose names were forgotten. Those subjects do not wake up after a century haunting the underworld ready to plunge ahead into a glorious future. Engaging with and using the experience of failure as a resource is crucial to the construction of a model of political subjectivity that we can all live with. The example of Pater's shrinking resistance suggests that we need to rethink the heroics of rebellion and to begin to imagine a politics that incorporates a history of forced exile. Such a "homeopathic" approach to political subjectivity incorporates rather than disavows the causes of social inequality. Given the ruination to which history's others are subject, we need to recognize and even affirm forms of ruined political subjectivity. I want to suggest that we need a politics forged in the image of exile, of refusal, even of failure. Such a politics might offer, to quote that beautiful loser Nick Drake, "a troubled cure for a troubled mind."[17]

3

The End of Friendship

Willa Cather's Sad Kindred

We are first of all, as friends, the friends of solitude, and we are calling on you to share what cannot be shared.

—Jacques Derrida, *The Politics of Friendship*

Willa Cather's 1936 collection of essays, *Not under Forty,* is prefaced by a note warning away young readers. The passage signals Cather's increasing literary and social conservatism; it also marks a break between her and her future audience. It reads:

> The title of this book is meant to be "arresting" only in the literal sense, like the signs put up for motorists: "ROAD UNDER REPAIR," etc. It means that the book will have little interest for people under forty years of age. The world split in two in 1922 or thereabouts, and the persons and prejudices recalled in these sketches slid back into yesterday's seven thousand years. Thomas Mann, to be sure, belongs immensely to the forward-goers, and they are concerned only with his forwardness. But he also goes back a long way, and his backwardness is more gratifying to the backward. It is for the backward, and by one of their number, that these sketches were written.[1]

Not under Forty offers a fairly complete statement of Cather's antimodernism. Throughout the book, Cather expresses her disdain for the new, the cheap, the fast, the mass-produced, and the "smart." No one speeding toward the future will have patience for this book, with its renunciations, its refusals, and its insistent orientation toward the past.

This note also makes legible Cather's powerful and lifelong ambivalence about the possibility of community and connection across time. The essays collected in the volume are works of literary criticism, and they range from statements of her aesthetics ("The Novel Démeublé") to reflections on individual works ("Joseph and His Brothers") to personal memoir and recollection ("A Chance Meeting," "148 Charles Street"). *Not under Forty* narrates Cather's attempts to forge connections with the literary and historical past by means of auratic, personal contacts with individuals and objects. She offers many examples of what Carolyn Dinshaw has described as "queer touches across time": she attempts to draw close to the past, to feel its warmth. At the same time, such approaches mostly take place in the shadow of death; they are, at best, a matter of chance, and the desire for intimacy is coupled with the threat of destruction and disconnection. Though Cather suggests that reaching the past might be a matter of easily drifting backward, the essays narrate a series of near misses and disappointments. The sign ROAD UNDER REPAIR to which Cather compares her title suggests that there may be no way to get there from here.

Cather repeatedly stages the pathos of her efforts to reach figures from the literary past; she also invites her readers to identify with those efforts, creating through allusion and personal narrative an intimacy with the reader. Still, it is not clear to what extent we are to share in her disappointments. By questioning the ability of anyone under forty years of age to read her book, Cather suggests that not only young people but also all future readers may be excluded. Of course, her refusal is partly ironic, as she does not exclude all future readers, only those middle-of-the-road readers who take such signs at face value.[2] Cather reaches out to readers who are exceptional—those who disidentify with the culture of the present and whose attention is turned toward the difficult and the outmoded. This exclusive invitation is not merely coy, however; Cather means to keep some readers out. Such a refusal raises the stark difficulty of forming a community of the backward: backwardness. The backward slide into the past, away from futurity, away from remembrance, away from us.

Cather's backwardness poses serious difficulties for contemporary critics hoping to forge a connection with her. Christopher Nealon has introduced the concept of "affect-genealogy" to account for the peculiarity and ambivalence of her historical longings, and to describe more generally how early twentieth-century queer subjects imagine communities across time. In this chapter, I take up Nealon's notion of "affect-genealogy" to think again through the problem of claiming Cather as

"one of ours" given her refusal of the future. This problem has been ex-
acerbated by a series of debates about whether or not it is legitimate to
name Cather as queer at all. Cather herself provides plenty of evidence
against such reading; although she dressed as a young man in her teenage
years, wrote love letters to her female friends in college, and lived with
her companion Edith Lewis for more than thirty years, she never identified herself with any emergent modern homosexual subcultures. In fact,
she was consistently hostile toward public expressions of same-sex desire. Cather has also been subject across the century to the usual denials
by literary critics. Although such refusals to read homosexuality as
meaningful in Cather's work have been largely addressed by feminist,
lesbian, and queer work over the past few decades, Joan Acocella's
polemic against this body of scholarship has had the effect of de-
queering Cather for a general readership.[3]

Identifying Cather as queer does not, however, solve the difficulty of
how to situate her in a queer literary genealogy. One still has to reckon
not only with Cather's notorious ambivalence toward gender and sexual
deviance but also with her backwardness—by which I mean not only
her turn toward the past but also her abiding interest in loneliness, historical isolation, and death. Recently, some critics have suggested that
we might consider friendship as an alternative way to frame intimacy
within Cather's works and as a model for understanding our own queer
relations with her. Such a turn makes sense not only in terms of Cather's
deep interest in friendship but also in terms of a turn to friendship in recent queer attempts to rethink intimacy beyond the family and the
couple.

Friendship does in fact seem to me the most promising way of understanding the idiosyncratic intimacies that define Cather's fiction. I
think, however, that we need a more complex and conflict-laden understanding of friendship in order to do justice to Cather's work.
Friendship is a highly idealized form of intimacy in queer studies and
in queer culture, and in this sense it cannot account for Cather's understanding of friendship as marked by betrayal, disappointment, loss,
and impossibility. Cather's backwardness suggests that she is a friend of
the backward; it also suggests that she may not be our friend, or not in
a way that we would recognize. In this chapter, I consider representations of friendship and relations across time in *Not under Forty* and in
Cather's 1925 novel *The Professor's House*. I also reflect on the history

and afterlife of female romantic friendship by turning to Cather's meeting with Sarah Orne Jewett, narrated in two essays in *Not under Forty.* Jewett is much more readily identified than Cather with an idealized version of nineteenth-century romantic friendship. Nonetheless, I find there are surprising resonances between Cather and Jewett's representations of friendship. Such unexpected continuities suggest that we may have overstated the importance of the break between nineteenth-century romantic friendship and modern homosexuality. It also suggests that the discourse of ideal friendship has flattened the real affective complexity of this bond. I gesture toward an alternative trajectory of queer friendship marked by impossibility, disconnection, and loss and turn to recent philosophical rethinkings of friendship in order to suggest that impossible or interrupted intimacy may offer a model for queer history both before and after the invention of modern homosexuality.

Our Good Friends

The recent interest in friendship in queer studies was preceded by lesbian-feminist attention to the history of female romantic friendship in the 1970s and early 1980s. This model of "primary intensity" between women, closely allied to Adrienne Rich's concept of the lesbian continuum, de-emphasized the erotic aspect of relations between women and privileged instead affective intensity, mutual support, and the freedom of self-definition.[4] At the moment of its ascendance, this model helped make sense of women's relationships both in the past and in the present. In her 1981 study, *Surpassing the Love of Men,* Lillian Faderman drew a direct line from the affective bonds of famous "couples" like the Ladies of Llangollen and Michael Field to the lesbian-feminist couples of the 1970s; at the same time, she lamented the "dark days," stretching from the advent of sexology to the rise of second-wave feminism. Faderman speculated that the "romantic friends of other eras would probably have felt entirely comfortable in many lesbian-feminist relationships."[5] Whether or not this was true, it was certainly the case that many lesbian-feminists took comfort by imagining themselves in the romantic friendships of the past.

The idealized image of passionate, gender-separatist, and possibly-maybe sexual relations between women did not survive the sex wars of the 1980s or the general darkening in tone of lesbian representation in the 1990s. Terry Castle's dismissal of the Ladies of Llangollen in her 1993 book, *The Apparitional Lesbian,* gives some idea of how deeply the discourse of romantic friendship was discredited during that time. Although these retiring Scottish ladies were once seen as icons of romantic lesbian bliss, Castle considers "this insufferable old pair" only to wonder if "it may not indeed be time to revise the often cloying 'romantic friendship' model."[6] In the past couple of decades, critics and historians have launched an attack on the idealized discourse of female friendship on several fronts: not only was it very likely that these ladies were "doing it" all along, but this limited, upper- and middle-class discourse could hardly account, they argued, for the full range of erotic and affective bonds between women before 1900.

It seems clear that this particular version of romantic friendship holds little appeal in the contemporary moment, when critical interest has turned away from the "profoundly female experience" of lesbianism to "gender trouble" and "sexual dissidence."[7] Yet while female romantic friendship has become increasingly marginal, attention to both the history and the philosophy of friendship has been reactivated in queer studies. Even in the midst of the turn to stigma, shame, and bad sex, friendship remains a kind of sacred space, a consistently idealized model of same-sex relations. In his late interview, "Friendship as a Way of Life," Michel Foucault laid down a foundation for this recent work as he invoked friendship as an alternative form of intimacy, a utopian space beyond the constraints of marriage and the family. In tracing the fluctuating fortunes of the friendship concept in gay, lesbian, and queer criticism, it is interesting to note that in this interview Foucault approvingly cites Faderman's *Surpassing the Love of Men.* In the intervening years, Faderman's work has been called utopian, desexualizing, and essentialist, while Foucault's work on friendship has been central to queer rethinkings of intimacy and the social.

Friendship plays an important role in queer history. Clearly idealized within a Greek homoerotic context, friendship in the West from the Renaissance to the nineteenth century constitutes a site for the exploration of same-sex intimacies relatively free from stigma. Jonathan Ned Katz's 2001 book, *Love Stories,* for instance, focuses on the alternative forms of intimacy explored by men in the nineteenth century, before the distinction between gay and straight was consolidated. Histories of same-sex relations "before homosexuality" hold out possibilities for a renewal of social and sexual relations in the present. Across the twentieth century, friendship provided an alternative to family and marriage for many gay people; the widespread notion of a friendship network as a gay or queer "family" arises from the historical exclusion of gay people from their birth families and from the institution of marriage. In contemporary gay and lesbian life, the valorization of friendship as a less obligatory and highly structured form of intimacy in queer culture spans great ideological divides: people who agree about little else tend to agree that an ethics of friendship as well as related forms of nonbiological kinship are among the greatest achievements of queer culture.[8]

Friendship also holds a particular appeal for queer theory. The field of queer studies emerges in part in the early 1990s out of a frustration with the limitations and exclusions of identity politics. Queer studies turns against the notion of fixed categories of sexual orientation and the essentialist gender categories that anchor them. In the collective effort to undermine a strict division between heterosexuality and homosexuality, queer scholars have looked to models of sexual and gender behavior that exceed the normative bounds of "modern gay identity." The history of friendship is a particularly attractive archive for the exploration of same-sex relations, partly because of the relative absence of stigma, and partly because of the relatively unstructured nature of friendship as a mode of intimacy.

In addition to these explanations for the queer interest in friendship, I think there is another one that has received less attention. Over the long course of Western history, friendship has been at the very top of the hierarchy of intimate relations; during that same period, same-sex desire and love have been among the most denigrated forms of intimacy. In the queer attention to friendship, there is a natural desire of the stigmatized to draw on the energies of what remains a powerfully idealized social form. The long philosophical tradition of friendship that sees this relation as a model of equality, reciprocity, and longevity proves almost irresistible to the bearers of a form of love understood to be nasty, brutish, and short.

According to a tradition reaching back to Aristotle, friendship is seen as an autonomous space, as free from the machinations of power as it is from the shocks of desire. Friendship is understood to be noninstrumental; its lack of a determinate end is one of the main factors distinguishing it from eros. Comparing "affection for women" and friendship between men in his essay on friendship, Montaigne writes that love is

> more active, more scorching, and more intense. But it is an impetuous and fickle flame, undulating and variable, a fever flame, subject to fits and lulls, that holds us only by one corner. In friendship it is a general and universal warmth . . . with nothing bitter and stinging about it. What is more, in love there is nothing but a frantic desire for what flees from us . . . As soon as it enters the boundaries of friendship, that is to say harmony of wills, it grows faint and languid. Enjoyment destroys it, as having a fleshly end, subject to society satiety. Friendship, on the contrary, is enjoyed according as it is desired.[9]

For Montaigne, love burns us, while friendship spreads a "general and universal warmth": friendship, or *philia*, moves away from eros and toward the universal love of the neighbor, *caritas*. It holds out the promise of an autonomous space away from the tremors of eroticism, and also from eros's relentless narrative logic of pursuit, consummation, and exhaustion. Being with the friend is an end in itself. There is no orgasm of friendship; wedding bells do not ring for friends.

The ideal of friendship has had a significant afterlife in queer thought. In "Friendship as a Way of Life," Foucault suggests cultivating a mode of existence in which friendship would be central. Questioning the tendency to always ask, "What is the secret of my desire?" Foucault writes, "Perhaps it would be better to ask oneself, 'What relations, through homosexuality, can be established, invented, multiplied and modulated?' " Friendship for Foucault is an alternative form of relation enabled by the advent of homosexuality. It is for this reason, he writes, that "homosexuality is not a form of desire but something desirable." Friendship holds out the promise of a "naked" relation, a fragile space outside of the institutional logics of marriage, "professional camaraderie," and routinized sexual encounters. The space Foucault describes, however, is hardly the transcendent space of eternal, harmonic, coupled friendship that Montaigne points to in his ambiently homoerotic essay. Friendship appears here as a relatively uncharted and labile space of relations traversed in multiple and unpredictable ways by desire. Foucault writes, "It's a desire, an uneasiness, a desire-in-uneasiness that exists among a lot of people." Foucault's motion of friendship draws on the philosophical canon of friendship, and it opens this discourse to disturbing and unexpected currents of desire and social refusal.[10]

The shift Foucault sketches away from homosexuality as a fixed identity to homosexuality as an undiscovered horizon of relational and ontological possibilities has had an enormous appeal for queer readers. His brief, suggestive remarks in this interview have been profoundly influential in the field. Still, queer writing on friendship tends to emphasize fairly familiar and reassuring qualities of friendship over uneasiness, desire, or the "improbable."[11] In a chapter titled "The Friendship Ethic" in *Same Sex Intimacies,* Jeffrey Weeks, Brian Heaphy, and Catherine Donovan approvingly cite Foucault and suggest that nonheterosexual friendship "continues to disrupt radically the conventional boundaries and separations in everyday life" and that such friendships "make life experiments possible."[12] The authors interview a diverse range of queer women and men, and present firsthand accounts of such life experiments. Yet the elements of what the authors ultimately describe as the friendship ethic— "care, responsibility, respect, and knowledge"—do not necessarily capture the uneasiness and the trouble that might be expected to accompany ongoing experimentalism. Rather, these characteristics represent a familiar catalogue of attitudes and behaviors associated with ethical treatment of the other.[13]

I do not want to suggest that nonheterosexual friendship networks are not characterized by experimentalism and by mutual care and respect. In many ways, such a description offers a good account of the kinds of alternative arrangements in which many queer people do actually find themselves. What I want to point to instead is the stabilizing role that this version of friendship plays in imagining queer existence and queer community. Friendship has played this role in an official capacity recently. In the activist call for alternatives to the same-sex marriage platform, friendship has been forwarded as a form of relation that is tied neither to the conjugal couple nor to blood kinship, but nonetheless presents a legible and generally appealing image of caring and intimacy.

In a section of the general statement of the organization Beyond Marriage entitled "The Longing for Community and Connectedness," the authors reflect on the inadequacy of the marriage form in meeting the needs of LGBT people.

So many people in our society and throughout the world long for a sense of caring community and connectedness, and for the ability to have a decent standard of living and pursue meaningful lives free from the threat of violence and intimidation. We seek to create a movement that addresses this longing.

So many of us long for communities in which there is systemic affirmation, valuing, and nurturing of difference, and in which conformity to a narrow and restricting vision is never demanded as the price of admission to caring civil society. Our vision is the creation of communities in which we are encouraged to explore the widest range of non-exploitive, non-abusive possibilities in love, gender, desire and sex—and in the creation of new forms of constructed families without fear that this searching will potentially forfeit for us our right to be honored and valued within our communities and in the wider world. Many of us, too, across all identities, yearn for an end to repressive attempts to control our personal lives. For LGBT and queer communities, this longing has special significance.[14]

With a nod to the historic exclusion of LGBT people from dominant forms of intimacy—marriage and the family—the Beyond Marriage statement acknowledges the specificity of queer longing for community. While such an acknowledgment might preface a call for the legalization of same-sex marriage, the statement actually risks this acknowledgment in the context of a call for a departure from limited and limiting forms of state-sponsored intimacy; it gestures toward an expanded and as yet unmapped field of relations. The risky utopianism of the Beyond Marriage movement is undeniable: they aim to address social exclusion and the special longing that it produces; at the same time, they resist the most obvious "solutions" to that longing. Such a move draws on the historical importance of friendship and alternative, nonbiological kinship for LGBT people. But such alternatives and the consolations that they provide have hardly been perfect. That fact—and not simply conservative conformism—accounts for the powerful appeal of gay marriage, and for the "special" quality of longing that queer people feel. The attempt to address that longing directly is blunted, in this statement, by the presentation of community as an unambiguous guarantor of intimacy and care.[15]

Such accounts do not admit the trouble and unease that are at the heart of friendship. In a well-known moment in "Friendship as a Way of Life," Foucault claims that it is not homosexual sex that poses a challenge to general social norms but rather new forms of homosexual intimacy. There is little to disturb in the expected image of "two young men meeting in the street, seducing each other with a look, grabbing each other's asses and getting each other off in a quarter of an hour." Foucault writes that "there you have a kind of neat image of homosexuality without any possibility of generating unease, and for two reasons: it responds to a reassuring canon of beauty, and it cancels everything that can be troubling in affection, tenderness, friendship, fidelity, camaraderie, and companionship" (136). Foucault's reflections on queer friendship gesture not only toward the possibility of new forms of intimacy and pleasure, but also toward an enhanced recognition of what can be troubling in affection and companionship. Because friendship has historically been a salve for queer forms of intimacy trouble, queer thought has generally presented friendship as trouble free. Yet that same history might allow us to think about queer ways of life and forms of intimacy that include trouble, and even make it central.

Together and Alone

One of Cather's most important representations of male friendship is the relationship between Godfrey St. Peter and his student Tom Outland in her 1925 novel *The Professor's House*. Although the Midwestern history professor has had a lifelong orientation toward the past—he has been engaged for decades in writing a multivolume account of the Spanish Conquest—he is initiated into backwardness by the appearance of this brilliant young student. Tom inspires a longing in St. Peter that he cannot account for but which eventually severs him from his family and from a larger sense of obligation to the social. The Professor freezes in his tracks. As Anna Wilson notes, the novel is characterized by a "will to stasis": the entire first section ("The Family") is organized around the Professor's reluctance to join his wife in the new house that he has built for them.[16] Clinging to the past, the Professor returns each day to work in the attic of the old house, refusing to sell the empty house and to break with the past. What is perhaps most striking about St. Peter's story is that Tom does not really begin to affect him until after his death.

All of Godfrey St. Peter's longings point toward the past, toward earlier moments in history and in his own life. Though such pleasures are best enjoyed alone, Godfrey is occasionally able to commune with others through the ambiguous pleasures of regret and melancholic longing. Normally, the members of his biological family are strictly excluded from such reveries. But at a performance of the opera *Mignon* that he attends with his wife, Lillian, he begins to recall an earlier time of "sweet, impersonal emotions."[17]

> "My dear," he sighed when the lights were turned on and they both looked older, "it's been a mistake, our having a family and writing histories and getting middle-aged. We should have been picturesquely shipwrecked together when we were young."
>
> "How often I have thought that!" she replied with a faint, melancholy smile.
>
> "You? But you're so occupied with the future, you adapt yourself so readily," he murmured in astonishment.
>
> "One must go on living, Godfrey. But it wasn't the children who came between us." There was something lonely and forgiving in her voice, something that spoke of an old wound, healed and hardened and hopeless.
>
> "You, you too?" he breathed in amazement. (78)

In the daily rhythms of family life, Godfrey withdraws completely from Lillian, who represents the exigencies of the present and the future—the imperative to go on living. In this moment of temporary reprieve, he is able to see his wife's loneliness—her disappointment and her unresolved mourning for past losses. Though Lillian does not say much (and most of what she says is negative), Godfrey reads in his wife's bearing and hears in her voice a welcoming backwardness. What he shares with her in this moment is not only an orientation toward the past or a shared set of losses but also a new closeness grounded in a fantasy of early death; he imagines a catastrophe that might have relieved them from the need to go on living. The connection that Godfrey feels to Lillian is circuited through lack; what brings them together is what they did not have (shipwreck) or might have had (shared death) rather than anything that they might actually share in the present (children, domestic space, the presence of the other).

While this fantasy brings husband and wife together for a moment, the novel suggests that marriage is too tied to the demands of the future—the necessity of making do and moving on—to accommodate this kind of intimacy in any sustained way. Godfrey's sense of communion with Lillian is soon broken; later that night, as he lies in bed, his mind returns to the image of a shipwreck, but now the image breaks away from the scene of his marriage:

That night, after he was in bed, among unaccustomed surroundings and a little wakeful, St. Peter still played with his idea of a picturesque shipwreck, and he cast about for the particular occasion he would have chosen for such a finale. Before he went to sleep he found the very day, but his wife was not in it. Indeed, nobody was in it but himself, and a weather-dried little sea captain from the Hautes-Pyrénées, half a dozen spry seamen, and a line of gleaming snow peaks, agonizingly high and sharp, along the southern coast of Spain. (78–79)

St. Peter's replaying of the shipwreck pulls him out of the scene of family life and recalls him to his youth, to the boat trip during which he conceived his history, *Spanish Adventurers in North America* (89). Without Lillian, he imagines a space of male homosociality, a landscape characterized by masculine hardness and abstraction. The company of silent men seems to offer an ideal alternative to the deadening routines of family life. At the same time, these men are in some way beside the point. Though it is clear that Lillian is "not in it," it is not immediately apparent that anyone else is either. Here, Cather evokes an impersonal erotic; though we eventually realize that the Professor is not alone on this fantasized or remembered ship, it nonetheless appears that the gleaming and uninhabitable snow peaks are as much the object of his desire as the spry seamen.

The family that is at the center of the novel's first section hardly ever affords St. Peter such rarefied pleasures; instead, they give him a headache. Scenes of male homosociality, by contrast, have an almost magical effectiveness in *The Professor's House*: they extract St. Peter from heterosexual domesticity, they release powerful creative energies, and they bring the present into contact with the past. St. Peter lives imaginatively in such worlds in his research; at the university, he experiences this charge in his rivalry with other professors and in the classroom. The only thing that compares to these group scenes is St. Peter's time alone: Cather's descriptions of his days working in the attic or swimming at the lake are, many of them, startlingly erotic. Because of this tension between the vitalizing company of other men and the metaphysical satisfactions of isolation, Tom Outland's ghost is St. Peter's perfect companion.

Tom, not incidentally the inventor of the Outland engine, is an apt conductor of the electric charge of male-male eroticism. St. Peter's friendship with Tom is the most important and perfect relationship of his life: apart from that, he insists that his "good years" were "largely wasted" (50). Tom appears almost as a figment of the Professor's solitary imaginings. The boy appears as if out of nowhere, without family and without connections, "so well fitted by nature and early environment to help [the Professor] with his work on the Spanish Adventurers" (39). Tom entrusts St. Peter with the story of his adventure among Indian ruins on the Blue Mesa in the American Southwest, adding to the Professor's store of fantasies. Even more obligingly, Tom suffers an early and picturesque death as a soldier in World War I. Through his death, Tom gives the gift of his absence, an absence that occupies St. Peter so intently that, during the summer his family is in France, he withdraws from his domestic obligations, from the social world, and, in the end, quite nearly, from the realm of the living.

The nature of the Professor's relationship with Tom is reflected in some measure by Lillian's jealous response to it. In a conversation that takes place after St. Peter refuses to join the family on a trip to France for the summer, however, Lillian suggests that the relationship has incited a more complex emotion in her.

> "Godfrey," she said slowly and sadly, "I wonder what it is that makes you draw away from your family. Or who it is."
> "My dear, are you going to be jealous?"
> "I wish I were going to be. I'd much rather see you foolish about some woman than becoming lonely and inhuman." (141)

While Lillian leaves unspoken the possibility of her jealousy over "some man," she suggests that it would actually be a relief to see Godfrey involved with anyone, instead of his being in a state of perpetual withdrawal—"lonely and inhuman." Nonetheless, the equivocation in her question to him about whether it is "a who or a what" that draws him away from his family is crucial. Godfrey responds to her query by saying that he has become used to living with ideas, yet, as Cather repeatedly indicates, it is not the Professor's work but rather his friendship with Tom that has come between Godfrey and his family. It remains unclear whether Tom is a who or a what for St. Peter.

During the summer, as he reads Tom's manuscript, Godfrey becomes more and more isolated. Allowing himself to be haunted by Tom, St. Peter embarks on a new friendship—with his boyhood self, "the original, unmodified Godfrey St. Peter" (239). The internal erotics of the Professor's relationship with this Kansas boy finally edge into something even more solitary. As he realizes that he does not want to live with his family again and that he has fallen out of love with his wife, Godfrey begins to fall even further: "Falling out, for him, seemed to mean falling out of all domestic and social relations, out of his place in the human family, indeed" (250). It is in this state that St. Peter falls asleep in his study with the stove on and, in an ambiguous and passive suicide, nearly achieves the end he has fantasized about earlier. He survives only because he is carried out of the room by Augusta, the family's seamstress, at which point he gives in to the demand to "go on living" and reluctantly rejoins his family.

Tom is the Professor's friend not only because he leaves him so utterly alone but also because he carries within him a history both of male intimacy and of extreme loneliness. The middle section of *The Professor's House* is given over to "Tom Outland's Story," Tom's first-person account of his time on the mesa. The account begins with a classic story of eroticized working-class male friendship between Tom and his friend Roddy Blake—what Scott Herring describes as a "Whitmanian model of friendship between dissimilar comrades."[18] Roddy and Tom, together with their friend Henry, eventually set up house while they are employed herding cattle. Describing the "shining cabin" they share, Tom comments that "the three of us made a happy family" (176). The happiness of this impromptu, all-male family is sharply contrasted, of course, with the misery of St. Peter's family relations in the novel's present.

Eve Kosofsky Sedgwick refers to Cather's lyrical descriptions of alternative intimacy along the American frontier as a "gorgeous homosocial romance."[19] Reading "Tom Outland's Story," it is hard to miss the romance or the beauty. Yet there is a sense in which this story does not really begin until this ideal male-male intimacy has been shattered. The romance is intensified when the men discover an intact but empty Indian village on top of the Blue Mesa. Tom and Roddy and Henry work together, sharing in a project of amateur anthropology. Their idyll is broken by Harry's sudden accidental death and, later, by what Tom understands as Roddy's betrayal. Tom leaves to go to Washington, D.C., to try to find a museum interested in the artifacts from the mesa. While he is gone, Roddy sells off the artifacts to a German trader, intending to split the money with Tom. Tom fiercely attacks Roddy, accusing him of having betrayed their friendship and their country. Roddy leaves the mesa and Tom never sees him again.

Although Harry's death and Roddy's departure mark an end to Tom's period of male-male intimacy, these events actually drive the transformation in him that is the real subject of his "Story." The scene of Roddy's departure marks the beginning of this transformation. After Tom forces him to leave, Roddy lowers himself off the mesa in darkness; as Tom watches, he is filled with a longing that will never again be satisfied.

> By this time my eyes had grown accustomed to the darkness, and I could see Blake quite clearly—the stubborn, crouching set of his shoulders that I used to notice when he first came to Pardee and was drinking all the time. There was an ache in my arms to reach out and detain him, but there was something that made me absolutely powerless to do so. He stepped down and settled his foot into the first fork. Then he stopped a moment and straightened his pack, buttoned his coat up to the chin, and pulled his hat on tighter. There was always a night draught in the canyon. He gripped the trunk with his hands. "Well," he said with grim cheerfulness, "here's luck! And I am glad it's you that's doing this to me, Tom; not me that's doing it to you."
>
> His head disappeared below the rim. I could hear the trees creak under his heavy body, and the chains rattle a little at the splicings. I lay down on the ledge and listened. I could hear him for a long way down, and the sounds were comforting to me, though I didn't realize it. Then the silence closed in. I went to sleep that night hoping I would never awaken. (224)

In this scene, Cather describes a version of what Walter Benjamin, in a very different context, would call "love at last sight." It is only as Roddy is leaving, as his body withdraws into a solitary hunch, his head dips out of sight, and the sound of his movement fades away, that Tom feels the force of his attraction to him. It is significant that Tom's response to Roddy's departure is marked by complete passivity: he longs to reach out for him but cannot move his arms; once he is really gone, Tom lies down in a passive suicidal stupor that doubles the professor's nearly fatal inertia at the end of the novel. Lying down to die in the face of the other's absence seems, at these moments, to be the highest expression of male-male love.

Tom, like the Professor, recovers from his swoon. As it turns out, it is his time alone on the mesa—like St. Peter's solitary summer—that defines what is most significant in his story. After Roddy's departure, Tom experiences a new sense of elation; he describes the "religious emotion" that overtook him in his final months there, what he calls a "filial piety" for the mesa itself (226–227). These months of solitude are the best moments of Tom's life. "I can scarcely hope that life will give me another summer like that one," his narrative reads. "It was my high tide. Every morning, when the sun's rays first hit the mesa top, while the rest of the world was in shadow, I wakened with the feeling that I had found everything, instead of having lost everything" (227). Against the backdrop of historical extinction, Tom experiences an unparalleled vitality—a fullness that is hardly to be distinguished from death. While "Tom Outland's Story" is in some sense a story of friendship, it is also a tale of "heartlessness" (228)—isolation, withdrawal, and communion with a world at once inhuman and dead. That this story is able to touch St. Peter and move him toward a similar state of isolation and inhumanity suggests the strange force of friendship for Cather: it is as much a solvent of human relations as it is a form of sociability.

Hermeneutic Friends

In his recent essay, "Catherian Friendship," Scott Herring argues that Cather "refuses the movement from friendship to homosexuality in order to wreck the designs of a legible urban sexual history, and to fracture the historical shift from passionate same-sex friendship to discernable homosexual (or, for that matter, heterosexual) identity."[20] As Herring points out, Cather's embrace of friendship as a model for same-sex relations presents a problem for contemporary critics hoping to claim her as a queer ancestor. Queer critics reading the suppressions, impossibilities, and failed relationships in Cather are tempted to fantasize for her characters, as Herring says, "happier endings" (66)—recognizably queer trajectories for their lonely and thwarted lives. Herring suggests that rather than writing Cather into the progressive history of twentieth-century sexuality, we might instead take seriously her refusal of this narrative—to see her as "uninterested in the novel formations of modern sexual identity" and as interested instead in "unforeseen designs for same-sex friendships" (68). Thus, rather than reading the relation between Tom and the Professor as a frustrated gay romance, we might take it at face value, as an alternative form of friendship.

Herring offers an important challenge to the progress narrative of twentieth-century gay and lesbian existence. He points to the backwardness of Cather's choice and its power to disrupt the taken-for-granted quality of queer life in the present. More contentious is Herring's suggestion that a turn from thwarted homosexuality toward friendship would be a way to interrupt fantasies of "happier endings" for Cather's characters. The alternative modes of friendship that Herring sees as the positive outcome of the "supposed failures" of more explicitly sexual same-sex relations in Cather's work might not satisfy certain desires for historical rescue—the desire, for instance, to give all the lonely queers of the past the gorgeous romance they deserve. Nonetheless, the "new alliances" that Herring points to lie at the endpoint of another queer narrative of progress: one that sees the "friendship ethic" as the highest achievement of queer culture.[21]

The idealization of queer friendship is central to Christopher Nealon's method of "affect-genealogy" in his book *Foundlings*. Nealon describes the way that twentieth-century gay and lesbian subjects attempt to find a place in history—to "feel historical"—by imagining alternative forms of community or queer kinship. For Nealon, queer texts are traversed by powerful longings that are both corporeal and historical; in their inarticulate hopes and desires, these texts gesture both toward impossible affiliations and a queer community across time. Nealon's chapter on Cather in *Foundlings* focuses on the desires that bring together the lonely and passionate outsiders that populate her fiction. Nealon reads Cather's prefatory note to *Not under Forty* as a dedication to her "perpetually vanishing friends," an attempt to articulate a community "somewhere between family and nation—a movement" (67–68).

Nealon considers the creation of affect-genealogies through powerfully invested practices of reading. "Foundling texts" anticipate future readers and are fully realized through a peculiarly invested practice of reception. Nealon meditates on Gertrude Stein's assertion in her 1903 story, "The Making of Americans," that "it takes time to make queer people."[22] Foundling texts "take time to make" as well. They are structured by a particular kind of temporal desire and take on their full meaning only with the emergence of a particular kind of reader. Nealon writes:

Because [foundling texts] do not properly belong either to the inert, terminal narratives of inversion or to the triumphant, progressive narrative of achieving ethnic coherence, they suggest another time, a time of expectation, in which their key stylistic gestures, choice of genre, and ideological frames all point to an inaccessible future, in which the inarticulate desires that mobilize them will find some "hermeneutic friend" beyond the historical horizon of their unintelligibility to themselves. (23)

Foundling texts express a desire for an "inaccessible future," for forms of life and community that are impossible in their own historical moment. These texts inhabit a "time of expectation," as they wait for the friends who will know how to read them.

Nealon suggests instead that such historical desires are crucial in making contact with the past. He writes, "These politics are bigger-hearted: they are an attempt to understand, through an identification with an ancestor, how history works, what it looks like, what possibilities it has offered in the past, and what those possibilities suggest about our ineffable present tense" (96). Contemporary readers attend to longings for futurity in these texts as a way to learn about history and its possibilities. By identifying with these often submerged or half-articulate desires, critics expand the horizon of historical possibility in foundling texts. In this sense, we might say that their "love" represents the outer limit of these texts' historical possibility.

Nealon offers a resonant and far-reaching account of the phenomenology of queer reading in the twentieth century. He attends to the ecstatic but often painful longing that queer readers bring to texts. But what strikes me as strange is that he should cast the love that passes between distant historical subjects as "big-hearted." It does not seem unreasonable to suggest that, given the profound historical isolation that queers feel, these longings for other times and other queer subjects would be shot through with ambivalence, aggression, and despair. Such ambivalence is crucial, I want to argue, to an understanding of the queer bonds that are formed across time. Although Nealon's explicit concern in *Foundlings* is with the impossibility of queer historical desires and with the difficulties of cross-temporal identification, in the end, his foundling texts are—thanks to the figure of the hermeneutic friend—more found than lost. Is there a sense in which a generous expanding of a work's historical horizons refuses the very difficulties—historical and affective—that it attempts, in its stubborn, backward way, to articulate?

Chance Meetings

Cather's essays in *Not under Forty* are shot through with the ambivalence and difficulty of making queer connections across time. The first essay, "A Chance Meeting," recounts Cather's accidental encounter with Madame Franklin Grout, the niece of Gustave Flaubert, in an old-fashioned hotel in Aix-les-Bains. The hotel is a place where time has been suspended. Cather writes:

> The hotel was built for the travelers of forty years ago, who liked large rooms and large baths, and quiet. It is not at all smart, but very comfortable. Long ago I used to hear old Pittsburghers and Philadelphians talk of it. The newer hotels, set up on the steep hills above the town, have the fashionable trade; the noise and jazz and dancing. (815)

Cather's description is marked by her usual disdain for the accelerated pace and cheap entertainments of modern life. To be sure, it is not only the comforts of large rooms and large baths and quiet that Cather appreciates at the Grand Hotel. Such an old-fashioned place is likely to attract old-fashioned people, and it is this locale that enables her chance encounter with Madame Grout.

Cather's understanding of chance in this encounter—and in the others she recounts in *Not under Forty*—recalls Walter Benjamin's discussion of chance in his account of Proust's *mémoire involuntaire* in his essay on Baudelaire. Benjamin cites Proust's statement that the past is "somewhere beyond the intellect, and unmistakably present in some material object (or the sensation which such an object arouses in us), though we have no idea which one it is. As for that object, it depends entirely on chance whether we come upon it before we die or whether we never encounter it." Benjamin glosses this passage in the following way: "According to Proust, it is a matter of chance whether an individual forms an image of himself, whether he can take hold of his experience. It is by no means inevitable to be dependent on chance in this matter. Man's inner concerns do not have their issueless private character by nature." For Benjamin, as for Cather, the conditions of modern life made such experiences dependent on chance rather than a part of everyday experience: one might count on having such experiences only in places relatively untouched by modernity.[23]

Cather's meeting with Madame Grout is threatened not only by the destruction of experience in modern life but also by the older woman's extreme physical frailty. Although she is lively and engaging, it is clear that her state is precarious. When Cather first discovers her interlocutor's identity, she responds with a physical touch: "I took one of her lovely hands and kissed it, in homage to a great period, to the names that made her voice tremble" (821). Through contact with Madame Grout, Cather kisses the past, trying to bring it near. At every moment, though, we understand the threat that hangs over their interaction. When Cather finally leaves the hotel, Madame Grout looks after her, "the powder on her face quite destroyed by tears" (829). Later, the package that Cather receives from Madame Grout (which originally contained a keepsake—a letter from Flaubert to George Sand) is torn to pieces, its contents missing. Finally the story ends, quite abruptly, with the news of Madame Grout's death. Rather than narrating that death, or describing her own reaction to receiving the news, Cather merely mentions that her friends in Paris sent her a newspaper clipping, which she reprints in full—it is Madame Grout's obituary.

Not under Forty is filled with such encounters—meaningful for Cather, but matters of chance, and often threatened by loss or disappearance. At the center of the volume are two essays, "148 Charles Street" and "Miss Jewett," both of which are concerned with Sarah Orne Jewett and Annie Fields. Cather's meeting with these two women shortly before Jewett's death was one of the most important events of her life; not only did it inaugurate a friendship and a brief, intense period of literary mentorship, it also represented a turning point in Cather's embrace of a female friendship based on the bond between Fields and Jewett. In "148 Charles Street," Cather remembers first seeing Fields and Jewett in their house together in 1908. As in "A Chance Meeting," Cather's contact with an older literary world is mediated through a face-to-face encounter. Annie Fields is a perfect connecting link between the past and the present: "At eighty she could still entertain new people, new ideas, new forms of art. And she brought to her greeting of the new all the richness of her rich past: a long, unbroken chain of splendid contacts, beautiful friendships."[24] Cather's presence and interest and memory are crucial in preserving this unbroken chain of "splendid contacts." But these memories are also sustained by the material location, 148 Charles Street, which so securely shuts out "the ugliness of the world, all possibility of wrenches and jars and wounding contacts" (842).

Cather's juxtaposition of "splendid contacts" inside their house with "wounding contacts" outside suggests that it is not only a connection to the literary past that Cather seeks here but also access to a mode of relationality. The intimate bond between Jewett and Fields is another kind of splendid contact that fascinates Cather. When Cather first arrives at 148 Charles Street, her friend Mrs. Brandeis asks that Cather be shown "the treasures of the house." Although those treasures are the ostensible subject of this essay, Cather relates her initial disinterest in those objects. She writes, "I had no eyes for the treasures, I was too intent upon the ladies" (839).

Cather's meeting with Jewett appears to many critics as a confrontation between a nineteenth-century model and an early twentieth-century model of female same-sex relations. Jewett has become an icon of Victorian romantic friendship; she famously befriended Annie Fields after the death of the latter's husband, and the two women lived together off and on for the next twenty-five years. By contrast, Cather is associated much more closely with the anxieties of sexual definition at the turn of the century in her taking on of a male persona, in her excoriation of Wilde after his trial, and in her at times virulent misogyny. Her biography seems shaken by the death throes of female friendship and the labor pains of a newly public "homosexual identity."

It is undeniable that the sexualization of relations between women at the turn of the century had profound effects; however, critics have tended to overstate the absolute nature of this historical break. The energies of romantic friendship are diffused throughout twentieth-century representations of female same-sex desire; at the same time, many anxieties that critics have associated exclusively with twentieth-century experience are legible in the earlier period. One reason we tend to think of this transition as a "clean break" is that we have thought this difference exclusively through the question of sexuality. I want to suggest that this emphasis on questions of sexuality, secrecy, and shame—on all the dynamics of the closet—overlooks a wider range of affective experience that links the two periods.

"Homosexuality" operates in very different ways in the texts of Cather and Jewett. Despite their differences, however, both authors are concerned with a particular form of temporality: the fractured temporality of "the end of friendship." Cather and Jewett betray a common concern with issues of duration, continuance, and succession. Considering a range of impossible or threatened friendships, Cather and Jewett anxiously explore the possibility of queer historical continuity. Staging meetings with the dead and also with those who are yet to be born, these figures weigh the odds of sustaining an "impossible" mode of desire.

Cather's most extended meditation on female friendship is "148 Charles Street." Her juxtaposition of the hostile world outside this house with the safe one inside underlines her idealization of the relationship shared between Fields and Jewett. The house serves here to protect a mode of relationality ("splendid contacts") that is threatened by the "wounding contacts" of the present. Despite the tranquillity of the interior scene at 148 Charles Street, however, this realm is not immune to threats from the outside. Cather suggests the frailty of this relation in a scene she recounts from Jewett and Fields' summer house in Manchester. She writes:

> At Manchester, when there were no guests, Mrs. Fields had tea on the back veranda, overlooking a wild stretch of woodland. Down in this wood, directly beneath us, were a tea-table and seats built under the trees, where they used to have tea when the hostess was younger—now the climb was too steep for her. It was a little sad, perhaps, to sit and look out over a shrinking kingdom; but if she felt it, she never showed it. Miss Jewett and I went down into the wood, and she told me she hated to go there now, as it reminded her that much was already lost, and what was left was so at the mercy of chance! It seemed as if a strong wind might blow away that beloved friend of many years. We talked in low voices. Who could have believed that Mrs. Fields was to outlive Miss Jewett, so much the younger, by nearly six years, as she outlived Mr. Fields by thirty-four! (844)

Cather attempts to sustain a connection with the form of relation shared by Jewett and Fields. Throughout the essay, Cather underlines her distance from the two women, while at the same time she draws close to them through an identification with loss. Jewett describes Fields's declining health and life possibilities, but for Cather it is a whole world— a set of affective and social possibilities—that is "on the verge of destruction." For Cather, romantic friendship is a "shrinking kingdom," a back garden that she surveys with a mixture of desire, longing, and regret. She demonstrates a mode of looking backward that is not exactly nostalgic, as the world that she longs for is not one of presence, but of absence, loss, and proleptic mourning. While Cather does not articulate this difficult and pessimistic historical vision herself, its implications are clearly audible in the older woman's concerned reflection: "much was already lost, and what was left was so at the mercy of chance!"

In this essay, the possibility of sustained human connection is itself understood as a threatened realm. The concern over Mrs. Fields's imminent death offers an image of the impossibility of stable human relations. At the same time, it serves as an allegory of Cather's own experience of historical loss. Female friendship was disappearing as Cather wrote, her anxiety about the demise of this affective mode is legible in her writings on Jewett and Fields. It is important to note, however, that Cather's longing here is for a structure of feeling she never fully inhabited.

Sad Succession

Cather belonged to neither the past nor the future of queer history; she experienced her own historical moment as impossible. Her distress in this essay is explicable in terms of a historical narrative that emphasizes her absolute difference from Jewett, which sees her as living out, in a particularly painful way, the difficulties of modern homosexual identity. But what is surprising, and significantly complicates this narrative, is the fact that this fragile temporality appears not only in Cather's writing about Jewett but also, quite powerfully, in Jewett's own writing. This scene from "148 Charles Street" could have been cribbed from Jewett herself: like Cather, Jewett thinks friendship through friendship's end.

Recent philosophical writing about friendship has tended to emphasize disruption and impossibility rather than equality and longevity. In *The Politics of Friendship,* Jacques Derrida speaks of the "collapse of the friendship concept," and follows thinkers like Maurice Blanchot and Jean-Luc Nancy in approaching friendship not through reciprocity or generosity; rather, he thinks about friendship in terms of the "disaster at the heart of friendship, the disaster of friendship or disaster *qua* friendship."[25] Derrida's work on friendship is conducted through his repeated meditation on the statement attributed to Aristotle, "O my friends! There is no friend," which Derrida understands as a statement of the impossibility of friendship. Friendship in modernity is aporetic, discontinuous, asymmetrical. Following Blanchot, Derrida imagines friendship as a "relation without relation," as he gestures toward a community "to come," a community that cannot be realized in the present.

Commenting on the work of Georges Bataille, Blanchot discusses such an exposure to the death of the other in *The Unavowable Community*. He writes that the "basis of communication" is

> exposure to death, no longer my own exposure, but someone else's, whose living and closest presence is already the eternal and unbearable absence, an absence that the travail of the deepest mourning does not diminish. And it is in life itself that the absence of someone else has to be met. It is with that absence—its uncanny presence, always under the prior threat of disappearing—that friendship is brought into play and lost at each moment, a relation without relation, or without relation other than the incommensurable.[26]

In his meditation on the relationship between friendship and the death of the other, Blanchot suggests a way that we might link this exposure to a rethinking of community. Jewett's fiction, with its exploration of the fragile temporality of friendships formed in the shadow of death, explores the possibility of a community formed in and through death.

The connection between individual and collective loss is the focus of a well-known episode from Jewett's novel *The Country of the Pointed Firs*. In the story, the narrator becomes fascinated with a dead woman, "poor Joanna," who, disappointed in love, secluded herself for the last decades of her life on a remote island. When the narrator is able to visit this island herself, she experiences a powerful identification with Joanna:

> There is something in the fact of a hermitage that cannot fail to touch the imagination; the recluses are a sad kindred, but they are never commonplace. Mrs. Todd had truly said that Joanna was like one of the saints of the desert; the loneliness of sorrow will forever keep alive their sad succession.[27]
>
> . . .
>
> I drank at the spring, and thought that now and then some one would follow me from the busy, hard-worked, and simple-thoughted countryside of the mainland, which lay dim and dreamlike in the August haze, as Joanna must have watched it many a day. There was the world, and here was she with eternity well begun. In the life of each of us, I said to myself, there is a place remote and islanded, and given to endless regret or secret happiness; we are each the uncompanioned hermit and recluse of an hour or a day; we understand our fellows of the cell to whatever age of history they may belong.

> But as I stood alone on the island, in the sea-breeze, suddenly there
> came a sound of distant voices; gay voices and laughter from a plea-
> sure-boat that was going seaward full of boys and girls. I knew, as if she
> had told me, that poor Joanna must have heard the like on many and
> many a summer afternoon, and must have welcomed the good cheer in
> spite of hopelessness and winter weather, and all the sorrow and disap-
> pointment in the world. (444–445)

Across infinite distances, across the boundary of death itself, the narrator forges a bond with Joanna, but the sad succession that includes
them is defined precisely by isolation and loss. In her enfolding of community and isolation, and of eternity and loss, Jewett offers an image of
the impossibility of resolving such contradictions.

Critics have tended to ignore this ambivalence and tension in Jewett's
work and have instead read it as a celebration of community. In a 1999
article entitled "'The Country of Our Friendship,'" Laurie Shannon
reads Jewett's fiction as an "intimist" project, which she defines as an
aesthetic, spiritual, and relational practice that takes the intimate space
of friendship as "a country, a creed, and a way of life."[28] Reading this
episode in *The Country of the Pointed Firs*, Shannon emphasizes the em-
bedding of this story within networks of sociability. She calls attention
to the final moments of this scene, when the narrator's thoughts for poor
Joanna are interrupted by the sound of "gay voices" from a passing boat
and contrasts this moment with the narrator's earlier observation that
"there is a place remote and islanded within each of us." Shannon
writes:

> Instead of situating community as transient and elusive, Jewett casts soli-
> tariness as a condition that is hard to preserve or even believe. The novel
> enshrines "gay voices," "laughter," and "pleasure" despite its sober re-
> spect for those who find its appeal resistible. The spectacular choice of
> Joanna sola and the experience her memory briefly triggers of standing
> alone, of being "islanded," emerge as objects of contemplation in what
> seems an inevitable "progress" toward friendship and redemption. (250)

In her reading of this scene and of *The Country of the Pointed Firs* as a
whole, Shannon emphasizes the reabsorption of negative affect by the
community and by the joyful experience of intimacy.

But is such a reading doing a service to the passage? The paradox at
the center of this episode is the incongruity of a shared isolation; it is

not at all clear, as Shannon argues, that community prevails, or that the islands of grief contained within the community are dissolved into it. Although these voices do reach the island, these sounds serve as signs of disconnection as well as connection: it is not hard to see how they might underline the unbridgeable distance between the island and the mainland. Though these voices may console, how much "progress" can they make against "all the sorrow and disappointment in the world"?

Star Friendship

In her preface to Jewett's work, published in 1925, Cather writes that *The Country of the Pointed Firs* "shine[s] with the reflection of its long, joyous future." Cather identifies Jewett's novel along with *The Scarlet Letter* and *Huckleberry Finn* as "three American books that have the possibility of a long, long life," and writes that she can "think of no others that confront time and change so serenely."[29] Shannon emphasizes this timeless, permanent quality of both Jewett's and Cather's work, concluding that it is through Cather that we have inherited Jewett's "serenity." For Shannon, Cather's "rallying move towards the constellation of Jewett's readership seems to propose a strategy of reading as an alternative to erotic hermeneutics, suggesting the proximities of intimacy and intimation within an intimist practice. It . . . replicates the stable and gratifying configuration Jewett herself made of affection and friendship—within her writing and out of it" (257). Reading Cather's meeting with Jewett in light of the profound anxieties about continuance that inform the rest of her work—and in light of her own refusal of futurity in *Not under Forty*—it is difficult to see this projection of a literary community as simply "stable and gratifying." The fantasy of long, joyous life—whether the life of a book or the life of a community—may have been gratifying to Cather: it seems to be gratifying to contemporary readers such as Shannon. But are we so certain that what Jewett passes down to us through Cather is a legacy of "serenity"?

These moments from Cather and Jewett form part of a history of shared anxieties about temporality, continuance, and the possibility of female friendship that extends from well before the turn of the twentieth century on through to the present day. Both Cather and Jewett turn toward the past—befriend it—in order to forge some kind of relation to the future. Their relation to the future is no more secure than their relation to the past, however. While we may try to give them the gift of modern sexual identity and queer community, what they have to give us is an inheritance of historical anxiety and longing.

I do not want to suggest that we give up reading the profound and complex historical allegories inscribed in such texts. Wherever we read of the desire to forge "vital genealogies" with other real and imagined queer subjects, though, it is important to recognize the extent to which such genealogies are not vital, but rather, ghostly, impossible, interrupted. Hope for alternative forms of relation and community is an important affect in the present, particularly as queers try to articulate alternatives to marriage as the dominant form of social life. As we consider the history of queer representation, it is crucial that we recognize how central the failure of community is in such representations. Such a recognition in turn asks that we expand our sense of what counts as a relationship and to rethink friendship as a compensation for the disappointments of love and desire. It also suggests that we might need to rethink what counts as legitimate or significant political emotions. We know that "hope for a better form of existence" counts as political, but what about feelings of loss, despair, anger, shame, and disgust, feelings represented so richly in many twentieth-century queer texts? Can we begin to think about mobilizing emotions like these?

In attempting to construct our own genealogies, we have tended to disavow the presence of such feelings both in these earlier representations and in our own relation to them. But I want to suggest that our attempts to forge literary, historical, affective, and political bonds with these texts demand a fuller recognition of the ambivalence at the heart of community. As we try to befriend these figures from the past, we would do well to remember the infinite distances contained within even the closest friendships. Nietzsche contemplates such immensities in his own meditation on the end of friendship in *The Gay Science*. He writes:

> We were friends and have become estranged. But that was right, and we do not want to hide and obscure it from ourselves as if we had to be ashamed of it. We are two ships, each of which has its own goal and course; we may cross and have a feast together, as we did—and then the good ships lay so quietly in one harbour and in one sun that it may have seemed as if they had already completed their course and had the same goal. But then the almighty force of our projects drove us apart once again, into different seas and sunny zones, and maybe we will

never meet again—or maybe we will, but will not recognize each other: the different seas and suns have changed us! That we had to become estranged is the law *above* us; through it we should come to have more respect for each other—and the thought of our former friendship should become more sacred! There is probably a tremendous invisible curve and stellar orbit in which our different ways and goals may be *included* as small stretches—let us rise to this thought! But our life is too short and our vision too meagre for us to be more than friends in the sense of that sublime possibility.—Let us then *believe* in our star friendship even if we must be earth enemies.[30]

Nietzsche here offers a vision of friendship's failure: it is possible only as star friendship, which is to say, through a transcendence so absolute as to be humanly impossible. The historical trajectory of such a friendship is so vast and so oblique as to forbid any knowledge of its past or future course. Nietzsche suggests that star friendship, rather than earth friendship, offers a model for an authentic relation to the figures of the past. We reach them only by opening ourselves to this sublime impossibility— by pledging ourselves to these friends we will never see again.

4

Spoiled Identity

Radclyffe Hall's Unwanted Being

> I sometimes have a queer feeling. I think: "Something very like this has
> happened before." The nasty things must not be repeated though.
>
> —Radclyffe Hall to Evguenia Souline, 30 July 1937

"Those who are failures from the start, downtrodden, crushed—it is
they, the weakest, who must undermine life among men."[1] Nietzsche's
diatribe against the "born failure" in *The Genealogy of Morals* anticipates
a common reaction to the downtrodden heroine of Radclyffe Hall's 1928
novel *The Well of Loneliness*. A few months after the novel's obscenity
trial, a verse lampoon entitled *The Sink of Solitude* appeared, mocking
the fate of "pathetic post-war lesbians."[2] The following year, Janet
Flanner, writing more coolly in the *New Yorker,* quipped that Hall's
"loneliness was greater than one supposed."[3] From the moment of its
publication, readers balked at the novel's melodramatic account of what
Hall called "the tragical problem of sexual inversion."[4] But the readers
who have reacted most adversely to the novel's dark portrait of inverted
life are those whose experience Hall claimed to represent. *The Well*, still
known as the most famous and most widely read of lesbian novels, is
also the novel most hated by lesbians themselves. In the years since gay
liberation, Hall's novel has been singularly out of step with the discourse
of gay pride. One reader voiced a common reaction when asked whether
or not she would recommend it: "I consider this book very bad news for
lesbians."[5] According to a model of readerly contagion not unlike the
poisoning effect of *ressentiment* that Nietzsche traces in the *Genealogy,*
this account of Stephen Gordon's life has been seen as a depressing spectacle that must undermine life among lesbians.

With its inverted heroine and its tragic view of same-sex relations, *The Well* has repeatedly come into conflict with contemporary understandings of the meaning and shape of gay identity. During the 1970s, the novel was attacked primarily for its equation of lesbianism with masculine identification; in the years of the "woman-loving-woman," it was anathema with its mannish heroine, its derogation of femininity, and its glorification of normative heterosexuality. Although the recent recuperation of butch-femme practices and the growth of transgender studies have sparked renewed interest in the book, Hall's embrace of the discourse of congenital inversion is still at odds with the antiessentialism of contemporary theories of sexuality. The dissemination of the Foucauldian notion of reverse discourse has also caused some critics to reconsider Hall's embrace of the language of inversion, but for many, such a revision has been insufficient to exonerate the novel. Though Hall does make congenital inversion "speak in its own name," her use of the term does not adequately absorb the stigma associated with this medical discourse. In this sense, *The Well* might be said to give reverse discourse a bad name.[6]

Behind such arguments with *The Well*'s ideology, one senses an underlying discomfort with the extreme sadness of the novel. The novel's association with internalized homophobia, erotic failure, and a stigmatizing discourse of gender inversion has allowed it to function as a synecdoche for the worst of life before Stonewall. So accepted is the link between *The Well* and this history of suffering that critics have found it convenient to refer to the "self-hating Radclyffe Hall tradition."[7] In her influential article "Zero Degree Deviancy," Catharine Stimpson takes *The Well* as the primary example in the tradition of "the dying fall," which she defines as "a narrative of damnation, of the lesbian's suffering as a lonely outcast." Such a narrative, Stimpson writes, "gives the homosexual, particularly the lesbian, riddling images of pity, self-pity, and of terror—in greater measure than it consoles."[8] Stimpson's attention to the text's "riddling" effects on the reader is typical of responses to the novel. Many readers understand the novel's dark portrait of lesbian life as not only an effect but also as a cause of our difficult history. Thus, Blanche Wiesen Cook, writing in 1979, fantasized about what it would have been like to grow up not having read *The Well*: "Unrequited love, tearful abandonment, the curse of it all might never have existed."[9]

It is helpful in considering such strong reactions to *The Well* to invoke the concept of "identity ambivalence" that Erving Goffman traces in his

1963 book *Stigma*. In this study of the social and psychological strategies of stigmatized individuals, Goffman describes the ambivalence that
these subjects feel when confronted with "their own kind." He writes:

> The stigmatized individual may exhibit identity ambivalence when he
> obtains a close sight of his own kind behaving in a stereotyped way,
> flamboyantly or pitifully acting out the negative attributes imputed to
> them. The sight may repel him, since after all he supports the norms
> of the wider society, but his social and psychological identification with
> these offenders holds him to what repels him, transforming repulsion
> into shame, and then transforming ashamedness itself into something
> of which he is ashamed. In brief, he can neither embrace his group nor
> let it go.[10]

The dynamic of identification and disidentification Goffman traces aptly
describes recent critical reactions to *The Well*. While few lesbian or
queer critics would claim to support "the norms of the wider society"—
the explicit aim of such criticism is often precisely to contest such
norms—they are nonetheless repelled by the figure of Stephen Gordon,
the type of the tragic lesbian. The repulsion she inspires in contemporary critics signals the effectiveness of these norms, which function
powerfully with or without our consent. But while critics have sought to
disavow the legacy of *The Well*, they have not, finally, been able to let
Stephen go. Rather, the vehemence of critics' rejection of her is a testa-
ment to the shame and repulsion she continues to inspire in lesbian
readers.

Hall offers an image of such "identity ambivalence" in *The Well* itself.
Stephen, however, is not the object of identity ambivalence but rather
its subject. Stephen's disavowal of the community of inverts is in fact
underwritten by her support of masculinist, aristocratic, nationalist
norms—the very standards by which she is judged an outcast and a
freak. Throughout the novel, she expresses her reluctance to spend time
in the company of "her own kind"; her fear of such a fate is signaled in
the ominously repeated phrase "like to like." Stephen stands at a remove
from the inverted men and women she encounters in the novel. Though
she is sympathetic to their plight, Stephen understands them to be
hopelessly degraded both by the hostility of the outside world and by
their exile from that world, from the salutary influences of family, tradition, and public life. During her sojourn in the queer underworld,

Stephen struggles heroically to maintain the "upper-world" values of honor, courage, and hard work.

Late in *The Well*, in a scene that reads like an allegory for the novel's recent critical reception, Stephen's fears of her own kind are confirmed. Reluctantly escorting her lover Mary Llewellyn on a tour of "the garish and tragic night life of Paris" (378), Stephen ends up at Alec's, "that meeting-place of the most miserable of all those who comprised the miserable army."[11] Her distress peaks when a young man in the bar hails her as "one of the family." Hall writes:

> A youth passed with a friend and the couple were blocked by the press of dancers in front of her table. He bent forward, this youth, until his face was almost on a level with Stephen's—a grey, drug-marred face with a mouth that trembled incessantly.
>
> "Ma soeur," he whispered.
>
> For a moment she wanted to strike that face with her naked fist, to obliterate it. Then all of a sudden she perceived the eyes, and the memory came of a hapless creature, distracted, bleeding from bursting lungs, hopelessly pursued, glancing this way, then that, as though looking for something, some refuge, some hope—and the thought: "It's looking for the God who made it."
>
> Stephen shivered and stared at her tightly clenched hands; the nails whitened her flesh. "Mon frère," she muttered. (388–389)

When Stephen is first confronted by the young man in the bar, she sees only the outward markers of his abjection—his trembling mouth, his pockmarked face. Repulsed, she attempts to block out his image. But Stephen's disidentification with the youth is underwritten by a powerful identification; when the boy addresses her as "ma soeur," she looks at his eyes and recalls another "hapless creature," the fox she saw hunted in her youth.[12] Stephen's initial contempt is softened by her knowledge that she, like the boy, is pursued by a hostile world. Stephen cannot finally renounce her identity group; in the end her repulsion turns to shame. She reluctantly avows her bond with him. Her head hanging in the prototypical attitude of shame, Stephen mutters "Mon frère." But her fists remain clenched, because she is still angered by the spectacle of the young man's suffering.

Though Hall does not describe the youth in the scene as acting "flamboyantly or pitifully," Stephen's anger toward him is incited by his "obviousness" as an invert, and by the traces of suffering he bears. Though she is allied with the values of the normal world, Stephen bears the marks of her inversion just as visibly. With her man's collar, her close-cropped hair, and her masculine build, Stephen is as "obvious" as they come. The signs of Stephen's suffering are just as clear: the lines around her mouth, her nicotine-stained fingers, and the livid scar on her cheek testify to Stephen's difficulties. But Stephen's resistance to identification with the boy is heightened rather than reduced by her similarity to him. Throughout the novel, Stephen attempts to differentiate herself from such "battered remnants of men" in order to shore up a sense of her own strength and well-being.

Though such a reaction may strike us as shameful, or even repulsive, it offers a remarkably apt image of the recent critical reception of the novel. Critics confronted with the spectacular sadness of the novel have responded with just such a mixture of identification and disavowal. Many critics have dismissed *The Well* altogether as "internally homophobic," a painful reminder of a vanished context. Others have attempted to read through the difficulties of the novel in order to project a happier ending for long-suffering Stephen. Such readings, though they offer some consolation, ignore Hall's deliberate attention throughout the novel to Stephen's sadness and to her utter failure to assimilate to her social context. In the intense affect still regularly generated by the novel, though, one can see its continuing relevance. Despite our resistance, *The Well* continues to hail contemporary readers with its own troubling "Ma soeur."

In the following reading of *The Well* and its reception by queer critics, I hope to show the importance of such troubling representations to any rethinking of the protocols of queer historiography. I argue that the need to turn the difficulties of gay, lesbian, and transgender history to good political use in the present has resulted in a lack of attention to the specificity and density of the historical past. The difficulty of *The Well*— its painstaking account of the social, psychic, and corporeal effects of homophobia—is an important reminder both of the losses of queer history and of the continuing difficulties of queer existence. In a reading of several key scenes, I consider Hall's representation of loneliness as a queer structure of feeling. I use contemporary criticism to read Hall's novel and, at the same time, use Hall's novel to read against the grain of queer criticism. Because I argue that negative feeling in *The Well* has constituted a blind spot for contemporary critics, it is primarily in the symptomatic resistances produced by the novel that I locate its most important contributions to the theory and practice of queer studies.

A Queer Feeling

The Well poses the problem of negative representation in a way that is hard to avoid. In response to such dark representations, critics have tended to emphasize the positive, celebrating moments of courage and pleasure in the record of the queer past. Such an affirmative political vision prevailed especially in the early years of gay liberation, when critics and historians searched the past for examples of same-sex love to serve as models for gay and lesbian life in the present. Many of these critics and historians focused on the distant past, before the institution of homosexuality as a mode of social and erotic organization. The cultures of same-sex love that were central to the postliberation historical imagination were notably free of homophobia as we know it.[13] But not all forms of affirmative historiography focused on wholly positive periods in the history of same-sex relations. Critics working in a mode that we might qualify as selectively affirmative sought to illuminate isolated moments of resistance in the larger story of homophobic oppression and violence. Queer life before Stonewall was not determined by shame and secrecy, these critics claimed, drawing attention to the power of previously debased pre-Stonewall cultures such as camp, drag, and butch-femme. Though many of these practices were at odds with the ideology of gay liberation and were bound up with the losses of queer history, these critics insisted on their importance as modes of resistance.

Since the move to queer studies with its focus on stigma, critics have begun to explore more fully the difficulties of the queer past. Despite their willingness to engage with disturbing topics, however, these critics still struggle with a fundamental paradox of queer criticism: how to incorporate a difficult or shameful past into the vision of a more promising future. In her seminal essay "Queer Performativity," Eve Kosofsky Sedgwick reflects on her decision to focus her discussion of Henry James's New York Prefaces on the stigmatizing utterance, "Shame on you." She writes:

> What's the point of accentuating the negative, of beginning with stigma, and for that matter a form of stigma—"Shame on you"—so unsanitizably redolent of that long Babylonian exile known as queer

childhood? But note that this is just what the word queer itself does, too: the main reason why the self-application of "queer" by activists has proven so volatile is that there's no way that any amount of affirmative reclamation is going to succeed in detaching the word from its associations with shame and with the terrifying powerlessness of gender-dissonant or otherwise stigmatized childhood. If queer is a politically potent term, which it is, that's because, far from being capable of being detached from the childhood scene of shame, it cleaves to that scene as a near-inexhaustible source of transformational energy. There's a strong sense, I think, in which the subtitle of any truly queer (perhaps as opposed to gay?) politics will be the same as the one Erving Goffman gave to his book *Stigma: Notes on the Management of Spoiled Identity*. But more than its management: its experimental, creative, performative force.[14]

Sedgwick realizes that "beginning with stigma" will seem perverse from the perspective of traditional gay and lesbian studies. But in her discussion of shame the term itself undergoes a striking transformation. The beginning of the passage locates shame in the outer reaches of exile, but Sedgwick brings it back into the fold. Shame's fortunes turn about midway through the passage, when Sedgwick raises and quickly dismisses the possibility that gay shame is useless for political purposes: "if queer is a politically potent term, which it is." Although Sedgwick contrasts queer politics to blandly affirmative gay politics, her own discussion of the term "queer" rests on an "affirmative reclamation" that is itself brazenly performative. Such a move is deeply indebted to traditional gay and lesbian politics, which also seeks to manage shame, to transform it into a usable resource. Though she argues for the importance of shame and stigma, Sedgwick is primarily concerned with the "transformational" capabilities of shame, with its "experimental, creative, performative force."

For critics interested in queer suffering, *The Well* is a rich, even a paradigmatic text. In its account of Stephen's experience of public stigma and private refusal, the novel offers a detailed and compelling account of her emotions, which swing wildly between shame, vulnerability, exaltation, bitterness, arrogance, pain, the sense of failure, *ressentiment,* self-hatred, and self-pity. Although the novel posed an unmistakable threat to an earlier tradition of affirmative historiography, its inexorable sadness seems to pose a similar challenge to contemporary queer critics. *The Well* has proved singularly resistant to queer theory's "futural imaginings"; it has been difficult to locate the political promise in this dark text. The novel's subtitle, in this sense, ought simply to be *Spoiled Identity*.

One sign that we have not fully encountered the difficulties of the past is that we do not have at the ready a critical vocabulary for describing the destitutions and embarrassments of queer existence. Yet *The Well* itself offers a stunningly rich and detailed account of such experiences. Critics who have read the novel have paid little attention to Hall's careful account of Stephen's experience; instead, they have sought to unmask the novel's various ideologies of misogyny and homophobia. Although such critiques are important, they have drawn attention away from the representation of homophobia and feeling in the novel. As Louis Althusser reminds us, it is impossible to remove ideology from the realm of experience: "when we speak of ideology we should know that ideology slides into all human activity, that it is identical with the 'lived' experience of human existence itself."[15] In Stephen Gordon, critics encounter the image of a queer subject who lives out ideology's effects in a particularly painful way; the novel is unrelenting in its specificity about this experience. *The Well* offers a meticulous account of the many outrages, failures, and disappointments that attend gender and sexual nonconformity in a homophobic world.

In the following reading of the novel, I argue that in her portrait of Stephen's "loneliness" Hall offers us a portrait of a complex and historically specific structure of feeling. Although loneliness is a traditional feature of twentieth-century gay novels, it is normally closely associated with the condition of being in the closet. For Hall, loneliness is only secondarily associated with the condition of "having a secret." Judith Halberstam has noted in this connection that Stephen's extreme visibility in the novel displaces questions of sexual secrecy and knowledge. She writes, "Stephen Gordon in no way lives her life as an open secret, and she in fact represents the unmistakable visibility of female sexual perversion when it appears in male clothing."[16] The novel is studded with incidents recounting Stephen's painful visibility in public.[17] As a result, loneliness is not primarily a question of epistemology in the novel but of ontology. Loneliness afflicts Stephen's being; it is deeply inscribed in her body. Rather than being contained by the strictures of the closet, Stephen is thwarted as she attempts to work out the difficulties of her vexed being. Loneliness in the novel is quite literally about being alone, about being an exile, and about bearing a stigmatized identity. But at the same time loneliness describes a condition of singularity, of occupying an unprecedented and uncharted place in the order of creation. Hall understands loneliness as a state of desolation, a deeply felt psychic and corporeal state of abandonment, refusal, and loss. It describes not only a way of life but also a state of being, a social experience insistently internalized and corporeal, felt to be both essential and permanent.

Critics tend to think about Hall's deployment of the discourse of inversion as a mistake or as an unfortunate consequence of her historical situation. But this essentialist discourse was extremely useful to Hall in her attempt to articulate loneliness as a structure of feeling. In the novel, Stephen Gordon's intimate and social alienation is underwritten by an ideology of failure. Loneliness is an effect of Stephen's experiences of public and private refusal; Hall traces the ways in which social experiences line up with the discourse of inversion and become sedimented in both the psyche and the body. In adopting this medical model of difference, Hall was able to describe the way negative social experiences are somatized. In the following reading of *The Well*, I investigate the way that stigma, though it is a social experience, appears to emanate, as if naturally, from Stephen's body. Thus, as her experience of refusal becomes part of the intimate landscape of the self, Stephen takes up the burden of representing larger social losses for those around her.

Intolerable Birthright

Stephen Gordon is a disappointment from the start. Hall describes her existence as an aberration, one of nature's mistakes; she underlines her difference by framing Stephen against a background of consummate perfection. The novel opens with a description of the family estate where Stephen is born:

> Not very far from Upton-on-Severn—between it, in fact, and the Malvern Hills—stands the country seat of the Gordons of Bramley; well-timbered, well-cottaged, well-fenced and well-watered, having, in this latter respect, a stream that forks in exactly the right position to feed two large lakes in the grounds.
>
> The house itself is of Georgian red brick, with charming circular windows near the roof. It has dignity and pride without ostentation, self-assurance without arrogance, repose without inertia; and a gentle

aloofness that, to those who know its spirit, but adds to its value as a home. (11)

The appearance of this "well-timbered, well-cottaged, well-fenced and well-watered" estate in the first sentence of *The Well* establishes a central contrast. While the neatly bifurcated stream that waters these grounds "forks in exactly the right position to fill two large lakes," Stephen's gender is split in a disturbing manner that renders her neither fully masculine nor fully feminine. Her gender transgression results in a kind of incompleteness that is ultimately unassimilable by the world of Morton. It is not just a house that Stephen loses in this novel of dispossession: the loss of Morton stands for the crushing psychic effects of Stephen's exile and all that the house represents.

Hall's conservative and nationalist tendencies are evident in this lament for the perfections of "such an homestead." *The Well* mourns the significant personal and social losses that inverts face because of society's hatred of them, but not least of such losses for Hall was the loss of class privilege.[18] What Stephen stands to inherit, along with the deed to Morton, is the sacred trust of the aristocracy: she, like her father, is fair-minded, honorable, and generous; she acts perfectly the part of the country gentleman—scholar, sportsman, and lover of nature. Barred from her inheritance both by her sex and also by her gender nonconformity, Stephen is forced from this rural life of gentle pleasures into a life of bohemian wandering. In contrast to the uncertainties of her life in London and Paris, Morton remains the sign of absolute value, the privileged site of continuity, human connection, and moral rectitude. The brick-and-mortar impassivity of the house exists in an endless narratorial present, seeming to watch over the events of the rest of the novel. Although Stephen goes on to use her inherited wealth to set up house elsewhere, the novel makes clear that her exile is an incurable state. Throughout *The Well*, Hall describes the situation of the inverted as radically unhoused: wanderers in the no-man's-land of sex, they are exposed to the unmitigated hostility of the "so-called normal" world.[19]

As this opening passage progresses, it sounds less like a description of an English country manor, and more like an inverted portrait—a photographic negative—of queer subjectivity. With Morton, Stephen loses an entire way of life, a subjectivity enabled by stability, permanence, and social acceptance. In Stephen's case, her exile and subsequent public exposure lead to a split in her being. On the one hand, she becomes less expressive, stonier, as she attempts to provide in her person a substitute for the sheltering indifference of the house. At the same time, she is unable to protect herself as she is cast adrift, and exposed to shifting tides of emotion. Thus, she loses access to the feelings associated with Morton, its aspect of "dignity and pride without ostentation, self-assurance without arrogance, repose without inertia." Though Stephen is not a purely desperate or lonely character—she experiences happiness, pride, joy, desire, and interest in the novel—she never approaches the tranquil self-respect that Morton projects. Such a burden is not without its pleasures: the novel is filled with descriptions of the voluptuous pride that Stephen takes in her appearance, her strength, and her abilities. But such prideful moments hover precariously near the abyss of shame into which she plunges at regular intervals.

In her dispossession, Stephen loses not only Morton but also her parents, whom Hall initially presents as being as perfect as their house. Sir Philip is "exceedingly well-favoured," "a lover and a dreamer" (12); Lady Anna is the "archetype of the very perfect woman, whom creating God has found good" (11). Such exquisite beings are practically guaranteed conjugal bliss, and Hall does not disappoint. She writes, "Seldom had two people loved more than they did; they loved with an ardour undiminished by time; as they ripened, so their love ripened with them" (12). In the midst of such an orgy of perfection, a note of longing is retroactively introduced by Stephen's conception: "Sir Philip never knew how much he longed for a son until, some ten years after marriage, his wife conceived a child; then he knew that this thing meant complete fulfillment, the fulfillment for which they had both been waiting" (12). While Philip and Anna had seemed to provide each other with complete happiness, the promise of a son rewrites the history of their marriage as a time of waiting for, rather than possessing, fulfillment.

Without considering the possibility that his firstborn might be a girl, Sir Philip names the child after St. Stephen and dreamily maps out the course of his heir's education and upbringing. Lady Anna suppresses her misgivings in deference to her husband; in time, she too begins to fantasize about playing with this phantom son in the meadows surrounding their house. In spite of their hopes, however, Stephen turns out to be a girl. Their only consolation is ultimately a bitter one; though biologically female, Stephen bears the impress of her parents' desire. This "wide-shouldered, narrow-hipped tadpole of a baby" (13) is born with a significant strain of masculinity, a tendency that becomes only more apparent with the passage of time. Stephen arrives not, as her father had hoped, to herald Sir Philip and Lady Anna's "complete fulfilment." Rather, her birth inaugurates in their lives a reign of incompleteness, discomfort, and loss. Thus, Stephen arrives as a kind of supplement, a third term that at once completes their union and exposes what is lacking in it.[20]

As if to fully manifest the logic of the supplement, Stephen arrives not as a real boy but as a failed or imitation boy. Rather than producing, according to desire, a perfect copy of her husband, Anna produces what she calls "a blemished, unworthy, maimed reproduction." Stephen closely resembles Sir Philip—her sensitive mouth, auburn hair, and hazel eyes are his—but she exaggerates the signs of physical lack in him, developing a replica "tiny cleft in her chin, so small that just at first it looked like a shadow" (13–14). Each outward resemblance between father and daughter reinforces Lady Anna's disappointment about the difference between them. Though Anna reproaches herself, telling herself that she ought to be "proud of the likeness," her child ultimately appears to her a caricature rather than a copy, an imitation "most unnatural and monstrous" (15).

Sir Philip is bitterly disappointed by the fact that his wife bears him a daughter, but he never expresses his anguish openly. Rather, seeing Lady Anna's grief, he "hides his chagrin" and maintains his idée fixe, insisting that they call the child Stephen anyway. Sir Philip raises Stephen as a boy, encouraging her to ride athwart, hunt foxes, lift weights, and read Greek; without question or comment, he comforts her on the many occasions when neighbors, playmates, servants, and her mother respond to her cross-gendered appearance with laughter and derision. Sir Philip takes pleasure in Stephen's masculine qualities, denying both her female body and the problems that her gender nonconformity causes her. Stephen incorporates her father's positive image of her, his pride in her masculine pursuits and his belief that she is part of nature. Sir Philip's protestation that Stephen is, in her own way, perfect, echoes Stephen's later self-justifications; over and against the evidence of monstrosity, Stephen too will insist that she is part of nature's scheme.

The novel suggests that Stephen inherits not only her strange gender identity from her parents but also her great capacity for negative feeling.

Stephen's early childhood is permeated by grief. Hall describes the scene immediately following Stephen's birth:

> Anna Gordon held her child to her breast, but she grieved while it drank, because of her man who had longed so much for a son. And seeing her grief, Sir Philip hid his chagrin, and he fondled the baby and examined its fingers.
>
> "What a hand!" he would say. "Why it's actually got nails on all its ten fingers: little, perfect, pink nails!"
>
> Then Anna would dry her eyes and caress it, kissing the tiny hand. (13)

Stephen incorporates the feelings of scorn and disappointment that her mother feels toward her in her youth; they surface later in the form of intense shame and self-hatred. One might also trace Stephen's feeling of exclusion or nonrecognition to her mother's refusal to interact with her directly. Her mother does not express her feelings of disappointment toward Stephen but routes them through her concern for Stephen's father. At the same time, Stephen seems to inherit directly her mother's habit of grief; crying while she feeds her, Lady Anna initiates Stephen into a lifetime of suffering.

Stephen's sense of self is keyed throughout the novel to a series of experiences of love granted and withdrawn. Stephen's ambivalent relationship with her mother sets the stage for this dynamic: Lady Anna shrinks from Stephen's infant touch, and Stephen's most intimate experience is structured by this refusal. Hall demonstrates the disastrous effects of such refusals on Stephen, who finds it difficult in the face of rejection to maintain a gendered sense of self. When her love goes unreciprocated, Stephen's gender inversion migrates toward abjection: with no one to perform her masculinity for, Stephen's loneliness becomes even more acute. In this sense, for Stephen, to be desired is to be.

Stephen's first traumatic encounter of failed love is with Collins, the housemaid. When Stephen first develops a crush on Collins, she "enters . . . a new world" that turns "on an axis of Collins" (18). To impress Collins, Stephen begins to dress up in the outfits of famous men from history. Hall writes, "This led to much foraging in the nursery rag-bag, much swagger and noise, much strutting and posing, and much staring in the mirror" (19). For Stephen, the very possibility that her love might be returned sends her into a frenzy of narcissistic self-display. Her confidence in these early scenes with Collins is impressive, as Stephen tells the house staff gravely, "Yes, of course I am a boy" (19). Through the powerful agents of costume, bodily performance, and erotic fantasy, Stephen effectively transforms herself into a cocky young man.

But Stephen's romance comes to a bitter conclusion when Stephen sees Collins kissing the footman in the garden. For several days leading up to the incident, Collins has been ignoring her; finally, Stephen happens upon the pair in the garden, where, Hall writes, "a really catastrophic thing happened."

> Henry caught Collins roughly by the wrists, and he dragged her towards him, still handling her roughly, and he kissed her full on the lips. Stephen's head felt suddenly hot and dizzy, she was filled with a blind, uncomprehending rage; she wanted to cry out, but her voice failed completely, so that all she could do was splutter. But the very next moment she had seized a broken flower-pot and had hurled it hard and straight at the footman. It struck him in the face, cutting open his cheek, down which the blood trickled slowly. (28)

The passage, with its attention to the roughness of the kiss between Henry and Collins, seems to adopt Stephen's perspective, for whom the encounter is truly catastrophic: the scene exposes Collins's preference for the footman; it also offers her first glimpse of adult sexuality. But the account shifts in and out of Stephen's perspective; we might also understand the word "catastrophic," beyond the range of Stephen's childish diction, to be Hall's gloss on the trauma of the incident. Although Hall might gently ironize Stephen's precocious ardor, she takes the incident's effects on Stephen's development seriously.

Stephen's position as the unwanted third in this scene is paradigmatic: throughout the novel, her desire is thwarted by a woman's turn toward a man. But Stephen's reaction to seeing this kiss in the garden is not simply a jealous one. Rather, she experiences the incident as a referendum on her very being. Just before the incident, Collins has indulged Stephen's belief that she is a boy; she has been an attentive audience to Stephen's performances and has flirted with her in an offhand way. When Stephen sees Collins kiss the footman, her precariously constructed masculinity comes crashing down. As a result, Stephen throws a jagged piece of pottery at Henry, leaving a wide gash on his face that slowly trickles blood. In this recasting of the primal scene, Stephen, enraged at the footman, symbolically castrates him. At the same time, she identifies with him; the version of masculinity that she takes up operates under the sign of this wounding. In later life, Stephen wears this sign on her body, in the scar on her own cheek.

Immediately after Stephen finds Collins with the footman in the garden, Sir Philip tells Stephen explicitly that he is going to treat her like a boy. Hall ends the chapter with a description of the quasi-contractual character of this shared disavowal. After telling Stephen not to speak to her mother about such incidents, but to come to him, Stephen looks at him: "She nodded, and Sir Philip saw his own mournful eyes gazing back from his daughter's tear-stained face. But her lips set more firmly, and the cleft in her chin grew more marked with a new, childish will to courage. Bending down, he kissed her in absolute silence—it was like the sealing of a sorrowful pact" (29). Although the scene with Collins has pointed up the tragic impossibility of Stephen's desires, Stephen here takes comfort from her father by taking up his strategy of fetishistic disavowal. Father and daughter together deny the fact that she is not a boy, and the fact that, as a result, she will be systematically barred from erotic and affective satisfaction.

The apparent contrast Hall draws between the Gordons' perfection and Stephen's freakishness does not hold up under scrutiny. Rather, Stephen seems to inherit the longing—the sense of incompleteness and lack—that her parents feel at her birth. By repetition, Stephen magnifies the flaws of this "most perfect" family. When she finally leaves Morton, Stephen takes the sexological texts from her father's study: "She had taken nothing with her from Morton but the hidden books found in her father's study; these she had taken, as though in a way they were hers by some intolerable birthright" (233). The novel suggests that Stephen inherits her "intolerable birthright"—her patrimony of loss, lack, and grief—from both God and the Gordons.

Desolate Body

Stephen's cross-gender identification is a particular site of shame and confusion for her and for her latter-day readers. In queer criticism her gender identity is the primary terrain where debates about her abjection or her sufficiency play out. With her avowed desire to be a man, her powerful gender dysphoria, and her romantic failure, Stephen represents the melancholic image of the butch lesbian that critics and activists have tried to overcome in recent years.

The stereotype of the melancholic butch—freak of nature, failed woman or failed man, rejected lover—is so powerful and so affectively charged that debates about cross-identification in queer and lesbian circles are often drawn irresistibly to it. Particular questions about Stephen's abjection center on her masculine identification and her desire to be a man. Such a desire is nearly taboo in contemporary lesbian discourse, though it has been addressed recently by transgender and transsexual critics. With the easing of phobic pressures on the figure of the masculine woman, critics have been more willing to accept and engage with Stephen's masculinity.

But even critics who have recognized Stephen's masculinity have consistently misrecognized her felt experience of inadequacy, longing, and lack. Reading Stephen retrospectively into happier narratives of cross-gender identification, these critics have failed to attend to Hall's descriptions of Stephen's intensely negative feelings. Their strongly idealist rereadings imagine a perfectibility belied both by Stephen's experience and by contemporary queer experience. An understanding of Stephen's loneliness is inseparable from an understanding of her aversive experience of her own embodiment.

Recent analyses of Stephen's experience of her body have focused on the novel's "mirror scene," first explored in depth by Teresa de Lauretis in her 1994 book *The Practice of Love* and later taken up by Judith Halberstam and Jay Prosser. Returning home from a shopping trip, having been rebuffed by her lover Angela Crossby, Stephen contemplates her naked image in the mirror:

> That night she stared at herself in the glass; and even as she did so she hated her body with its muscular shoulders, its small compact breasts, and its slender flanks of an athlete. All her life she must drag this body of hers like a monstrous fetter imposed on her spirit. This strangely ardent yet sterile body that must worship yet never be worshipped in return by the creature of its adoration. She longed to maim it, for it made her feel cruel; it was so white, so strong, and so self-sufficient; yet withal so poor and unhappy a thing that her eyes filled with tears and her hate turned to pity. She began to grieve over it, touching her breasts with pitiful fingers, stroking her shoulders, letting her hands slip along her straight thighs—Oh, poor and most desolate body! (186–187)

Stephen's confrontation with her image proves to be intensely alien-
ating. Unlike the child in Lacan's mirror scene, Stephen does not see an
image that is ideal or complete but rather one that is at odds with her
desired self-image and must be "dragged around" like a "monstrous
fetter." While incapable of giving birth to children, Stephen's body is tormented by excessive desires. At once lacking and too complete or self-
sufficient, this "desolate body" exists for Stephen as an object of pity
rather than of admiration.

De Lauretis, in her avowedly "perverse" reading, interprets Stephen's
scene in terms of the Freudian theory of fetishism. Describing Stephen's
body as "faulty and faulted, dispossessed, inadequate to bear or signify
desire," de Lauretis captures the sense of nonfit, lack, and inadequacy
that defines Stephen's experience of her gender. In a reading that explicitly resists the "traditional reading of Stephen's masculinity complex,"
de Lauretis interprets this scene as a moment of Stephen's longing for
the lost female body:

> Because it is not feminine, this body is inadequate as the object of de-
> sire, to be desired by the other, and thus inadequate to signify the fe-
> male subject's desire in the feminine mode; however, because it is mas-
> culine but not male, it is also inadequate to signify or bear the subject's
> desire in the masculine mode.[21]

De Lauretis recasts Stephen's famous "castration complex" as a longing
for the prohibited female body. According to her reading, Stephen's
problem is not the absence of the phallus; rather, she argues, it is the
presence of the paternal phallus in Stephen's body "which renders the
female body (the mother's, other women's, and [her] own) forever inaccessible to Stephen" (212). What is essential in de Lauretis's theory of
desire is not the presence or absence of the phallus, but rather having a
body that the mother desires.[22] Given the conundrum of Stephen's
identity, she proposes a theory of "lesbian fetishism," which describes
the way that a lesbian fetish—which she defines as "any object, any sign
whatsoever, that marks the difference and the desire" (228) between lesbian lovers—substitutes for the phallus.

In his 1998 book *Second Skins* Jay Prosser argues that efforts to read
The Well as a lesbian novel have been "a case of trying to fit a square peg
into a round hole" (168). In "configuring inversion as a metaphor for
homosexuality," he argues, "we have left out what sexual inversion in

sexology and in Hall's novel are most literally about: . . . gender inversion, cross-gender identity." Prosser imagines gender inversion as a precursor to transsexual subjectivity, a longing for biological, psychic, and sexual transformation not yet medically available to the subjects in the case histories. Like Stephen herself, Prosser understands Stephen's gender trouble as "a failure to be real" (161–162), her difficulties a matter of "gender ontology" rather than social acceptance. Prosser treats Stephen sympathetically, taking her descriptions of her experience at face value. By interpreting *The Well* as, in effect, a case history, Prosser avoids reading Stephen's experience as a matter of "false consciousness" and provides an important counterbalance to the dominant mode of response to the novel.

According to Prosser, de Lauretis's perverse theory of lesbian desire erases Stephen's explicit and deeply felt longing for masculinity. Prosser insists that "the mirror scene is not a moment of sexual perversion—the perverse desire of the mannish lesbian—but of sexual inversion" and further argues that what Stephen sees in the mirror is "the inverted body of the pretransition female-to-male transsexual." For Prosser, the scene brings Stephen face to face with her ontological lack: the mirror shatters Stephen's illusion of her maleness and reflects back to her "the reality of her failure to be a real man" (161). Though Prosser's approach to *The Well* is important in countering dismissive or censuring responses to Stephen's masculinity, his literal interpretation of Stephen's desire to "be a real man" blinds him to the larger place of gender in the novel. Though Stephen understands herself as castrated or physically lacking, the people around her also often understand her as "insufficiently" castrated because she does not accede to her feminine role. Stephen's mother seems most often outraged not by the fact of Stephen's failure to be a man but by her overt masculinity—her failure to be a "normal woman." In taking Stephen's self-description at face value, Prosser treats her self-description as if it were unfiltered by ideology.[23]

In *Female Masculinity*, Judith Halberstam also critiques de Lauretis for her failure to acknowledge Stephen's desire to be masculine. But Halberstam avoids Prosser's literalism and his understanding of gender ontology in the novel. For Halberstam it is "social disapproval" rather than the lack of biological maleness that is the cause of Stephen's loneliness. Halberstam also takes issue with what she understands as de Lauretis's biologism. De Lauretis's theory of fetishism is itself an effort to explain how the female body can and does bear desire in the masculine mode; I understand de Lauretis to be describing Stephen's experience of her gender rather than making a definitive statement on the structure of female (masculine) desire. But Halberstam adamantly resists the notion that Stephen is lacking in relation either to femininity or to masculinity. She asserts that "nowhere . . . does the narrative even hint at . . . the inadequacy of Stephen's masculinity" and argues for the sufficiency of the female body to bear desire in a masculine mode.

For Halberstam, the mirror scene is a sign not of Stephen's hatred of the sight of her body but of her disidentification with femininity and nakedness. In diametric opposition to Prosser's claim that for Stephen "neither looking like nor feeling like constitute being" (161), Halberstam argues that the novel is structured by an "epistemology of the wardrobe," "a dressing that is not exactly cross-dressing and that positions itself against an aesthetic of nakedness" (99). Through such means, Halberstam suggests, Stephen performs her nonontological but nonetheless satisfying and real female masculinity. While Halberstam's reading interrupts stereotyped notions about the sadness or inadequacy of the figure of the butch lesbian, it does not account for Stephen's constant and deeply felt sense of lack. While it may be true that it is social disapproval that makes Stephen feel like a loser, she nonetheless experiences her loneliness as a bodily feeling of lack. Halberstam's desire to affirm the possibility of a successful and satisfying female masculinity draws attention away from Stephen's affective and corporeal experience.

Prosser suggests, finally, that it is the "repeated failure of lesbian relations more than any other feature that thwarts the attempt to read the novel as lesbian" (166). Crucially, he acknowledges Stephen's lack and the pain associated with it, but he is able to do so, perhaps, only because he has another narrative in mind for her. Confronted with Stephen's ontological problem, Prosser suggests an ontological cure: the technological modification of Stephen's being. Prosser takes the novel's failure to provide a happy lesbian ending as a failure to be a lesbian novel. (Might one also argue, then, that *Romeo and Juliet* is not about straight people?) Prosser goes on to suggest that narratives that "don't quite fit, which exceed or resist their homosexual location . . . might find belonging in a transsexual context" (168). Despite his understanding of Stephen's self-division and her difficulty in existing between the sexes, Prosser assimilates her story to a redemptive narrative that, through means of the modern technology of sexual reassignment surgery, solves her problem in the present. Thus his own critical practice works in concert with the genre of the transsexual autobiography, in which "all life events in the autobiographies seem to lead toward the telos of the sex-changed self. This gendered coherence is inextricable from the narrative coherence of the genre" (116). Prosser admits that such a tidy tale of progress is a back-formation, a kind of order possible only in retrospect, but that is precisely what allows him to rewrite Hall's novel as a body narrative of transsexuality.

Put off by the darkness of Hall's account of Stephen's gender trouble, each of these critics attempts to assimilate Stephen's narrative to a later, happier narrative of gendered existence. But Stephen is beyond the reach of such redemptive narratives. Throughout she struggles with the question of how to give and receive love, a question inseparable from the unresolvable nature of her gender identity. Stephen cannot steer a clear course between the masculine and the feminine: any attempt to re-solve her sense of nonfit into a longing for either masculinity or femi-ninity misses a crucial aspect of her experience. Of course these feelings are ideological, but they are also real. Stephen is doomed to experience her own body as essentially unlovable; the reasons for this failure are crushingly specific—her sense of failure and longing has everything to do with being a mannish woman before the war in rural, quasi-aristocratic England. And yet this does not mean that a change in cir-cumstances would render Stephen perfectly happy, perfectly satisfied. Despite our present sense of expanding possibilities for gendered em-bodiment, the melancholic trace in Stephen's experience of herself is im-possible to wish away.[24]

Unwanted Being

The relationship between gender formation and loss is at the heart of Judith Butler's work on the melancholy of gender. In the introduction to *The Psychic Life of Power,* Butler underscores the crucial role of loss in subject formation and the assumption of gender:

> Is there a loss that cannot be thought, cannot be owned or grieved, which forms the condition of possibility for the subject? Is this what Hegel called "the loss of the loss" . . . ? Is there not a longing to grieve—and, equivalently, an inability to grieve—that which one never

was able to love, a love that falls short of the "conditions of existence"? This is a loss not merely of the object or of some set of objects, but of love's own possibility: the loss of the ability to love, the unfinished grieving for that which founds the subject. (24)

Butler considers "the loss of the loss" primarily in connection with her theory of heterosexual gender melancholia, in which she posits the foreclosure of same-sex attachments as the basis for normative gender identifications. This theory, which follows from Freud's reflection on melancholic incorporation in *The Ego and the Id,* allows Butler to consider the founding loss at the heart of both normative and nonnormative gender identifications. Such an understanding of the tenuous nature of all gender identifications accords, as we have seen, with Hall's representation of gender identity in *The Well;* Hall repeatedly links Stephen's abject experience of gender to the gender anxieties and failures of the "so-called normal." But in *The Well,* such anxieties, once activated, stick to Stephen, transforming her into a despised creature. We might think of Butler's attempt to resituate such losses at the foundation of normative gender identity as a way of easing the burden of stigmatization that attaches to people like Stephen.

Though she has considered the relationship between the performativity of drag and heterosexual gender melancholia at length, Butler is much more hesitant to extend this theory to a description of cross-gender identification. As Butler points out herself, there is a risk in speaking of gender melancholia in relation to figures who are already so closely allied in popular consciousness with melancholia. Discussing the figure of "the melancholic drag queen," Butler writes:

Where there is an ungrieved loss in drag performance *(and I am sure that such a generalization cannot be universalized),* perhaps it is a loss that is refused and incorporated in the performed identification, one that re-iterates a gendered idealization and its radical uninhabitability. This is *neither a territorialization of the feminine by the masculine* nor an *"envy" of the masculine by the feminine,* nor a sign of the essential plasticity of gender. What it does suggest is that gender performance allegorizes a loss it cannot grieve, allegorizes the incorporative fantasy of melancholia whereby an object is phantasmatically taken in or on as a way of refusing to let it go.

The above analysis is a risky one because it suggests that for a "man" performing femininity or for a "woman" performing masculinity (the latter is always, in effect, to perform a little less, given that femininity is often cast as the spectacular gender) there is an attachment to and a loss and refusal of the figure of femininity by the man, or the figure of masculinity by the woman. Thus, it is important to underscore that drag is an effort to negotiate cross-gendered identifications, but *that cross-gendered identification is not the exemplary paradigm for thinking about homosexuality*, although it may be one. (235, emphasis added)

In this passage, one can hear Butler speaking back to a series of stigmatizing narratives about queer and transgendered people. Butler is anxious that her theory of gender melancholia work to disrupt rather than reinforce the habitual association of cross-gender identification, homosexuality, and melancholy.

The narratives that Butler resists here sound strikingly like her own theory of gender melancholia. In her theory of blocked identifications there is a surprising and persistent echo of the received understandings of the melancholy of both homosexuality and cross-gender identification. Her theory of gender as founded on loss and foreclosed desires chimes in particular with pathologizing descriptions of butch subjectivity. For instance, Halberstam writes regarding the stone butch in *Female Masculinity*: "the stone butch has been characterized as more blocked, more lacking, and more rigid than all other sexual identities" (112). Rather than pursuing the connections between the melancholic drag queen or the sad stone butch and her theory of gender melancholia, Butler explores the melancholia of all gender identifications, both normative and nonnormative. Her aim is a reversal of terms, so that heterosexual identifications will be understood as being the most blocked, lacking, and rigid of identifications. "In this sense," she writes, "the 'truest' lesbian melancholic is the strictly straight woman, and the 'truest' gay male melancholic is the strictly straight man" (235).

While the political importance of her attempt to disrupt the identification between gender cross-identification and melancholy is clear, Butler refuses to consider how gays and lesbians might actually live out their experiences of the melancholy of gender. Hall's representation of Stephen's subject formation offers a painfully slow-paced and explicit account of such an experience. In a crucial scene Hall describes Stephen's reaction, directly after she has been betrayed by Angela and lacerated by her mother for her "unnatural" desires, to another shattering experience of refusal:

> As though drawn there by some strong natal instinct, Stephen went
> straight to her father's study; and she sat in the old arm-chair that had
> survived him; then she buried her face in her hands.
>
> All the loneliness that had gone before was as nothing to this new
> loneliness of spirit. An immense desolation swept down upon her, an
> immense need to cry out and claim understanding for herself, an im-
> mense need to find an answer to the riddle of her unwanted being. All
> around her were grey and crumbling ruins, and under those ruins her
> love lay bleeding; shamefully wounded by Angela Crossby, shamefully
> soiled and defiled by her mother—a piteous, suffering, defenceless
> thing, it lay bleeding under the ruins. (203)

Utterly abandoned, her loneliness at a peak, Stephen takes refuge in the
study of her dead father. The study is a particularly charged site of
meaning in the novel; Sir Philip has spent late nights here reading the
books on inversion that he has locked away from his wife and daughter.
Later, when he is crushed under a tree, he is taken to his study to die,
unable at the end to utter the secret that is so much on his mind.
Stephen's occupation of her father's study in this scene serves to underscore her continuing identification with him and her disidentification
with her mother—which is, according to the copy of Krafft-Ebing she is
about to discover, precisely her "problem." The fact that Stephen is
drawn to the study by a "strong natal instinct" would seem to indicate
that Stephen's melancholy here is not only a delayed mourning for her
father but also a preexisting structure of gender melancholia activated
by his death and by her mother's refusal. In addition, the rhetoric of
encryption in this scene evokes Stephen's melancholic incorporation
of the image of her dead father. The fact that Stephen discovers "the
secret of herself" in her father's study is apt, because it is here that he
has brooded most over the image of Stephen's—and his own—failed
masculinity.

Stephen's confrontation with her mother constitutes a curious
restaging of the oedipal crisis. While Stephen has desired her mother
throughout the novel with relative impunity, it is only after the death of
Sir Philip that Lady Gordon herself forbids Stephen access to her. While
the Gordon family scene reproduces the oedipal geometry—with
Stephen in the starring role of son—Lady Gordon's prohibition here
runs counter to the oedipal logic of prohibition. The mother is not for-
bidden to Stephen on account of the taboo against incest; rather,

Stephen here again encounters what Butler describes as a foreclosure of a "modality of desire." Lady Gordon's "No" is articulated as a homosexual prohibition: she bars access to Angela and, by implication, to herself, telling Stephen that she has always been disgusted by her touch. But it is interesting to note that this homosexual prohibition is articulated primarily as a prohibition against gender inversion. "Above all," says Lady Gordon, "this thing is a sin against the father who bred you, the father whom you dare to resemble" (200). This relocation of the homosexual prohibition to Stephen's gender identity has the result of anchoring lack securely in her body, which readily produces itself as the site of loss and castration.

On the one hand, the difficulties presented by Stephen's loneliness are epistemological: she feels "an immense need to find an answer to the riddle of her unwanted being." But, on the other hand, with the resonant phrase "unwanted being," Hall underlines the ontological aspect of Stephen's loneliness. The phrase both describes the experience that she has just weathered—her rejection by Angela and her mother—and points to a more general social fact: Stephen bears an unwanted identity, a social subjectivity constituted by public refusal and scorn. Her public and private experiences of refusal are reinforced by the ontological language of inversion, the pathologizing discourse that renders her very being excessive. The word "unwanted" resonates throughout the novel, for it describes how personal rejections are internalized, so that they form the core of Stephen's being. A description of a transitory event becomes a fixed quality, an essential aspect of identity. Unwanted from birth, Stephen becomes an "unwanted being": it is her utter abandonment by all those who might have recognized or desired her that makes her loneliness so acute. Such an experience is dictated as well by a more general social logic. The refusals that Stephen undergoes follow from the assumption that she is unfit for love and life. Thus, Lady Anna and Angela reject her as a matter of course. For Stephen, however, the sting of erotic rejection casts her even further into despair because it coincides with a general expectation of failed love.

Hall stages this scene of Stephen's total abjection against a backdrop of "grey and crumbling ruins." Neither public nor private, this allegorical landscape figures the catastrophic collapse of the distinction between the two spheres. Ruins stand in here for the experience of refusal and for Stephen's ruined subjectivity. The "landscape of ruins" that Hall evokes in this passage recalls a moment from Butler's discussion of gender melancholia. She writes: "In melancholia, not only is the loss of an other or an ideal lost to consciousness, but the social world in which such a loss became possible is also lost. The melancholic does not merely withdraw the lost object from consciousness, but withdraws into the psyche a configuration of the social world as well" (181). In this scene, Stephen's interior world is revealed as the site of such a devastated social landscape. Significantly, Hall moves from a discussion of Stephen's self to a description of "her love," the love that lies bleeding under the ruins ("a piteous, suffering, defenceless thing, it lay bleeding under the ruins"). The antecedent to this "it" is buried earlier in the passage: in this final, uncanny moment, not only Stephen's love but Stephen herself is pinned under the ruins. Naming Stephen an "it," Hall enacts her abjection linguistically, metamorphosing her into a piece of crushed flesh.

We might say that, for queer subjects, the loss that is disavowed in heterosexual gender melancholia is lived as a real social and affective experience. Butler's speculation about the constitutive loss at the heart of all gender identifications resonates remarkably with the phenomenology of Stephen's "unwanted being." In the landscape of ruins surrounding her heroine, Hall offers an image of the crushing convergence of the social, psychic, affective, and corporeal factors that determine Stephen's inability to be loved. Butler's project has allowed us to understand gender melancholia as a condition associated not only with nonnormative gendered embodiments but also with gender as such. The antihomophobic charge of this project is undeniable. And yet such a project is incomplete without an account of what it feels like to live out the melancholia structuring all sexual and gender identity.

The Forsaken

> Worse, it was traditional to feel this way.
>
> —John Ashbery, *Girls on the Run*

Stephen's final act in *The Well* is to sacrifice her lover Mary to her old friend Martin. Though Mary loves her and wants to stay with her, Stephen decides that Mary should marry Martin to have access to all the things that Stephen feels she could never give her: "children, a home that the world would respect, ties of affection that the world would hold sacred, the blessed security and the peace of being released from the world's persecution" (430). In a move that has deeply troubled lesbian and queer critics, Stephen seals her own lonely fate, accepting her role as martyr and tragic lover as she affirms the priority of this heterosexual union. It is now, Hall writes, that Stephen "must pay very dearly indeed for that inherent respect of the normal which nothing had ever been able to destroy, not even the long years of persecution . . . She must pay for the instinct, which in earliest childhood, had made her feel something akin to worship for the perfect thing which she had divined in the love that existed between her parents" (430).

At the end of the novel, Stephen is utterly abandoned, crushed by the refusal that she herself has engineered. Standing alone in her room, Stephen's desolate interior space is thronged by "unbidden guests," a ghostly procession of the "lost and terrible brothers from Alec's" (436). Hall writes:

> Oh, but they were many, these unbidden guests, and they called very softly at first and then louder. They were calling her by name, saying: "Stephen Stephen!" The quick, the dead, and the yet unborn—all calling her, softly at first and then louder. Aye, and those lost and terrible brothers from Alec's, they were here, and they were also calling: "Stephen, Stephen, speak with your God and ask Him why he has left us forsaken!" She could see their marred and reproachful faces with the haunted, melancholy eyes of the invert—eyes that had looked too long on a world that lacked all pity and all understanding: "Stephen, Stephen, speak with your God and ask Him why He has left us forsaken!" And these terrible ones started pointing at her with their shaking, white-skinned, effeminate fingers: "You and your kind have stolen our birthright; you have taken our strength and given us your weakness!" They were pointing at her with white, shaking fingers. (437)

At the moment of her most intense suffering, Stephen is confronted with a ghostly procession of the inverted. As if in response to her earlier disavowal of these abject figures, the most miserable of all the miserable army return, demanding recognition. In this apocalyptic last scene, Stephen comes face to face with the pain—including her own and Mary's—that she has disavowed over the course of the novel. It is precisely against such pain that Stephen had wished to guard herself in her earlier confrontation with the boy at Alec's. But at the end of the book, these haunted, reproachful figures overwhelm her, accusing her with their shaking, white, effeminate fingers, and asking her—twice—why she and her God have left them forsaken.

As she resisted the boy at Alec's, Stephen attempts to resist the onslaught of the miserable army. But they are too many for her—"they are coming on." Stephen capitulates in an orgy of grief and anguish:

> Rockets of pain, burning rockets of pain—their pain, her pain, all welded together into one great consuming agony. Rockets of pain that shot up and burst, dropping scorching tears of fire on the spirit—her pain, their pain . . . all the misery at Alec's. And the press and the clamour of those countless others—they fought, they trampled, they were getting her under. In their madness to become articulate through her, they were tearing her to pieces, getting her under. (436–437)

In this terrible moment of possession, Stephen is utterly transfigured by her experience of searing pain. At the end, Hall writes, Stephen's "barren womb" bears fruit, as these "countless others" inhabit Stephen's desolate interior space. The collective voice of these lost brothers rings through Stephen, "a demand like the gathering together of great waters." In the end, in spite of herself, Stephen cries aloud with their voice, "Acknowledge us, oh God, before the whole world. Give us also the right to our existence!" (437). Though Stephen to the last has continued to disavow her kind, this final moment of agony reconnects her to their suffering, allowing her to speak on their behalf, to represent them to God and the world.

If the earlier scene at Alec's offers an allegory for the critical disavowal of Stephen Gordon, *The Well*'s final scene imagines the consequences of such a disavowal. When the ghostly army of inverts accuses Stephen of "stealing their birthright," they point to her refusal to ally herself with them. In spite of her persecution, Stephen continues to worship the normal and to distance herself from those "battered remnants of men whom the world" has "stamped under." The miserable army reproaches Stephen for taking only the strength and not the weakness of these subjects. This accusation has come to ring strangely across the years, as Stephen herself has been abandoned by contemporary critics. The novel's final scene points to the costs of attending to the strength and never to the weakness—the fear, the suffering, and the self-hatred—of those who have come before us.

In attempting to chart our course by the lights of the queer subjects who preceded us, there is always a temptation to disavow their suffering. We tend to read history off of the successes of the past and to see in its failures only ideology at work. Proceeding in the mode of affirmation, we have constructed a genealogy that steps from stone to stone, looking for high points of pride, gender flexibility, and resistance. Of course, such forms of wishful thinking can be very effective in bringing about political transformation: as Elizabeth Grosz writes in relation to feminism, "any oppositional political movement . . . involves a disavowal of social reality so that change becomes conceivable and possible."[25] But political change can happen not only through the disavowal of loss, but also through cleaving to it.

We need a genealogy of queer affect that does not overlook the negative, shameful, and difficult feelings that have been so central to queer existence in the last century. We have been used to thinking of such affects as pure waste, the inevitable by-products of our historical tough luck. But as long as homophobia continues to structure our public and private lives, and books like *The Well* continue to be so eerily familiar, we cannot do without an analysis of the intimate effects of homophobia. Although it is painful to recognize our continuity with figures like Stephen Gordon, it is through such shaming acts of identification that we can come to terms with the difficulty of queer history and with its continuing legacy in the present. Such a reckoning is necessary, for without it we cannot remember history's failures, or do justice to our own experience in the present. Celebration will only get us so far, for pride itself can be toxic when it is sealed off from the shame that nurtured it.

In an essay published in 2000, Christopher Castiglia suggests that individual and collective acts of memory are central to queer existence. Castiglia's essay captures the ambivalence of memory for queer communities, which are strengthened through acts of retrospection, but whose legacy is often one of loss. At the end of the article, Castiglia writes, "To look back is, after all, to refuse the imperative laid down at the destruction of Sodom."[26] The significance of Castiglia's invocation of this story is made evident by the story itself: "Then the Lord rained on Sodom and Gomorrah sulfur and fire from the Lord out of heaven; and he overthrew those cities, and all the Plain, and all the inhabitants of the cities, and what grew on the ground. But Lot's wife, behind him, looked back, and

she became a pillar of salt" (Gen. 19.24–26). Lot's wife looks back on a
scene in which all of her past attachments have been destroyed. In doing
so, she refuses the imperative of the law and responds instead to the call
of what the law has destroyed. The fear, of course, is that in looking
backward, we will be paralyzed by grief, and grief will overwhelm politics. But grief is politics, to the extent that politics is inseparable from
history.

5

Impossible Objects

Sylvia Townsend Warner and the Longing for Revolution

> And how do I desire it? he thought. I want to feel it on every side, more abundantly. But I want to die first.
>
> —Sylvia Townsend Warner, *Mr. Fortune's Maggot*

A persistent doubt about whether or not sexuality has a history is one of the most significant challenges faced by scholars in the field of the history of sexuality. The field has constituted itself against such disbelief, against claims that sexuality is too private and too idiosyncratic to constitute an object of sustained historical inquiry; that the evidence for a history of same-sex relations is slender; and that any look at the history of queer experience is inevitably a projection of a current state of affairs, a matter of "special pleading."[1] Despite the growth of this discipline over the last several decades, the validity of the history of sexuality as an object of study can still never be assumed, but must always be argued. The construction of queer existence as an "impossible object" of historical inquiry suggests an analogy between the epistemological disadvantage of queer studies in the academy today and the epistemological disadvantage of individual queers, those "impossible people" who, over the course of the last century, have been marginalized not only through moral censure but also through silence and disregard. In this sense, we might say that the history of the field recapitulates the history of the community; the demand for the recognition of queer history as a viable practice is charged with a long history of similar claims for the viability of certain "hard to believe" modes of existence and desire. The inventiveness of a whole range of queer historical practices might be understood as a result of the paired necessities of having to "fight for it" and to "make it up."[2]

Through such highly charged encounters, the past itself is transformed: it becomes, in the words of Leila Rupp, a "desired past"—not a neutral chronicle of events but rather an object of speculation, fantasy, and longing.[3] This chapter explores the encounter between history and fantasy in Sylvia Townsend Warner's 1936 novel *Summer Will Show* and considers the link between historical fantasy and the revolutionary imagination. Written in the years leading up to the Spanish Civil War, the novel chronicles the growing intimacy between two women against the background of the failed Paris revolution of 1848. Warner turns her attention to dissident political and sexual desires and to the fate of social outsiders in a volatile historical moment. At the same time, the novel's own narrative structure is uneven and jagged. In attempting to give narrative shape to impossible desires—queer desire and the desire for revolution—the novel departs from the linear temporality of progressive history.

The ostensible subject of *Summer Will Show* is the desire for a workers' revolution and for the transformation of everyday life. While the transformative energies of revolution are invoked in the novel, these energies are short-circuited again and again. Through exploring revolution and its failures, Warner imagines a form of expectancy linked to a vision of history as permeated by loss. She imagines a revolution fueled by despair and by desire. Warner's figuring of the revolution as an "impossible object of desire" is significantly at odds with a forward-looking, scientific Marxism, but it is at the heart of the novel's attention to a politics of affect.

At the center of such reflections in the novel is the bohemian artist Minna Lemuel. Orphaned by a pogrom in Lithuania, Minna makes a living as a storyteller in Paris, while supporting the work of the revolution. On the night of the February uprising, a salon in her apartment is interrupted by workers demanding carriages for the building of a barricade in the street. As Minna looks on from her window, her new friend Sophia Willoughby feels a sense of flatness in the proceedings; she casts a glance at Minna, who says:

> You think I am not very enthusiastic? I have not given them my carriage, have not exclaimed . . . Perhaps you think I am not very sincere. But if you have ever longed for a thing, longed for it with all that

is noblest in you and worked for it with all that is most base and most calculating, you would understand with what desolation of spirit one beholds the dream made flesh.[4]

The setting of *Summer Will Show* is, like that of many of Warner's other novels, a failed revolution. Minna speaks these words to Sophia in the early days of the uprising, before the alliance between the workers and the bourgeoisie was broken. The desolation that her comment registers is not a response to the failure of a particular dream, although it proleptically invokes the collective disappointment to come. At this point, however, Minna suggests a more general disappointment—the desolation that comes with the realization of any dream.

The subject of the novel is revolutionary hope; at the same time, Warner traces a number of darker feelings—desolation, despair, regret, fear—that attach to the desire for social transformation. Gillian Beer captures this element of Warner's fiction well, noting that she is "rare among writers of the 1930s in producing work at once skeptical about belief and wholehearted in its relish of the possible. The Utopian reach of her fictions of the 1930s is, over and over again, undermined sardonically from within."[5] Tracing this mixture of utopianism and disappointment throughout Warner's writing, Beer argues that in these novels "escape is investigated rather than celebrated. The hoped-for alterity—of island life in *Mr. Fortune's Maggot* (1927), of revolution in *Summer Will Show* (1936), of Spain in *After the Death of Don Juan* (1938)—is bared to view, with all its catastrophic losses" (76–77).[6] In its narration of a failed revolution, the novel suggests the compatibility of political activity and feelings of despair. In fact, despair in the novel appears as a kind of resource: as much as hope, it is necessary to make change happen.[7] Such a structure of feeling is grounded, I would argue, in a history of queer experience: in the association of same-sex desire with the impossible and in a history of longing for recognition in an impossible elsewhere. Linking revolutionary longing to this history of queer longing, Warner explores the dark affects that fuel social change.

While the novel fits to a degree in a tradition of utopian political fiction, its orientation is toward the past rather than the future. *Summer Will Show* does not project an achieved social world toward which it is tending. There are few indications of a perfected social world to come. Above all, it is clear that such a future is not the moment in which Warner is writing in the 1930s. The postrevolutionary world that the novel imagines is characterized by loss, violence, and disappointment; the failures of this historical revolution illuminate the failures of the present rather than setting off its successes. More often, though, the "other world" that the novel invokes is not a future world at all. Warner's revolutionary imagination is bound not to the redeemed world but to the damaged world that it aims to repair.

Impossible Histories

Critical responses to *Summer Will Show* tend to present it in extremely polarized terms: they see it either as a Marxist novel—concerned with class politics and relatively uninterested in questions of romance, fantasy, and sexuality—or as a sapphic text in which the workers' revolution becomes secondary to Warner's representation of an intimate relation between two women.[8] The novel obeys many of the dictates of the historical novel as Georg Lukács outlined it in his work of the 1930s; it returns to a crucial moment of social upheaval and explores the "historical psychology" of its characters—the historicity of their "inner motives and behaviour."[9] Work that has emphasized this aspect of the novel has tended to disregard its plot of same-sex desire. For instance, in her introduction to the 1986 Virago reprint of *Summer Will Show*, Claire Harman asserts that "lesbianism was not Sylvia Townsend Warner's theme in this book," and that the novel's plot of "anarchic" love forms the backdrop to its central concern—class politics.[10] Terry Castle has made the strongest argument for the fantastic element of the novel in her article "Sylvia Townsend Warner and the Counterplot of Lesbian Fiction." Castle argues that *Summer Will Show* is aligned with Warner's more explicitly fantastic fiction (such as her popular first novel, *Lolly Willowes*); according to her reading, the novel breaks with conventions of verisimilitude in order to imagine a world in which lesbian love would be unexceptional, a part of everyday life.

Janet Montefiore attempts to reconcile these two critical approaches, but fails.[11] She ends by suggesting that the difference between these two readings "is, finally, political": "for [Castle's] lesbian-feminist reading, what is important about the book is that it goes beyond plausibility; it 'dismantles the real, as it were, in a search for the not-yet-real, something unpredicted and unpredictable.' My own socialist-feminist interpretation values the novel for the way it enables the reader to share in the transformation of a woman's consciousness, not only of her erotic desires . . . but of the material world of political struggle . . . These opposed interpretations are, so far as I can see, irreconcilable: either *Summer Will Show* engages with history, or it does not" (212).

Such a description does not capture the complexity of the place of history in the novel. *Summer Will Show* is probably best described as a historical novel imbued with strong elements of fantasy. Although it is possible to describe its peculiar tone as the product of a confluence of genres, what is at stake in the novel is a rethinking of history as itself bound up with fantasy. History in the novel is not simply a neutral chronicle of events; nor is it a ground for the working out of the dynamics of class conflict. Rather, history—like the future—is a medium for dreaming about the transformation of social life. Such dreams bear little resemblance to the predictions of a scientific Marxism: they are wild dreams, desires so powerful that they disrupt the linear temporality of progressive history. Castle describes such temporal warping as an effect of desire in her treatment of sexuality in the novel. For Warner, however, desire for another "impossible" world aims to transform not only sexual relations but all aspects of the social. While the presence of a fantastic element within history has become a familiar concept in recent queer historiography, Warner borrows from intimate experience to introduce this fantastic element into a representation of class struggle.

When *Summer Will Show* opens, Sophia Willoughby is living alone with her two children on her family estate. Conservative and independent, she is estranged from her husband and isolated from those around her. In the novel's first pages, Sophia and her two children spend a hot summer afternoon walking up to the lime kiln on the property; Sophia's children have developed whooping cough and, repeating the treatment that her parents gave her, she takes them to breathe the fumes of the kiln. Soon after, the routine at Blandamer is upset by the arrival of Sophia's nephew Caspar, the illegitimate son of an uncle working in the West Indies. Sophia is seduced by his beauty and falls into a "holiday frame of mind" (43). Soon, however, she recovers her composure and begins to feel that Caspar's presence is a threat to domestic tranquility; she accompanies him to a nearby boarding school and drops him off. When she returns, the children have fallen ill; as it turns out, the encounter with the kiln man has left them with fatal cases of smallpox.

Sophia's husband Frederick returns from Paris to see the children, who die soon thereafter.

The death of the children marks a turning point in the novel. In a state of numbing grief, Sophia decides to try to have another child. First she walks to the lime kiln one night and makes an overture to the man who had infected her children; after he rejects and insults her, she decides that she will travel to Paris to find Frederick and have another child with him. When she arrives, she fails to find Frederick at his hotel and so finds her way to Minna's apartment, where a mixed company of artists, bohemians, and revolutionaries is gathered together. At first put off by the disorder of the scene, Sophia is soon absorbed by the story that Minna is telling of her parents' death by pogrom. When workers arrive requesting carriages for the barricades, all the guests leave except Sophia, who sleeps over. The women spend the whole next day talking and begin an intimacy that occupies the rest of the narrative. Sophia becomes increasingly estranged from Frederick, who eventually cuts off access to her money; she moves in with Minna, and begins working for the Communists.

Late in the novel, Caspar reappears; he has left boarding school, and Frederick has paid his subscription in the counterrevolutionary force of the Gardes Mobiles. Sophia once again shuffles him off, asking him to move out of the apartment. The novel ends several months after it began, during the failed June uprising. Minna and Sophia go to fight together on the barricades; Caspar reappears for the last time, and stabs Minna with his bayonet. Sophia herself is captured, and though nearly executed, she is released at the last minute. She searches for Minna's body without success, at last returning to their apartment alone. In the final moments of the novel, Sophia sits down and begins to read the pamphlet she had been distributing the day before—it is *The Communist Manifesto*.

The choice of 1848 is important in terms of the generic status of the novel. It was, to begin with, a turning point in the history of class relations. The revolution of 1848 seemed to promise a productive alliance between the bourgeoisie and the working class; however, in the bloody suppression in June, these hopes were crushed, and the counterrevolutionary force of the bourgeoisie was revealed. It was also an important date in the history of sexuality. The birth of modern homosexuality is usually dated to the term's appearance in medical literature later in the century; however, the importance of the figure of the lesbian as a counter in French literary and artistic circles should not be underestimated. It was, after all, Charles Baudelaire's midcentury Sapphic writings that led Walter Benjamin to name the lesbian the "heroine of modernity." Reading Lukács as well as Marx's *Eighteenth Brumaire of Louis Napoleon,* Thomas Foster describes the way that 1848 fell short of its revolutionary potential, remarking that "the February revolution released desires for emancipation that European society was not ready to fulfill or at least created a social space where these desires could be expressed, and for Warner that social space includes lesbian desire" (548).

The conjuring of unfulfilled desires in the revolution of 1848 has made it one of the most ghostly and fantastic moments in modernity. In the opening of the *Manifesto* that is cited at length at the end of Warner's novel, Marx and Engels call for a manifestation of the dream of Communism: "A spectre is haunting Europe—the spectre of Communism. All the powers of old Europe have united in a holy alliance to exorcise this spectre . . . It is high time that the Communists should lay before the whole world their point of view, their aims and tendencies, and set against this spectre of Communism a Manifesto of the Party itself" (cited in Warner, 406–407). What Marx and Engels call for is the dream made flesh: the replacement of ghostly potential with manifest reality. Like so many crucial moments in modernity, 1848 split reality in two: a future taken up with the progressive realization of this dream and a past in which the ghost of what might have been continues to walk.

What is fantastic in *Summer Will Show* is linked both to utopian longings and to a fixation with the past—a willingness to be haunted. As Christopher Nealon has argued, the saturation of historical "experience" with historical fantasy is characteristic of queer representation in the twentieth century.[12] Here, the return to the unfinished revolution of 1848 and to the interrupted intimacy of Sophia and Minna offers Warner a means of opening history to currents of speculation, fantasy, and desire.

Tragic Praxis

The novel takes on questions of genre and the relation between "historical faithfulness" and fantasy in Minna's narration of her childhood in Lithuania. This story is a piece of historical fiction set into the 1848 present of the novel. In this account, Minna describes her political awakening; in this sense, her narrative serves not only as a model for Sophia's imminent awakening but also as an allegory of the emergence of the historical within the novel itself.

Before describing the murder of her parents, Minna recalls the spring when her mother took her out to see the river breaking up in the thaw. The scene, which will soon reappear under a radically different aspect, at first appears a transparent symbol of revolutionary freedom:

> On either side it was still frozen, the arched ice rearing up above the water like opened jaws. But in the center channel the current flowed furiously, and borne along on it, jostling and crashing, turning over and over, grating together with long harsh screams, were innumerable blocks of ice. As the river flowed its strong swirling tongue licked furiously at the icy margins, and undermined them, and with a shudder and a roar of defeat another fragment would break away and be swept downstream. It was like a battle. It was like a victory. The rigid winter could stand no longer, it was breaking up, its howls and vanquished threats swept past me, its strongholds fell and were broken one against another, it was routed at last.
>
> I wept with excitement, and my mother comforted me, thinking I was afraid. But I could not explain what I felt, though I knew it was not fear. For then I knew only the wintry words of my race, words such as exile, and captivity, and bondage. I had never heard the word Liberty. But it was Liberty I acclaimed, seeing the river sweeping away its fetters, tossing its free neck under the ruined yoke. (122–123)

The passage describes the taking up of a landscape into allegory. In the image of the raging river with its "icy margins," the young Minna reads a whole narrative of the inevitable defeat of the "rigid winter" by the irrepressible force of "Liberty." While her mother is only able to read her emotion as fear—seeing it only in the framework of the "wintry words of [her] race"—Minna remembers feeling an emotion that she could not name, which promises to break her out of a Jewish narrative of diasporic endurance and move her toward a socialist narrative of redemption.

Continuing her narrative, Minna flashes forward to the next spring, when she sees the aftereffects of her dream of liberty made flesh. In this return to the scene of this awakening, everything looks different: it is a pestilence year, and a fog hangs over the landscape. The "thunders and crashings" of the previous year can still be heard at the riverbank, but the scene is quite different. Although the first view of the river offered an image of a landscape wholly absorbed into allegory, in the second view, allegory has reverted back into material reality. The river itself is visible again, along with the raw materials that go into the production of human liberty:

> A mist hung over the water, flowing with the river, the glory of the year before was not there. Then, as I looked, I saw that on the hurried ice-blocks there were shapes, men and horses, half frozen into the ice, half trailing in the water. And in the ice were stains of blood. Last year, I remembered, it had seemed like a battle, like a victory. Had there been blood and corpses then, and I had forgotten them? The full river seemed to flow more heavily, when ice-block struck against ice-block they clanged like iron bells. (124–125)

In this passage, the ideal of liberty precipitates out into its constituent parts: dead men, horses, and spilled blood. This second thaw makes visible the losses that constitute any victory. Here, especially, it is the flesh of horses on which the reality of these metaphors of liberty is realized. In the first spring, the river is figured as a wild horse, rearing up between its banks and finally "sweeping away its fetters, tossing its free neck under the ruined yoke." The next year, the corpses of horses, frozen into ice along with their riders, are carried downstream. The violent rhetoric of the first passage—the jolting and crashing, the fury, the screams and howls—is here materialized in the form of human and animal remains, victims frozen into a grisly legibility. Such an engagement with loss is modeled in Minna's story, and she insists throughout the novel on the durability of suffering. Revolutionary consciousness in *Summer Will Show* is imagined as a desire for an impossible redemption—a total transformation of society that cannot and yet must take place.

This moment in Minna's narrative reflects a tragic view of political action that Raymond Williams articulated in his 1966 book *Modern Tragedy*. Williams understands revolution as "the inevitable working through of a deep and tragic disorder."[13] Identifying this revolutionary violence as a tragic necessity, Williams cautions against a utopianism that would overlook the costs of such struggles. Responding to the enemies of revolution, Williams writes:

This tragic aspect of revolution, which we are bound to acknowledge, cannot be understood in such ways. We have still to attend to the whole action, and to see actual liberation as part of the same process as the terror which appals us. I do not mean that liberation cancels the terror; I mean only that they are connected, and that this connection is tragic. The final truth in this matter seems to be that revolution—the long revolution against human alienation—produces, in real historical circumstances, its own new kinds of alienation, which it must struggle to understand and which it must overcome, if it is to remain revolutionary. (82)

Williams's treatment of liberation has a good deal in common with Minna's recasting of the ideal of liberty as an icy panorama of dead flesh. Williams cautions against an idealizing discourse of liberation that would "cancel the terror" that liberation demands. Resisting the temptation of hardening into a new form of alienation means sustaining an open-ended engagement with loss.

In *Summer Will Show,* radical social change is imagined as tragic or catastrophic; at the same time, its gains are anything but certain. In the novel, Warner takes a step away from the progressivist logic of Marxist revolutionary teleology, imagining revolution as an object of fantasy; the longing it inspires is impossible to satisfy. In his reading of the novel, Robert L. Caserio discusses Warner's distance from Marx, and her emphasis on human fragility. He writes:

For Warner, Marx's analytic road to liberty is superior to any other; yet when she follows the road to its end, she reverses Marx's ultimate evaluations. Marx ends with a reallocation of capitalist powers that values the phenomenon of power itself and makes power identical with freedom. In contrast, Warner suggests that the value of the liberty Marx alone leads us to is that it frees us to face an inevitable vulnerability in human affairs and orders. ("Celibate Sisters," 269–270)

According to Caserio's reading, the endpoint of liberation would be to release subjects into an exposure to human fragility. One might add that *Summer Will Show*'s attention to vulnerability and the inevitability of loss points toward a different form of politics.

Gillian Beer writes that Warner's "works in the 1930s are imbued with the major historical events and dread of the time: the persecution of the Jews and of other groups such as gypsies and gays, the sense of betrayal and yet of the necessity for secret organizations, the willingness to be active, the dry despair in the face of overwhelming Fascist forces."[14] Warner's antifascist politics may draw on a different political imaginary, one that is linked specifically to Judaism in the novel. Throughout her fiction, Warner is concerned with the experience of those marked visibly and classified as "other" in modernity: homosexuals, Jews, the poor, gypsies, the disabled, women, people of color, colonial subjects. She considers not only the transformation of society through class revolt but also the oppression of despised minorities. It may be more difficult to conjure a hopeful attitude toward the future in relation to such regimes of stigmatization and denigration. Such repetitive narratives of racial hatred— grounded in "facts" of human nature like the hatred of outsiders—are resistant to visions of social progress.[15]

If the young Minna disavows the "wintry words of [her] race" when she sees "liberty" in its idealized form, the second view of the river may make these words—exile, and captivity, and bondage—seem more useful. Departing from the forward-looking, progressive, and linear view of liberty that she saw in the river the first time, in her second view Minna sees the repetitive nature of the seasons: the river may burst it bounds, but come next winter, it will freeze up again. Part of a cycle of inevitable repetition, spring will always come again, each time somewhat different—but always bearing news of the ravages of the winter.

What Will Be

The epigraph of the novel becomes more legible in light of these considerations. It reads: "Winter will shake, Spring will try, / Summer will show if you'll live or die." The passage describes an uncertain struggle with adversity: winter is the darkest moment, but spring will still test the resources of the vulnerable "you" to whom the couplet is addressed. But summer is crucial: it is summer that will show definitely if you will live or die. Although the verse is written in a simple future tense, it invokes the novel's peculiar version of the future perfect. Summer will show whether the wounds you have sustained prove fatal—it will show if you will have made it through or not. In its engagement with the backwardness, the imperfection of the future perfect, this novel suggests that whether you make it or not, countless others will have already died— and that putting flesh on the bones of this dream of survival means seeing yourself among them.

Minna models such an engagement with loss throughout the novel, and she insists on the durability of suffering. This aspect of her politics is linked to her "romantic" revolutionism, and is explicitly contrasted to the scientific socialism of the character Ingelbrecht, a stand-in for Engels. Caserio describes Minna's revolutionism as a combination of "defeatism and utopism" that loses sight of "the specificity of the present material moment of history" (266). Whether "defeatism and utopism" necessarily block a perception of present material circumstances bears more discussion; nonetheless, it is clear that Minna's idiosyncratic revolutionary desires and regrets dominate the novel. Although the novel offers a partial critique of her position, it also traces Sophia's progressive identification with her as the path of her awakening to politics. Sophia becomes more and more like Minna until she finally takes her place, living in her apartment, becoming, like her, an unclassed woman who lives in exile and is haunted by the past. In the end, Sophia's hopes for the future are motivated by loss: by the failure of the uprising and by her grief over Minna's death.

This mix of "defeatism and utopism" recalls other backward-looking revisions of Marxism. In particular, Minna's haunted expectancy recalls the melancholic utopianism of Walter Benjamin's "Theses on the Philosophy of History." That essay constitutes another revisionist account of the revolution of 1848 through a critical engagement with Marx's *Eighteenth Brumaire of Louis Napoleon*. Benjamin dissents from the progressivist logic of Marxist dialectical history, suggesting that it is not by burying the past but rather by being haunted that one can change the course of history. That essay famously ends with an invocation of "Messianic time" in Jewish mysticism. Benjamin describes the way that prophets remained in a constant state of expectancy without forming a definite image of a redeemed future. In such a state, "every second of time was the strait gate through which the Messiah might enter."[16] The revolutionary consciousness that Benjamin invokes is a desire for an impossible historical redemption—the longing for a transformation of society that cannot and yet must take place.

Warner describes such an impossible form of expectation not only in *Summer Will Show* but also at the end of *After the Death of Don Juan* (1938). This allegorical novel, written in the aftermath of the fascist victory in the Spanish civil war, considers the relation between the aristocracy, the church, and the peasants. Again, Warner chose another failed revolution as the scene for this historical novel; the novel ends in a brutal scene in which hired soldiers hunt down and kill all the peasants who have revolted in the small village of Tenorio Viejo. In the final scene of the novel, two of the revolutionaries wait out their final moments in the schoolhouse. Ramón and the more militant Diego know that they are about to die; they also know that their revolt will be forgotten, since no one is left who might tell their story.

Ramón has been mortally wounded; he stares at a map in the classroom and talks with Diego as he bleeds to death.

> "What are you looking at, Ramón? What do you see?"
> "So large a country," said the dying man. "And there in the middle of it, like a heart, is Madrid. But our Tenorio Viejo is not marked. I have often looked for it. It is not there, though. It is too small, I suppose. We have lived in a very small place, Diego."
> "We have lived in Spain," said the other.
> "Aye."
> His gaze left the map and turned to the face bent over him. They looked at each other long and intently, as though they were pledged to meet again and would ensure a recognition.[17]

The map is one that Ramón has studied many times, hoping to find a place there, or to make one. In his last moments, this dream is crushed as Ramón realizes that Tenorio Viejo is not there and that it never will be. In contrast to Madrid, this small place is not marked and what happens there does not count.[18]

Diego's simple but enigmatic answer is that they have lived "in Spain." This comment suggests that Ramón and Diego have been part of history, if anonymously, and it holds out hope for another kind of collectivity, still to be achieved. That such a collectivity will be achieved is anything but assured: what it will mean to have lived in Spain depends on a future that is barred to them. In the end, Ramón turns away from that future; there is nothing left in the world for him to study or to wish for, except the face of his friend. The affective intensity of this moment is almost unbearable as the scope of their revolutionary hopes and disappointments is narrowed down to a single point. At the end of the novel, the long look that they give each other is all the history they have left. Still, in the grips of despair, they project that moment of mutual recognition forward into the future, "as though they were pledged to meet again." The mood is decidedly subjunctive, though. Like Benjamin's soothsayers, they can promise nothing; all they have to offer is the depth of their longing.

The Uses of Despair

Summer Will Show explores the paradox of how one can be a revolutionary—sustain revolutionary hope—in light of profound losses and the despair that is the effect of such losses. In a moment late in the novel, Sophia and Minna walk along the bookstalls in Paris; Sophia's attention is drawn to the opening stanza of a poem by Marvell, "The Definition of Love." Though they are destitute at this point in the novel, Minna buys the book because she feels "an obligation toward it." The stanza reads:

> My love is of a birth as rare
> As 'tis for object strange and high:
> It was begotten by despair
> Upon Impossibility.

Summer Will Show traces the narrative of a "strange and high" love—an implausible union "begotten by despair upon Impossibility." This verse aptly describes the relation between Sophia and Minna, which is begotten out of Sophia's despair, and which might seem "impossible" for any number of reasons: Sophia and Minna begin as rivals, wife and mistress to the same man; they are marked by differences in class, political allegiance, and ethnic background; and their love is marked by the historical impossibility of same-sex relations.

The "strange and high" object also appears as the dream of a worker's revolution and the total social transformation that it would entail. In this sense, Warner borrows the historical image of same-sex love in order to describe the women's affective relation to the desired object of revolution. Revolution in *Summer Will Show* is also begot by despair upon impossibility: it appears in the novel as an analogue for the "impossible object" of same-sex desire. Warner borrows from the lexicon of queer feeling: because of the long-standing link of same-sex desire with the impossible, queer experience is characterized by extremes of feeling: the vertiginous joy of an escape from social structures; at the same time, a despair about the impossibility of existing outside of such structures. Revolution in the novel is both that which must happen and that which cannot happen; Warner describes the mixture of hope and despair that is produced by attachment to such an impossible object.

Rather than seeing this impossibility as pure loss, Warner suggests this impossibility as a resource. Invoking the rhetoric of reproduction, the poem describes the speaker's love as the product of a union between despair and impossibility. This rare birth is not a consummation; despair's embrace of impossibility does not yield an assured future. And yet, the poem insists that such a rare birth is preferable—stranger, higher—than a love born out of hopefulness. In this sense, intimate experience in the novel offers a model for an alternative form of political feeling, a non-utopian expectancy: a kind of hope without reason, without expectation of success.[19] Such a form of political affect may be the kind of feeling we need to learn how to use in contemporary politics, when hope in its old idealizing and utopian form—of optimism—seems to have lost its hold on many of us.

It does not make sense to talk about the death of the dream of Marxist revolution in the 1930s as it does at the beginning of the twenty-first century. In *Specters of Marx*, Jacques Derrida dates the "eschatological themes of the 'end of history,' of the 'end of Marxism,' . . . and so forth" to the 1950s—still twenty years after the publication of *Summer Will Show*.[20] Warner did not seem to be suffering from such feelings at the time: shortly after finishing the novel she joined the Communist Party and traveled to Spain with her lover Valentine Ackland. Yet the novel insistently explores the limits of revolutionary enthusiasm, pointing to a range of other, darker feelings that go into the making of social change.

Gillian Beer suggests that we might read Warner's novels as "experiments in affect" (77). *Summer Will Show* offers a combination of intense joy and total devastation; it opens with "hope for a better future" and at the same time leaves its reader with a hollow sense of despair. I would suggest that such experiments are ways of investigating not only the range of human emotions but also the means of inciting the desire for social change. We have tended to think that such desires can only be fueled by hope, but Warner suggests that political motivation—like so many other kinds of motivation—may be opaque, irrational, and indirect. In private life, we are used to the idea that we may not want what we think we want. That insight animates one of Warner's diary entries, written the day after she became lovers with Ackland: "My last day, and our first. It was a bridal of earth and sky, and we spent the morning lying in the hollowed tump of the Five Maries, listening to the wind blowing over our happiness, and talking about torpedoes, and starting up at footsteps. It is so natural to be hunted and intuitive. Feeling safe and respectable is much more of a strain."[21] Warner's novel is remarkable in that it exposes such mixed feelings in the realm of "real" politics, suggesting that intimate experience offers a model—albeit a complicated one—for thinking the social.

The final scene in *Summer Will Show* gestures emphatically to the link between intimate and public politics. After searching in vain, Sophia returns to Minna's apartment, which has served throughout the novel as a revolutionary cell—a laboratory for experiments in affect. Sophia's aristocratic aunt Léocadie is waiting for her, and she tries to recall her to her "old manner of living" (402). Sophia is unmoved; after her aunt leaves, she turns to face the empty apartment:

> Ah, here in this empty room where she had felt such impassioned happiness, such freedom, such release, she was already feeling exactly as she had felt before she loved Minna, and wrapping herself as of old in that coward's comfort of irony, of cautious disillusionment! How soon her blood had run cold, how ready she was to slink back into ignominy of thought, ignominy of feeling! And probably only the pleasure of disagreeing, the pique of being thought shabby and deplorable, had kept her from returning to the Place Bellechasse. She looked round her, dragging her gaze over the empty, the soiled and forlorn apartment. There was the wine that Minna had left for her, the slippers she had tossed off, sprawling, one here, one there, and on the table where she had thrown it down and forgotten it, the fifth of the packets which Ingelbrecht (yes, he was dead too) had entrusted to her. She took up one of the copies, fingered the cheap paper, sniffed the heavy odor of printers' ink, began to read.
>
> "*A spectre is haunting Europe . . .*"
>
> She seated herself; and leaning her elbows on the table, and sinking her head in her hands, went on reading, obdurately attentive and by degrees absorbed. (405–406)

In one sense, it is possible to read this moment as a transition from personal to collective experience: Sophia loses her lover, but gains a party.[22] The intensely personal nature of her final encounter with *The Communist Manifesto* does not support such a reading, for we find Sophia sinking down into a posture of absorbed reading that turns away from the street and the collective. Her relation to the physical text—her touching and smelling of its pages—recalls her ambivalent attraction to Minna's body early in the novel. Rather than a replacement of a bad object with a good object, the ending seems to suggest that one's relation to a collectivity might be based on the model of erotic love. It is through loving Minna that Sophia sees her glimpse of freedom; to forsake her would only lead to coldness—ignominy of thought and ignominy of feeling. Instead, Warner suggests that waiting for Minna might serve as a model for waiting for the revolution. Rather than looking forward to a brighter future, Sophia remains in the ruined present, the signs of her loss all around her. Sinking down, she allows herself to be haunted by her dead lover and by the words of the dead revolutionary Ingelbrecht.

Before her death, Minna herself serves as the exemplar of this alternate form of expectancy: attentive to the losses of the past and to the inevitable violence of the revolution, she invites ghosts rather than exorcising them. When she is asked about the good the revolution might do, she responds, "What good? None, possibly. One does not await a revolution as one awaits the grocer's van, expecting to be handed packets of sugar and tapioca" (147). Minna waits for the revolution as one waits for the beloved: with hope and with despair, but without certainty.

Epilogue
The Politics of Refusal

> I must make the final gesture of defiance, and refuse to let this be absorbed
> by the final story; must ask for a structure of political thought that will take
> all of this, all these secret and impossible stories, recognize what has been
> made out on the margins; and then, recognizing it, refuse to celebrate it; a
> politics that will, watching this past say "So what?"; and consign it to the
> dark.
>
> —Carolyn Kay Steedman, *Landscape for a Good Woman*

This book traces a tradition of backwardness in queer representation
and experience. Backwardness means many things here: shyness, ambivalence, failure, melancholia, loneliness, regression, victimhood, heartbreak, antimodernism, immaturity, self-hatred, despair, shame. I describe
backwardness both as a queer historical structure of feeling and as a
model for queer historiography. In telling a history of early twentieth-
century representation that privileges disconnection, loss, and the refusal of community, I have tried to bring my approach to the past in line
with dark, retrograde aspects of queer experience. If the gaze I have
fixed on the past refuses the usual consolations—including the hope of
redemption—it is not, for that reason, without its compensations. Backwardness can be, as Willa Cather suggests, deeply gratifying to the backward. Particularly in a moment where gays and lesbians have no excuse
for feeling bad, the evocation of a long history of queer suffering provides,
if not solace exactly, then at least relief.

I have tried to resist the criterion of utility as a standard of judgment
for the feelings and experiences that I describe. I have argued that the

146

pressure within queer studies to make use of bad feelings has not allowed
for sustained engagement with the stubborn negativity of the past:
critics have ignored what they could not transform. Still, despite my
hesitancy about alchemizing queer suffering, I do want to think in the
final pages about the relation between backwardness and the queer future. It is not the aim of this book to suspend absolutely the question of
the future; that is Lee Edelman's project in *No Future,* and although I see
its value, I am interested in trying to imagine a future apart from the
reproductive imperative, optimism, and the promise of redemption. A
backward future, perhaps.

There are forms of queer negativity that are in no sense "good for politics." There are others—self-hatred, despair, refusal—that we have yet to
consider because their connection to any recognizable form of politics is
too tenuous. Still, many of these unlikely feelings are closely tied to the
realities of queer experience past and present; a more capacious understanding of political aims and methods might in fact draw on such experiences. As many critics have argued, the politics of gay pride will only
get us so far. Such an approach does not address the marginal situation of
queers who experience the stigma of poverty, racism, AIDS, gender dysphoria, disability, immigration, and sexism. Nor does such an approach
come to terms adequately with sexual shame—with the way that the closet
continues to operate powerfully in contemporary society and media. Finally, the assertion of pride does not deal with the psychic complexity of
shame, which lingers on well into the post-Stonewall era.

While critics and activist groups have attempted to cultivate a politics
of the negative in recent years, the great problem to be reckoned with in
such approaches is the problem of political agency. Many of the queer
figures that I have considered in this book are characterized by damaged
or refused agency. Is it possible that such backward figures might be capable of making social change? What exactly does a collective movement of isolates look like? What kind of revolutionary action can we expect from those who have slept a hundred years?

Left Melancholy

Walter Benjamin's "angel of history" is a preeminently backward figure,
an emblem of resistance to the forward march of progress. In his "Theses

on the Philosophy of History," Benjamin sketches a scene that recalls the image of Lot's wife gazing back on the destruction of Sodom:

> A Klee painting named "Angelus Novus" shows an angel looking as though he is about to move away from something he is fixedly contemplating. His eyes are staring, his mouth is open, his wings are spread. This is how one pictures the angel of history. His face is turned toward the past. Where we perceive a chain of events, he sees one single catastrophe which keeps piling wreckage upon wreckage and hurls it in front of his feet. The angel would like to stay, awaken the dead, and make whole what has been smashed. But a storm is blowing from Paradise; it has got caught in his wings with such violence that the angel can no longer close them. The storm irresistibly propels him into the future to which his back is turned, while the pile of debris before him grows skyward. This storm is what we call progress.[1]

History in Benjamin's description is a "single catastrophe," a pile of wreckage that just keeps getting bigger. He suggests that while most people are content to forget the horrors of the past and move on toward a better future, the angel resists the storm of progress. By turning his back on the future and fixing his gaze on this scene of destruction, the angel refuses to turn the losses of the past, in Adorno and Horkheimer's terms, into the material of progress. The angel longs to redeem the past—"to make whole what has been smashed"—but he cannot. As he tries to linger with the dead, the wind tears at his wings, carrying him, against his will, into the future.

Benjamin emphasizes the violence to which the angel is exposed in his failed attempt at redemption. Like Lot's wife, the angel faces backward; like Odysseus, however, he keeps moving forward while he looks backward. Benjamin suggests that taking the past seriously means being hurt by it. He is damaged both by the horrible spectacle of the past and by the outrage of leaving it behind.

The angel of history has become a key figure in recent work on loss and the politics of memory, trauma, and history. In contemporary criticism, Benjamin's sacrificial witness functions as something like an ethical ideal for the historian and the critic. Yet this figure poses difficulties for anyone thinking about how to effect political change. What are we to do with this tattered, passive figure, so clearly unfit for the rigors of the protest march, not to mention the battlefield? The question is how to imagine this melancholic figure as the agent of any recognizable form of activism. At the heart of the ambivalence about the angel of history is a key paradox of political life. Although historical losses instill in us a desire for change, they also can unfit us for the activity of making change. If we look back, we may not be able to pull ourselves away from the spectacle of Sodom in flames.

Wendy Brown warns against the potential dangers of such an orientation in her essay "Resisting Left Melancholy." Brown discusses the possibilities for sustaining hope after the "death of Marxism." In a reading of Benjamin's article "Left Melancholy," Brown attempts to make a distinction between productive and paralyzing forms of political melancholia. Left melancholy is a form of nostalgia for an expired past—a way of clinging to a broken and outdated dream of class revolution. To this form of melancholy she opposes a productive clinging to historical loss, which is what she sees in the allegory of the angel of history.

Brown asks a series of questions about how to imagine the future after the breakdown of historical master narratives. She considers our feelings about the future when we no longer believe in the inevitability of historical progress and when our dreams for a global revolution have died. What do dreams of freedom look like after the ideal of freedom has been smashed? Brown diagnoses a pervasive despair on the Left, a melancholic attachment to earlier forms of politics that has proved disastrous for responding to contemporary political conditions.

Brown's diagnosis of this structure of feeling is apt, and this essay is a crucial exploration of the state of contemporary affective politics on the Left: rather than adopting a position that simply condemns apathy as a cop-out, a failure of nerve, she tries to map the response to losses on the Left as a melancholic response. Brown comes to diagnose, not to punish. Melancholic leftists cling to the lost objects because of actual feelings of love, actual desire for radical social change: the problem with their politics is not the attachment but rather the paralyzing effects of melancholic incorporation and disavowal. Contemporary critics and activists should attend to her suggestion that the "feelings and sentiments— including those of sorrow, rage, and anxiety about broken promises and lost compasses—that sustain our attachments to Left analyses and Left projects ought to be examined."[2] Brown's call for an investigation into these feelings sounds, however, at times more like a request that such feelings should not exist. She writes:

> What emerges [in the present moment] is a Left that operates without either a deep and radical critique of the status quo or a compelling alternative to the existing order of things. But perhaps even more troubling, it is a Left that has become more attached to its impossibility than to its potential fruitfulness, a Left that is most at home dwelling not in hopefulness but in its own marginality and failure, a Left that is thus caught in a structure of melancholic attachment to a certain strain of its own dead past, whose spirit is ghostly, whose structure of desire is backward looking and punishing. (463–464)

Whereas Brown is writing in one sense from the perspective of a Left melancholic, someone trying to think of alternative political structures of feeling given the contemporary context, here her critique seems to shade into the kind of chin-up neoliberal polemics that she abhors. Although that essay sets out to think about the affective consequences of historical losses, in a passage such as this one Brown points to these bad feelings themselves as the problem. Why would this essay, so sympathetic to melancholic politics, make a final call for the dissolution of melancholy into mourning? Although I think Brown sets out to widen the range of political affects, thinking about the political usefulness of feelings like regret and despair, in the end she returns to what is invariably invoked as the only viable political affect: hope for a better future.

Despite Brown's claims to the contrary, it is difficult to distinguish between "good" and "bad" melancholy; melancholia itself cannot be sealed off from more problematic feelings and attitudes such as nostalgia, depression, and despair. The anxiety to draw a *cordon sanitaire* around politically useful affects is legible in many quarters; one could certainly argue that Benjamin's own diatribe against left melancholy is fueled by anxieties about the political valence of his own melancholic identification. Such anxieties are also legible in his "Theses," where Benjamin's tiger leaping into the past seems to serve as a revolutionary, can-do alibi for the angel of history and where the historical materialist is distinguished from the historicist because he is "man enough to blast open the continuum of history" (262).

It is much easier to distinguish between productive and paralyzing melancholia on paper than it is in psychic life, where even the best feelings can go bad—and they give no warning. If we are serious about engaging with the terrain of psychic life—and at the same time, challenging a progressivist view of history—then it seems crucial that we begin to take the negativity of negative affect more seriously. Bad feelings such as rage, self-hatred, shame, despair, and apathy are produced by what Lauren Berlant calls the routine "pain of subordination." Tarrying with this negativity is crucial; at the same time, the aim is to turn grief into grievance—to address the larger social structures, the regimes of domination, that are at the root of such pain. But real engagement with these issues means coming to terms with the temporality, the specific structure of grief, and allowing these elements of negative affect to transform our understanding of politics. We need to develop a vision of political agency that incorporates the damage that we hope to repair.

Carla Freccero, returning to Benjamin's angel, considers such an approach in *Queer/Early/Modern*. Throughout her book Freccero considers the political possibilities in what she calls "queer spectrality"; she argues that allowing oneself to be haunted can open up a "reparative future" (102). Exploring the ethics and politics of melancholia, Freccero finally wonders about the implications of her theory for the question of political agency.

> If this spectral approach to history and historiography is queer, it might also be objected that it counsels a kind of passivity, both in [Leo] Bersani's sense of self-shattering and also potentially in the more mundane sense of the opposite of the political injunction to act. In this respect it is also queer, as only a passive politics could be said to be. And yet, the passivity—which is also a form of patience and passion—is not quite the same thing as quietism. Rather, it is a suspension, a waiting, an attending to the world's arrivals (through, in part, its returns), not as a guarantee or security for action in the present, but as the very force from the past that moves us into the future, like Benjamin's angel, blown backward by the storm. (104)

Freccero specifically links passivity to queer politics, suggesting that a passivity that is "not quite" quietism might constitute an alternative approach to the problem of agency. Although some might argue that Benjamin confuses the issue of seeing atrocity with the need to do something about it (confusing the historical materialist with the revolutionary), Freccero ventures to suggest that the angel himself might be a model political actor.

The consequences of such a shift are clearly troubling to Freccero, who follows this suggestion with a footnote in which she responds to Brown's concern about political passivity.

> Wendy Brown, in *Politics Out of History,* notes that the angel is paralyzed and helpless and that it is therefore incumbent upon us to seize the moment, to interrupt the storm. She describes Benjamin's understanding of the agents of this process in what seem to me to be humanist terms, in that we are indeed the agents of history who do the interrupting. In using this image, I want first to suspend the definition of the storm, which in Benjamin's text is "what we call progress," and also, if possible, to suspend the question of agency within the image. What, after all, we might ask, is an angel? (147, n.105)

In this remarkable final note, Freccero performs an exemplary act of backwardness, clinging to the "paralyzed and helpless" figure of the angel even as Brown urges action. Far from "seizing the moment," Freccero—like Benjamin's angel, or like one of Pater's shy and shrinking figures—begs for a reprieve. Resisting the rhetorical force of Brown's call to arms, she heads underground, and suspends each of the key terms in the passage—progress, agency, angel. The queer exemplarity of this move has nothing to do with any traditional sense of political agency; rather, queer activism here consists in evasion, latency, refusal, and in turning Brown's injunction back on itself. What is to be done? We don't know, just as we don't know what an angel is.

Backward March

In his 1999 book, *Disidentifications,* José Esteban Muñoz offers a tongue-in-cheek version of what a queer, backward activism might look like. Recounting a joke that he shares with a friend, Muñoz describes plans for a "gay shame day parade":

> This parade, unlike the sunny gay pride march, would be held in February . . . Loud colors would be discouraged; gay men and lesbians would instead be asked to wear drab browns and grays. Shame marchers would be asked to carry signs no bigger than a business card. Chanting would be prohibited. Parade participants would be asked to parade single file. Finally, the parade would not be held on a central city street but on some backstreet, preferably by the river.[3]

Through this image of silent, orderly marchers filing through the backstreets of the city, Muñoz suggests that the shame and self-hatred associated with life in the closet persist in the contemporary moment.

These imaginary figures, joined in abjection, have not "yet" decided against the logic of their exclusion.

Although Muñoz is clearly joking in this evocation of a gay shame march, his joke has become more relevant to discussions of queer feeling and politics in the past several years. Muñoz's book came out one year after the activist collective Gay Shame formed in New York City. The movement drew on impulses that were also important to Muñoz's work and to that of many other queer scholars at the time: a sense that the transformational possibilities of gay pride had been exhausted, and that it had instead become a code name for assimilation and for the commodification of gay and lesbian identity. In particular, Gay Shame was disgusted with the new look and feel of gay New York. Gay Shame San Francisco (perhaps the most important offshoot of the original movement) narrates the history of the group on their Web site.

> Gay Shame emerged at a very specific moment in New York City history. It was June 1998, the height of Mayor Giuliani's reign of terror known officially as the "Quality of Life" campaign, during which rampant police brutality against unarmed people of color was the norm, community gardens were regularly bulldozed to make way for luxury housing, and homeless people were losing services and shelter faster than Disney could buy up Times Square . . . Gay Shame emerged to create a radical alternative to the conformity of gay neighborhoods, bars, and institutions most clearly symbolized by Gay Pride. By 1998, New York's Gay Pride had become little more than a giant opportunity for multi-national corporations to target-market to gay consumers . . . The goal of Gay Shame was to create a free, all-ages space where queers could make culture and share skills and strategies for resistance, rather than just buying a bunch of crap.[4]

The emphasis of Gay Shame was on the shame of gays selling out, on antisex zoning laws, and the gay move to the mainstream that was turning the movement into just another excuse for buying "a bunch of crap." Rather than focusing on shame per se (as a feeling), the movement focused on the shamefulness of gay pride (and gay consumerism and gay gentrification and gay mainstreaming more generally).

Each year on the day of the gay pride march, Gay Shame San Francisco holds a march, where nothing is for sale and protesters voice their opposition to the mainstreaming of gay life. The tone of the Gay Shame events is a far cry from the quiet backstreet march described by Muñoz,

however. Gay Shame San Francisco practices rowdy in-your-face forms
of direct action: though they embrace shame as a counterdiscourse to
pride, they do not act ashamed.[5] Gay Shame San Francisco has in fact
made explicit their understanding of the relation between gay shame
and activism in statements they made in the wake of a conflict that took
place at the 2003 Gay Shame conference at the University of Michigan.
Like Gay Shame the activist movement, the conference responded to the
cultural moment of gay normalization but in a somewhat different way.
The main statement for the conference read as follows:

> The purpose of the conference is to inquire into various aspects of les-
> bian and gay male sexuality, history, and culture that "gay pride" has
> had the effect of suppressing. The conference intends to confront the
> shame that lesbians, gay men, and "queers" of all sorts still experience
> in society; to explore the transformative impulses that spring from
> such experiences of shame and to ask what affirmative uses can be
> made of these residual experiences of shame now that not all gay
> people are condemned to live in shame.[6]

This statement argues, from a queer academic perspective, what critics
including Eve Kosofsky Sedgwick, Michael Warner, and Douglas Crimp
(among others) have understood as the political potential of shame. As
is perhaps to be expected, the conference focused less on matters of
real estate, zoning, and class war than the activist movement; instead,
the focus was primarily on issues of representation, culture, and experience.[7]

Members of the Gay Shame collective were invited to the conference
and they appeared on the Gay Shame Activism panel during the second
day. The panel was marked by conflict, and eventually fights broke out
between members of the panel and the audience. In the wake of the conference, Mattilda (Matt Bernstein Sycamore) published an attack on the
conference titled "Gay Sham."[8] Mattilda accuses the organizers of the
conference of inviting Gay Shame San Francisco only as fetish objects or
token representatives to stand in for radical queer activism. In the aftermath of the conference, the Gay Shame Web site offers an exhortation
specifically aimed at academics seeking to write about gay shame. Under
the heading "Gay Shame & Academia," the authors write:

> If you are writing a paper, GAY SHAME offers plenty of materials on-
> line and hopefully our meetings are great sources of inspiration. We

hope that once your paper has been turned in that you remember to unleash your defiance on the world for all to see. GAY SHAME challenges you to step away from the classist pillars of theoretical "discourse" and celebrate direct action deviance (see HOW TO START A DIRECT ACTION page for ideas).[9]

During the conference, many academics in the audience responded to Gay Shame's critique by arguing that they were also activists, and that the distinction is not so easily drawn. Gay Shame San Francisco was not impressed. The question as they saw it was not whether different professors or academics "did activism." Rather, it was a more direct conflict about the fact that academics are, by and large, a professional class and so have very different aims as well as different ways of articulating those aims.

It is interesting to note how little tension there is between shame and action in Gay Shame San Francisco's rhetoric. The organization is not interested in feeling shame, or in the feeling of shame, although the tone of their material is dependably dark. Rather, they deploy shame: against gay landlords in San Francisco as well as against radical academics who do not back their theories up with direct action. Through their tactics at the Gay Shame conference and afterwards, GSSF activated (somewhat successfully) what we might call leftist academic shame—the feeling that results from diagnosing social ills without doing anything about them.

Still, despite Gay Shame San Francisco's hard line about the relationship between feeling, thought, and direct action, the Web site features an interesting acknowledgment of the affective difficulties of activism, which they diagnose as post action depression:

P.A.D.S. (Post Action Depression Syndrome)

After your first action, you may find yourselves experiencing a wide range of extreme responses: mania, ecstasy, dizziness, lightheadedness, nausea, dysphoria, vomiting, rage, enlightenment, empowerment, inspiration, disappointment, confusion, numbness, betrayal, vulnerability, euphoria, sensitivity, awareness, invulnerability, wanderlust or enchantment. This is common. It is important to continue organizing. Brainstorm future projects to help keep the group focused, effective and inventive. Don't be worried if people hate you—when you take an unpopular stance (and we certainly hope you do), expect to be unpopular.

This may be a great time to collectively write a statement of purpose in order to communicate the group's politics. This may help build consensus within the group, encourage more people to get involved and create future actions that work together to build a sustainable culture of resistance. A statement of purpose may give the group focus and direction in order to work toward future actions that articulate the politics of the group in as many relevant directions as possible. Of course, this may also lead to arguing endlessly over differences instead of building an environment where direct action can flourish, so proceed with caution, creativity, glamour, intrigue and clamor.[10]

Gay Shame San Francisco offers a stunning account of the complex and ambivalent feelings that activism (and social opposition more generally) inspires. While insisting on the importance of direct action, the statement also offers an account of the potential pitfalls—the bad feelings and broken connections—that can inhibit such action. The statement ends, appropriately enough, with a directive, but also with a warning: "Proceed with Caution"—the implication being that "getting stuck" is a danger that comes with the territory.

Feeling Bad, Acting Up

Both the Gay Shame movement and the depression march recall a longer history of queer activism in which bad feelings were central. In tracing such a history I would point not only to certain risky and disorganized forms of protest in the gay liberation movement but also to the insistence on bad feelings in the early days of queer activism. Acknowledging damage—and incorporating it—was crucial to the turn to queer politics and queer studies in the late 1980s. With the AIDS crisis raging, Reagan in office, and homosexuality recriminalized in the *Bowers v. Hardwick* decision, damage was all around. The activist group Queer Nation (an offshoot of the group ACT UP) was formed in response to this atmosphere of crisis. In one of their pamphlets from 1990, they discuss their choice of the word "queer," emphasizing the importance of "trouble" to the concept.

Queer!
Ah, do we really have to use that word? It's trouble. Every gay person has his or her own take on it. For some it means strange and eccentric and kind of mysterious. That's okay, we like that. But some gay girls

and boys don't. They think they're more normal than strange. And for others "queer" conjures up those awful memories of adolescent suffering. Queer. It's forcibly bittersweet and quaint at best—weakening and painful at worst. Couldn't we just use "gay" instead? It's a much brighter word and isn't it synonymous with "happy"? When will you militants grow up and get over the novelty of being different?

Why Queer . . .

Well, yes, "gay" is great. It has its place. But when a lot of lesbians and gay men wake up in the morning we feel angry and disgusted, not gay. So we've chosen to call ourselves queer. Using "queer" is a way of reminding us how we are perceived by the rest of the world. It's a way of telling ourselves we don't have to be witty and charming people who keep our lives discreet and marginalized in the straight world. (Anonymous Queers, 1990)

The idea that queer could be reclaimed from its homophobic uses and turned to good use—while still maintaining its link to a history of damage—was crucial to the development of a queer intellectual method in the late 1980s and early 1990s. While queer studies borrowed from the general approach of queer activism at the time, it did not always fully embrace the "forcibly bittersweet" tone of the movement.

Another Queer Nation pamphlet from 1990, *An Army of Lovers Cannot Lose,* borrowed its title from the 1970 Statement of the Male Homosexual Workshop at the Revolutionary People's Constitutional Convention. In this statement, the authors emphasize their relation to the old days of gay liberation and their distance from the current ethos of gay assimilation: "being queer means leading a different sort of life. It's not about the mainstream, profit-margins, patriotism, patriarchy, or being assimilated. It's not about executive director, privilege and elitism. It's about being on the margins, defining ourselves; it's about gender-fuck and secrets, what's beneath the belt and deep inside the heart; it's about the night" (Anonymous Queers, 1990). It is important to note that the mainstream indicated here is the mainstream of gay and lesbian organizing—as is indicated by the allusion to "executive director," not "CEO." It was this aspect of the queer movement that Michael Warner underlined in his definition of queer as "against the regimes of the normal" in his introduction to the 1993 volume *Fear of a Queer Planet.*[11]

The statement also emphasizes the importance of feelings, both good and bad, in the constitution of the movement. This was a movement that hit below the belt; that did not disavow the long history of secrecy but made it central; that was "about the night." The pioneers of queer organizing saw suffering and shame as essential to social transformation. Such a focus linked them with some of the most interesting moments in the movement for gay liberation and with the efforts of s/m and butch-femme lesbians to get their dissident desires on the radar screen during the late 1970s and 1980s. As well, it linked them with a longer history of queer abjection that was also, they insisted, a crucial legacy.

At the heart of the queer movement was not only the question of the history of identity and the meaning of slurs but also the problem of feeling bad—of "waking up in the morning feeling angry and disgusted." Queer politics broke with the progressive utopian historical vision of some versions of gay liberation and second-wave feminism. At the same time that conditions for the most privileged gays and lesbians were improving, it was hard to hold on to optimistic historical narratives during the darkest days of the AIDS crisis. Queers focused instead on the ongoing problem of homophobia and its material and psychic effects. Typical of this moment is the "Dyke Manifesto" distributed by the New York Lesbian Avengers at the 1993 march on Washington. The poster on which the manifesto is printed features an opening address— "Calling All Lesbians! Wake Up!" Written over the entire poster in red are three words: POWER SEX ACTIVISM. Recalling the revolutionary rhetoric of earlier movements, the Avengers' manifesto also gives voice to negative and retrogressive tendencies at odds with the utopian call to action. In small print, they write that Lesbian Avengers "ARE OLD FASH-IONED: PINE, LONG, WHINE, STAY IN BAD RELATIONSHIPS."[12]

What place pining, longing, and whining (or staying in bad relationships, for that matter) might have in radical activism is not clear. Nevertheless, it is true that many activist movements—and some critics—find the question worth exploring. Ann Cvetkovich's 2003 book, *An Archive of Feelings*, makes backward feelings central. Cvetkovich considers the relation between lesbian public cultures and trauma; she pays particular attention to a form of trauma that has been difficult to discuss in lesbian contexts: childhood sexual abuse. Looking at a range of materials both popular and elite, Cvetkovich explores the way that queercore bands, lesbian artists, and zinesters have negotiated the intimate damage of misogyny and homophobia.

Early in the book, Cvetkovich discusses her use of the term "trauma" and comments that the book is both about bad feelings and informed by the experience of feeling bad:

> As a name for experiences of socially situated political violence, trauma forges overt connections between politics and emotion. Sexual acts, butch-femme discourse, queer transnational publics, incest, AIDS and AIDS activism, grassroots archives—these are some of the sites of lesbian public culture where I have not only found the traces of trauma but ways of thinking about trauma that do not pathologize it, that seize control over it from the medical experts and forge creative responses to it that far outstrip even the most utopian of therapeutic and political solutions . . . The kinds of affective experiences that I explore here are lost in discourses of trauma that focus only on the most catastrophic and widely public events . . . I want to place moments of extreme trauma alongside moments of everyday emotional distress that are often the only sign that trauma's effects are still being felt. Trauma discourse has allowed me to ask about the connection between girls like me feeling bad and world historical events.[13]

Cvetkovich's book is centrally concerned with trauma. Although she is interested in examples of subjects who seize control over trauma and who forge creative responses to it, the bad feelings do not drop out during this process. Rather, the nontherapeutic approach to trauma that she describes suggests a wild utopianism—a hopefulness in despair—that is reminiscent of the politics of despair Sylvia Townsend Warner describes in *Summer Will Show*. For her examples, Cvetkovich turns to artists and activists whose work is bound up with the everyday experience of feeling bad.

Cvetkovich is involved with an academic and activist organization, the Public Feelings Project, that has attempted to create a political movement that takes seriously such apparently useless feelings. The Chicago-based "feeltank" associated with the group organizes an annual depression march. The protesters march in bathrobes and slippers, carrying signs that say, "Depressed? It might be political," and passing out fake prescriptions for Prozac. The point of an event like this is not only that the political landscape is bad but also that it makes you feel bad, and that it may make you less capable of taking action, or of taking action in a way that accords with traditional understandings of activism. Whether such backward forms of activism can make a difference in the present remains to be seen; it seems clear that movements that attempt to ignore such feelings or wish them away will have to deal with them sooner or later. The history of political depression is long; furthermore, it is a feeling that thrives in exile.

What Is an Angel?

In *Feeling Backward*, I have argued that "feeling bad" has been a crucial element of modern queer experience but that it has not been adequately addressed in histories of queer representation or in writing about queer politics. For some critics, however, work in queer studies has been too focused on bad feelings and negativity in recent years. In her recent work Elizabeth Freeman argues that the turn to suffering in queer studies has made it impossible to imagine a politics of pleasure:

> So far, a simultaneously psychoanalytic and historicist loss—perhaps replacing or subsuming structuralist lack—has emerged as one of fin de siècle queer theory's key terms . . . I would like to suggest, however, that this powerful turn toward loss—toward failure, shame, negativity, grief, and other structures of feeling historical—may also be a prema-ture turn away from a seemingly obsolete politics of pleasure that could, in fact, be renewed by attention to temporal difference. This is, melancholic queer theory may acquiesce to the idea that pain—either a pain we do feel or a pain we should feel but cannot, or a pain we must laboriously rework into pleasure if we are to have any pleasure at all—is the proper ticket into historical consciousness.[14]

For Freeman, feeling pain about gay and lesbian history is an unwanted duty, a responsible activity that blocks access to the real pleasures that feeling (up) the historical record can afford. She suggests that with a shift of focus "we might imagine ourselves haunted by ecstasy and not just by loss; residues of positive affect (erotic scenes, utopias, memories of touch) might be available for queer counter- (or para-) historiogra-phies" (66).[15]

Freeman is undoubtedly right to suggest that the queer historical record is chock full of untapped pleasures. It is also the case that bad feelings have a certain prestige within academic discourse both because of their seriousness and also because of their relation to long philosoph-ical traditions of negativity ("lack" becomes "loss"). Yet her suggestion that melancholic queer theory "acquiesces, however subtly, to a Protestant ethic in which pleasure cannot be the grounds of anything productive at all" (59) does not account for the stigmatized and unproductive forms of queer suffering that this book, at least, takes as its subject. Many of the bad feelings under review here—self-pity, despair, depression, loneliness, remorse—are in fact bound up with pleasure, with precisely the sort of pleasure that gets regularly excoriated as sentimental, maudlin, nostalgic, self-indulgent, and useless. I would suggest that part of the reason that these feeling-states continue to be denigrated is that they are associated with pleasures—even ecstasies—so internal that they distract attention from the external world. While melancholia or the sense of failure may borrow some prestige from philosophical accounts of negativity, when it comes to enlisting feelings for queer political projects, these ones are picked last.[16]

The main problem with such feelings is that they are not good for action—they would seem to disqualify the person who feels them from agency or activity in any traditional sense. Judith Halberstam has recently made an argument on behalf of negative feelings that are closely tied to action. In a forum on "The Antisocial Thesis in Queer Theory" published in *PMLA* and in her ongoing work on failure, Halberstam details the affective archive of what she sees as a "truly political negativity, one that promises . . . to fail, to make a mess, to fuck shit up."[17] Drawing on Cvetkovich's *An Archive of Feelings* and responding to Lee Edelman's *No Future*, Halberstam proposes an archive of negative political feelings that includes "rage, rudeness, anger, spite, impatience, intensity, mania, sincerity, earnestness, overinvestment, incivility, and brutal honesty" as well as "dyke anger, anticolonial despair, racial rage, counterhegemonic violence, [and] punk pugilism" (824). While there is no doubt that these underappreciated feelings have their place in political life, and that unruly behavior has been at the heart of many breaks in the social fabric, I have been interested in *Feeling Backward* in forms of failure that are less closely tied to action. While feeling bad *can* result in acting out, being fucked up can also make even the apparently simple act of "fucking shit up" seem out of reach.

In this same forum, Lee Edelman offers a critique of Halberstam's article that suggests that she misunderstands negativity, seeing it not as an antagonism internal to the social order itself but as a positive aspect of social life. He writes, "Affirming . . . as a positive good, 'punk pugilism' and its gestural repertoire, Halberstam strikes the pose of negativity while evacuating its force."[18] Although the conflict that emerges between Edelman and Halberstam might be understood as a product of unreconcilable methodological differences—and an attendant disagreement about the constitution of the social—they do have something important in common: they share a commitment to a notion of negativity that is equated with destructive force. Edelman ups the ante in his conclusion when he introduces a hammer into the fistfight: the "spurious apostles of negativity hammer new idols out of their good, while the aim of queer negativity is rather to hammer them into the dust. In the process, though, it must not make the swing of the hammer an end in itself but face up to political antagonism with the negativity of critical thought" (822).

Although I agree with Edelman that making the "swing of the hammer" the sine qua non of political negativity is not a good idea, I do not think that is because the concepts of "gestural repertoire" and "stance" are not important for political life. In fact, it is the question of the recognized or allowed styles of political subjectivity that has concerned me throughout this book. This debate argues eloquently for the need for an expanded gestural repertoire.[19] I am interested in feelings at some distance from those identified by Philip Fisher as the "vehement passions," feelings on the model of anger and wonder that indicate "an aroused and dynamic spirit."[20] It is the lack of vehemence and lack of dynamism that make the backward feelings I survey here difficult to imagine as political. They make clear the need to imagine and work toward an alternative form of politics that would make space for various forms of ruined subjectivity: Walter Pater's shrinking refusal of the "gift" of public homosexual identity; Willa Cather's melancholic identification with impossible or lost forms of community, and her antagonism toward the future; the "spoiled identity" and loneliness of Radclyffe Hall's Stephen Gordon; and Sylvia Townsend Warner's grief-stricken revolutionary activism. These accounts are almost unrecognizable as versions of political subjectivity. Although we may have become attuned over the past several years to forms of radical politics that are not celebratory, we still have not yet begun to imagine a politics that allows for damage.

Given the scene of destruction at our backs, queers feel compelled to keep moving on toward a brighter future. At the same time, the history of queer experience has made this resolute orientation toward the future difficult to sustain. Queers are intimately familiar with the *costs* of being queer—that, as much as anything, makes us queer. Given this state of affairs, the question really is not whether feelings such as grief, regret, and despair have a place in transformative politics: it would in fact be impossible to imagine transformative politics without these feelings. Nor is the question how to cultivate hope in the face of despair, since such calls tend to demand the replacement of despair with hope. Rather, the question that faces us is how to make a future backward enough that even the most reluctant among us might want to live there.

Notes

Introduction

1. In the debates over the turn from gay to queer, the politics of affirmation were central. See, for instance, this quote from the section of the 1990 pamphlet *Queers Read This* entitled "Why Queer?": "Ah, do we really have to use that word? It's trouble. Every gay person has his or her take on it. For some it means strange and eccentric and kind of mysterious. That's okay, we like that. But some gay girls and boys don't. They think they're more normal than strange. And for others 'queer' conjures up those awful memories of adolescent suffering. Queer. It's forcibly bittersweet and quaint at best— weakening and painful at worst. Couldn't we just use 'gay' instead? It's a much brighter word and isn't it synonymous with 'happy'?" From *Queers Read This: I Hate Straights* (Leaflet distributed in June 1990 at a gay pride parade in New York City by Anonymous Queers). Reprinted in *The Columbia Reader on Lesbians and Gay Men in Media, Society and Politics*, ed. Larry Gross and James D. Woods (New York: Columbia University Press, 1999), 588–594.

2. Michel Foucault, *The History of Sexuality*, vol. 1, trans. Robert Hurley (New York: Vintage, 1978), 101. Although George Chauncey and others have challenged Foucault's account of the invention of homosexuality, pointing to nonelite sources of modern homosexual identity, the concept of reverse discourse remains central to contemporary queer thought and representation. Whether or not one agrees with Foucault's historical narrative in detail, the implication that homosexual identity is reclaimed from social scorn still holds. Disqualification might come from above in the form of the medical attribution of pathology or it might come from below in the form of slurs and violence; in any case, though, insult retains its centrality in gay

and lesbian lives. The term "homosexuality" itself—whether tricked out as the less clinical and more cheerful "gay" or downgraded to the nastier "queer"—retains the trace of its origin in the laboratory. George Chauncey, *Gay New York: Gender, Urban Culture, and the Making of the Gay Male World, 1890–1940* (New York: Basic Books, 1994). For the importance of insult in the making of gay identity, see Didier Eribon, *Insult and the Making of the Gay Self,* trans. Michael Lucey (Durham, NC: Duke University Press, 2004).

3. This quote from Carson McCullers's novel *The Member of the Wedding* is the source of the title for Rachel Adams's chapter on that book in *Sideshow U.S.A.* Rachel Adams, *Sideshow U.S.A.: Freaks and the American Cultural Imagination* (Chicago: University of Chicago Press, 2001).

4. For an example of the queer critique of progressivist history, see Jennifer Terry, "Theorizing Deviant Historiography," *differences* 3:2 (1991): 55–74.

5. This structuring ambivalence is evident in two excellent articles on melancholia and queer representation. In "Turning Back," Angus Gordon agrees with Michael du Plessis that there is no essential connection between homosexuality and melancholia, even as he avows that the concept is for him "an irresistible heuristic metaphor." See Michael du Plessis, "Mother's Boys: Maternity, Male 'Homosexuality,' and Melancholia," *Discourse* 16 (1993): 145–173; and Angus Gordon, "Turning Back: Adolescence, Narrative, and Queer Theory," *GLQ* 5:1 (1999): 1–24. I have been influenced by Gordon's discussion of melancholia, childhood, and the disavowal of the losses of the closet in my own account of turning back. Also see Elspeth Probyn, "Suspended Beginnings: Of Childhood and Nostalgia," in *Outside Belongings* (London: Routledge, 1996), 93–123, for an affirmative but nonetheless quite dark discussion of queer nostalgia. On melancholia in relation to the losses of queer history (and particularly in relation to lesbian historiography), see Valerie Traub, *The Renaissance of Lesbianism in Early Modern England* (Cambridge: Cambridge University Press, 2002). I discuss Traub's theory of historical melancholia in Chapter 1.

6. Although critics have discussed the negativity of isolated texts or traditions, bad feelings run throughout—and might be said to define—queer representation. See, for instance, Catharine Stimpson's discussion of the tradition of the "dying fall" in "Zero Degree Deviancy: The Lesbian Novel in English," *Critical Inquiry* 8 (1981): 363–379, and Christopher Nealon's account of the literature of inversion in the introduction to *Foundlings: Lesbian and Gay Historical Emotion before Stonewall* (Durham, NC: Duke University Press, 2001), 9–10. See also Carolyn Allen, *Following Djuna: Women Lovers and the Erotics of Loss* (Bloomington: Indiana University Press, 1996); Leo Bersani, *Homos* (Cambridge, MA: Harvard University Press, 1995); and Dianne

Chisholm, *Queer Constellations: Subcultural Space in the Wake of the City* (Minneapolis: University of Minnesota Press, 2005). Feelings of isolation, ambivalence, shame, and loneliness turn up not only in blistering works by the avant-garde or in maudlin accounts of homosexual tragedy: they are also legible in tales of triumph and fulfillment.

7. I take the phrase "archive of feeling" from Ann Cvetkovich's *An Archive of Feelings: Trauma, Sexuality, and Lesbian Public Cultures* (Durham, NC: Duke University Press, 2003).

8. For a discussion of the story of Lot's wife in terms of the feminist movement and the problem of "recovered memory," see Janice Haaken, *Pillar of Salt: Gender, Memory, and the Perils of Looking Back* (New Brunswick, NJ: Rutgers University Press, 1993). For a specifically queer use of this figure, see Christopher Castiglia, "Sex Panics, Sex Publics, Sex Memories," *boundary 2* 27:2 (Summer 2000): 149–175.

9. Dipesh Chakrabarty, *Habitations of Modernity: Essays in the Wake of Subaltern Studies* (Chicago: University of Chicago Press, 2002), ix.

10. The importance of temporality and particularly what Johannes Fabian calls the "denial of coevalness" in the constitution of modernity has been taken up in a range of recent works. See Johannes Fabian, *Time and the Other* (New York: Columbia University Press, 1983). For a good general account of such work see Rita Felski, "New Cultural Theories of Modernity," in *Doing Time: Feminist Theory and Postmodern Culture* (New York: New York University Press, 2000), 55–76. A list of works on the concept of alternative modernities might include Arjun Appadurai, *Modernity at Large: Cultural Dimensions of Globalization* (Minneapolis: University of Minnesota Press, 1996); Homi Bhabha, *The Location of Culture* (London: Routledge, 1994), especially the conclusion, "'Race,' Time and the Revisions of Modernity"; Dipesh Chakrabarty, *Provincializing Europe: Postcolonial Thought and Historical Difference* (Princeton, NJ: Princeton University Press, 2000) and *Habitations of Modernity*; Brent Edwards, *The Practice of Diaspora: Literature, Translation, and the Rise of Black Internationalism* (Cambridge, MA: Harvard University Press, 2003); Rita Felski, *The Gender of Modernity* (Cambridge, MA: Harvard University Press, 1995); Dilip Parameshwar Gaonkar, *Alternative Modernities* (Durham, NC: Duke University Press, 2001); Paul Gilroy, *The Black Atlantic: Modernity and Double Consciousness* (Cambridge, MA: Harvard University Press, 1993); Ranajit Guha, *History at the Limit of World-History* (New York: Columbia University Press, 2002); Michael Hanchard, "Afro-modernity: Temporality, Politics, and the African Diaspora," *Public Culture* 11 (1999): 245–268; Timothy Mitchell, ed., *Questions of Modernity* (Minneapolis: University of Minnesota Press, 2000); Michael North, *The Dialectic of Modernism: Race, Language, and Twentieth-Century Literature* (New York:

Oxford University Press, 1994); Joseph Roach, *Cities of the Dead: Circum-Atlantic Performance* (New York: Columbia University Press, 1996); Gayatri Spivak, *A Critique of Postcolonial Reason: Toward a History of the Vanishing Present* (Cambridge, MA: Harvard University Press, 1999).

11. For a discussion of the ways that lesbians are associated with the belated and the anachronistic in narrative, see Annamarie Jagose, *Inconsequence: Lesbian Representation and the Logic of Sexual Sequence* (Ithaca, NY: Cornell University Press, 2002). Her chapter on Virginia Woolf's *Mrs. Dalloway* is particularly relevant. She describes the way in which Clarissa's love for Sally Seton is relegated to an "almost historic period" (98); meanwhile, Miss Kilman, who embodies "the excessively unpalatable figuration of homosexuality in the present tense" (99), is at once abjected and associated with a primitive or prehistorical past.

12. Djuna Barnes, *Nightwood* (New York: New Directions, 1937), 40.

13. For accounts of camp, see Esther Newton, *Mother Camp* (Chicago: University of Chicago Press, 1979); David Bergman, *Camp Grounds: Style and Homosexuality* (Amherst: University of Massachusetts Press, 1993); Morris Meyer, *The Politics and Poetics of Camp* (New York: Routledge, 1994); Matthew Tinkcom, *Working Like a Homosexual: Camp, Capital, Cinema* (Durham, NC: Duke University Press, 2002); Susan Sontag, "Notes on 'Camp'" (1964), in *Against Interpretation: And Other Essays* (New York: Picador, 2001); D. A. Miller, "Sontag's Urbanity," *October* 49 (Summer 1989): 91–101. For a consideration of the importance of childhood traumas and pleasures in contemporary subcultures that emphasizes the backward tendencies in queer culture, see Cvetkovich, *Archive of Feelings.*

14. For a recent queer use of this figure of turning back, see Mark Turner's book on the culture of cruising, *Backward Glances* (London: Reaktion, 2003). Broadview Press has also recently released an anthology of gay American writing entitled *Glances Backward,* edited by James Gifford. Another form of backwardness that has received a lot of attention in queer studies is the importance of shame and shyness in queer world making. In her work on Henry James, Eve Kosofsky Sedgwick suggests that we might define queerness in relation to shyness: "Some of the infants, children, and adults in whom shame remains the most available mediator of identity are the ones called . . . shy. ('Remember the fifties?' Lily Tomlin used to ask. 'No one was gay in the fifties; they were just shy.') Queer, I'd suggest, might be usefully thought of as referring in the first place to this group or an overlapping group of infants and children, those whose sense of identity is for some reason tuned most durably to the note of shame." See Eve Kosofsky Sedgwick, *Touching Feeling: Affect, Pedagogy, Performativity* (Durham, NC: Duke University Press, 2003), 63. See also Eve Kosofsky

Sedgwick, *Shame and Its Sisters* (Durham, NC: Duke University Press, 1995); Michael Warner, *The Trouble with Normal: Sex, Politics, and the Ethics of Queer Life* (1999; Cambridge, MA: Harvard University Press, 2000); D. A. Miller, *Place for Us: Essay on the Broadway Musical* (Cambridge, MA: Harvard University Press, 1998); Jennifer Doyle, Jonathan Flatley, and José Esteban Muñoz, eds., *Pop Out: Queer Warhol* (Durham, NC: Duke University Press, 1996); Jose Esteban Muñoz, *Disidentifications: Queers of Color and the Performance of Politics* (Minneapolis: University of Minnesota Press, 1999).

15. For an account of Hall's private reflections on her identity as an invert, see the letters collected in *Your John: The Love Letters of Radclyffe Hall,* ed. Joanne Glasgow (New York: New York University Press, 1999).

16. Max Horkheimer and Theodor W. Adorno, *Dialectic of Enlightenment: Philosophical Fragments,* ed. Gunzelin Schmid Noerr, trans. Edmund Jephcott (Stanford, CA: Stanford University Press, 2002), 25–26.

17. Lauren Berlant, "The Subject of True Feeling," in *Feminist Consequences: Theory for the New Century,* ed. Elisabeth Bronfen and Misha Kavka (New York: Columbia University Press, 2001), 126–160.

18. Rei Terada, *Feeling in Theory: Emotion after the Death of the Subject* (Cambridge, MA: Harvard University Press, 2003).

19. Raymond Williams, "Structures of Feeling," in *Marxism and Literature* (Oxford: Oxford University Press, 1985), 132.

20. I have been influenced in my understanding of such transits between the individual and the social by Nealon's work on "feeling historical" in *Foundlings.* He suggests that we might think of "sexuality as a mode of address, as a set of relations, lived and imagined, that are perpetually cast out ahead of our 'real,' present-tense personhood, as a kind of navigation, or proleptic sketch of historical futures" (180). I discuss Nealon's work at greater length in Chapters 1 and 3.

21. Sianne Ngai, *Ugly Feelings* (Cambridge, MA: Harvard University Press, 2004), 6, 26.

22. See Sedgwick, *Touching Feeling,* esp. 35–65.

23. Warner, *Trouble with Normal,* 35–36.

24. Douglas Crimp, "Mario Montez, for Shame," in *Regarding Sedgwick: Essays on Queer Culture and Critical Theory,* ed. Stephen M. Barber and David L. Clark (New York: Routledge, 2002), 66. For a critique of gay shame as a form of nostalgia typical of white queer studies, see "What's Queer about Queer Studies Now?" ed. David Eng, Judith Halberstam, and José Esteban Muñoz, special issue, *Social Text* 84/85 (October 2005).

25. From my transcription of *The Children's Hour,* directed by William Wyler (1961).

26. Patricia White, *unInvited: Classical Hollywood Cinema and Lesbian Representability* (Bloomington: Indiana University Press, 1999). See White's fascinating reading of the transition from connotation to denotation in Hollywood's representation of lesbianism. Analyzing the relation between *The Children's Hour* and Wyler's 1936 version of the Lillian Hellman play, *These Three,* White argues that because the prohibition on homosexuality in cinema also meant a ban against explicit representations of homophobia, the direct treatment of lesbianism in film often had disastrous consequences for screen lesbians like Martha. White aptly describes the ambivalence of the modern-day viewer toward such representations; "modern day viewers want to see Martha, but they don't want to see her dead." Many negative or stereotypical representations from the past have been reappropriated through the mode of camp. Today, cult images such as that of the lesbian vampire, the evil madam, or the butch prison warden have largely lost their negative charge, and are now more likely to provoke laughter than tears. Though it is never certain what makes some images and not others available for camp reappropriation, images that have been reclaimed tend to be those that reflect, in an excessive or ambivalent way, values that are acceptable or even desirable within the contemporary context. In a moment when butch style and hypersexuality are embraced within lesbian culture, spectacular figures such as these are not considered threatening or offensive. Through the mode of camp or hero worship, these once-debased figures are transformed into icons by subjects who recognize them as incomplete, premature, or distorted images of themselves. But certain images—of Martha Dobie on the couch, of Miss Kilman at the café in Virginia Woolf's *Mrs. Dalloway,* or of Stephen Gordon in front of the mirror in *The Well of Loneliness*—remain resistant to appropriation. See White's discussion of the complexity of lesbian reception in her reflections on "retrospectatorship" in the final chapter of *unInvited.*

27. All citations from *The Celluloid Closet* are from my transcription of the film, directed by Rob Epstein and Jeffrey Friedman (1995).

28. While self-hatred and shame are themselves understood to be outmoded emotions in the current political situation, Bright reflects on the stubborn resistance of such feelings to narratives of progress. In a culture saturated by the discourse of pride, feelings of shame and self-hatred are themselves shaming. If such negative feelings were explicable within the hostile climate of the earlier part of the century, they seem inappropriate today; queer subjects who avow these feelings are subject to charges of 'internalized homophobia.'

29. There is of course a great deal of evidence one might muster to counter the claim that today girls like Martha universally "fight for their budding preference." On the significance of teen suicide, see Eve Kosofsky Sedgwick's

essay "Queer and Now," in *Tendencies* (Durham, NC: Duke University Press, 1993); for an important critique of the use of the tragic teen as a grounding figure for queer theory, see Gordon, "Turning Back."

30. Judith Butler, "Critically Queer," in *Bodies that Matter: On the Discursive Limits of "Sex"* (New York: Routledge, 1993), 223.

31. Miller, *Place for Us,* 26.

32. Virginia Woolf, *To the Lighthouse* (New York: Harcourt, Brace and World, 1927), 300.

33. Lee Edelman, *No Future: Queer Theory and the Death Drive* (Durham, NC: Duke University Press, 2004), 143.

34. For a related reading of the antihomophobic possibilities of a psychoanalytic account of sexuality, see Tim Dean, *Beyond Sexuality* (Chicago: University of Chicago Press, 2000). Dean argues that not only Lacan's interpreters but Lacan himself did not always see the most radical implications of his theories: "Lacan's axiom that 'there is no sexual relation' counters the heterosexist assumption of complementarity between genders; yet Lacan's explanations of this axiom are couched in terms of each gender's failure to relate to the other, rather than in terms of sexual relationality's failure as such, independent of gender" (17).

35. For an illuminating and contentious discussion of this tradition, see "The Antisocial Thesis in Queer Theory," published in 2006 in *PMLA,* which features short essays that came out of a panel at the 2005 MLA in Washington, DC. In this exchange, Robert L. Caserio (the convener of the original panel), Lee Edelman, Judith Halberstam, José Esteban Muñoz, and Tim Dean reflect on the ten-year anniversary of the publication of Leo Bersani's *Homos.* The thesis of Bersani's book, argued primarily through readings of Freud, Proust, Genet, and Gide, is that there is an inherent asociality in gay desire. "Forum: Conference Debates. The Antisocial Thesis in Queer Theory" *PMLA* 121.3 (May 2006): 819–828.

36. Bersani, *Homos,* 108.

37. Walter Pater, "Diaphaneitè," in *The Renaissance: Studies in Art and Poetry* (Oxford: Oxford University Press, 1986), 157.

38. Joan Acocella, *Willa Cather and the Politics of Criticism* (New York: Vintage, 2002). This book was based on an article that appeared in *The New Yorker* on November 27, 1995 ("Cather and the Academy," pp. 1156–1171).

39. For a helpful account of the ambivalent reception of the novel, see *Palatable Poison: Critical Perspectives on "The Well of Loneliness,"* ed. Laura Doan and Jay Prosser (New York: Columbia University Press, 2001).

40. I take up the politics of negative affect at greater length in the epilogue. See David Eng, *Racial Castration: Managing Masculinity in Asian America* (Durham, NC: Duke University Press, 2001); Anne Anlin Cheng, *The*

Melancholy of Race: Psychoanalysis, Assimilation, and Hidden Grief (New York: Oxford University Press, 2002); Edith Wysochrod, *An Ethics of Remembering: History, Heterology, and the Nameless Others* (Chicago: University of Chicago Press, 1998); Ann Cvetkovich, *An Archive of Feelings*; Avery F. Gordon, *Ghostly Matters: Haunting and the Sociological Imagination* (Minneapolis: University of Minnesota Press, 1997); Douglas Crimp, *Melancholia and Moralism: Essays on AIDS and Queer Politics* (Cambridge, MA: MIT Press, 2004); Judith Butler, *Gender Trouble* (New York: Routledge, 1999) and *The Psychic Life of Power* (Stanford, CA: Stanford University Press, 1997). For a collection of recent work on this topic, see David Eng and David Kazanjian, eds., *Loss: The Politics of Mourning* (Berkeley: University of California Press, 2003).

41. All quotes are from my transcription of *Without You I'm Nothing*, directed by John Boskovich (1989).

42. Elizabeth Freeman, "Packing History, Count(er)ing Generations," *New Literary History: A Journal of Theory and Interpretation* 31:4 (Autumn 2000): 743.

1. Emotional Rescue

1. Carolyn Dinshaw, *Getting Medieval: Sexualities and Communities, Pre- and Postmodern* (Durham, NC: Duke University Press, 1999), 35.

2. Louise Fradenburg and Carla Freccero contextualize this shift in queer studies in a broader shift in historicist work more generally: "One way that current historicisms might seem to differ from their predecessors is by their very habit of analyzing the pleasurable and/or political investments in the production of truth-effects." Louise Fradenburg and Carla Freccero, eds., *Premodern Sexualities* (New York: Routledge, 1996), xvii. For work in queer affective historiography, see David Halperin, *How to Do the History of Homosexuality* (Chicago: University of Chicago Press, 2002); Dinshaw, *Getting Medieval*; Nealon, *Foundlings*; Carla Freccero, *Queer/Early/Modern* (Durham, NC: Duke University Press, 2006); Scott Bravmann, *Queer Fictions of the Past: History, Culture, and Difference* (Cambridge: Cambridge University Press, 1997); Freeman, "Packing History, Count(er)ing Generations"; Traub, *The Renaissance of Lesbianism*; Cvetkovich, *An Archive of Feelings*.

3. The affirmative turn might be understood as a structural feature of not only queer history but of marginal or minority history more generally.

4. Roland Barthes, *A Lover's Discourse: Fragments*, trans. Richard Howard (New York: The Noonday Press, 1978), 16–17.

5. Roland Barthes, *Roland Barthes by Roland Barthes,* trans. Richard Howard (Berkeley: University of California Press, 1977), np.

6. In this caption, Barthes is citing Jacques Lacan, who defines the concept of demand as the demand for love. For Lacan too, demand constitutes a kind of hinge between desire and need. Before the moment of the mirror stage, the infant's need is still attached to objects and capable of satisfaction; once the child enters the realm of the symbolic, he becomes the subject of desire. Desire exists under the law of the signifier; it is radically detached from objects and can for this reason never be satisfied. Demand for Lacan is linked to the imaginary; it represents a moment when the subject is no longer a subject of need but is not yet a subject of desire.

7. The equivocal nature of this image is perhaps best evoked with reference to a linguistic slippage between the definitions of "demand"—"to ask for with authority; to claim as a right"—and "demanding"—"claiming more than is generally felt by others to be due" (*The Random House College Dictionary,* rev. ed.). It is interesting to note an obsolete meaning of "demand": "Countermand; opposition to a command, desire, or wish; demand" (*Oxford English Dictionary*). In this outdated sense of the word, demand is not an imperious order but rather a form of resistance or deferral.

8. Rolling Stones, "Emotional Rescue" on *Emotional Rescue* (Virgin, 1980).

9. For a point of comparison, see E. P. Thompson's great work of historical recovery, *The Making of the English Working Class* (New York: Vintage, 1963/1966), 12–13. Thompson states in his preface that his aim in writing the book is to "rescue" the poor, deluded, obsolete, outmoded, and "backward-looking" workers of the Industrial Revolution, those "casualties of history" who threaten to be forgotten by the "enormous condescension of posterity." In the next paragraph, Thompson subtly changes course, suggesting that history's losers may not need us as much as we need them. Thompson argues that history should not be read "in the light of subsequent preoccupations": "after all, we are not at the end of social evolution ourselves. In some of the lost causes of the people of the Industrial Revolution we may discover insights into social evils we have yet to cure."

10 Sappho, *If Not, Winter: Fragments of Sappho,* trans. Anne Carson (New York: Knopf, 2002).

11. Renée Vivien, "Dans les lendemains," *Oeuvre poétique complete de Renée Vivien, 1877–1909,* ed. Jean-Paul Goujon (Paris: Régine Deforges, 1986), 164. Translation mine.

12. In such cross-historical relays, aging takes on tremendous importance as an embodied historical practice. Cf. Nealon's discussion in *Foundlings* of Gertrude Stein's assertion that it "takes time to make queer people" (23) as

well as his discussion in his chapter on lesbian pulp fiction of how the bodies of pre-Stonewall lesbians "age into history" (175).

13. In this sense, we can understand Vivien's project of reclamation as evidence of Joan DeJean's claim in *Fictions of Sappho* that the indeterminacy of Sappho's textual corpus allowed her to be all things to all people. "A final meaning of translation is close to transference in the psychoanalytic sense. Fictions of Sappho are, at least in part, a projection of the critic's/writer's desires onto the corpus, the fictive body, of the original woman writer." Joan DeJean, *Fictions of Sappho, 1546–1937* (Chicago: University of Chicago Press, 1989), 3.

14. Perhaps the most influential piece of writing in this field is Foucault's late, short interview, "Friendship as a Way of Life," in which he proposes homosexuality as a means for inventing and multiplying new forms of relationship. Michel Foucault, "Friendship as a Way of Life," in *Essential Works: Foucault 1954–1984*, vol. 1, *Ethics, Subjectivity, and Truth,* ed. Paul Rabinow (New York: The New Press, 1997), 136. See also Kath Weston, *Families We Choose: Lesbians, Gays, Kinship* (New York: Columbia University Press, 1991); Jeffrey Weeks, Brian Heaphy, and Catherine Donovan, *Same Sex Intimacies: Families of Choice and Other Life Experiments* (New York: Routledge, 2001); Judith Butler, *Antigone's Claim: Kinship between Life and Death* (New York: Columbia University Press, 2000) and "Is Kinship Always Already Heterosexual?" *differences: a journal of feminist cultural studies* 13.1 (2002): 14–44; Lauren Berlant and Michael Warner, "Sex in Public," in *Intimacy,* ed. Lauren Berlant (Chicago: University of Chicago Press, 2000); David Eng, *Queer Diasporas/Psychic Diasporas* (forthcoming); Castiglia, "Sex Panics"; Samuel Delany, *Times Square Red, Times Square Blue* (New York: New York University Press, 1999); Warner, *The Trouble with Normal.*

15. Miranda Joseph, *Against the Romance of Community* (Minneapolis: University of Minnesota Press, 2002), viii.

16. Bravmann, *Queer Fictions,* 96.

17. Dinshaw cites Bravmann's *Queer Fictions* as well as critical work on community by critics such as Jean-Luc Nancy and Giorgio Agamben and social theorists Joshua Gamson and Cindy Patton. See *Getting Medieval,* p. 222, nn. 68 and 69.

18. Nealon also balances the longing for community with various forms of resistance to community in *Foundlings*. The poles of community and anticommunity in his book are assigned to what he describes as the "ethnic model" and the "inversion model" in the gay and lesbian literary tradition. The straightforward claiming of gay ancestors is a feature of the ethnicity model and is characterized by such practices as making lists of famous homosexuals (a "prime and lonely strategy" [6]). The inversion model is marked by

an emphasis on individual pathology; texts grouped under this heading include Djuna Barnes's *Nightwood,* Marcel Proust's *Remembrance of Things Past,* and André Gide's *The Immoralist.* Nealon remarks that these texts seem "allergic to anything like the contemporary model of community" (9). Nealon locates "foundling texts" as between these two traditions, although in several places, these texts with their longings for queer historical community seem closer to the ethnicity model—though they do evince less confidence about the possibility of making contact with other gay and lesbian subjects. For a fuller discussion of Nealon's foundling historiography, see Chapter 3.

19. Dinshaw, "Got Medieval?" *Journal of the History of Sexuality* 10.2 (2001): 202–212, 203.

20. For a discussion of Barthes that addresses both of these questions, see D. A. Miller, *Bringing Out Roland Barthes* (Berkeley: University of California Press, 1992).

21. Cited in Dinshaw, *Getting Medieval,* 46.

22. Pursuing an understanding of queerness as an absence of or an aversion to sex might include figures deemed unnatural for their lack of a natural desire—a host of saints, dandies, frigid women, isolated children, and awkward teens. Although the absence of sex is certainly an important aspect of queer historical experience, it has not received much critical attention, perhaps for the somewhat banal reason that it is not very sexy. "Touch-a touch-a touch-a touch me"—the title of a song from *The Rocky Horror Picture Show* (the line forms a sex-positive and perverted couplet with "I want to be dirty")—appears as a section heading in Ann Pellegrini's review of *Getting Medieval;* one can see how this phrase offers a more apt motto for sexuality studies than *Noli me tangere.* Ann Pellegrini, "Touching the Past; or, Hanging Chad," *Journal of the History of Sexuality* 10.2 (2001): 185–194, 190.

23. Willa Cather, "Katherine Mansfield," in *Not under Forty,* collected in *Willa Cather: Stories, Poems, and Other Writings,* ed. Sharon O'Brien (New York: The Library of America, 1992), 878.

24. Cherríe Moraga, *Loving in the War Years* (Cambridge, MA: South End Press, 2000), 115.

25. Traub, *The Renaissance of Lesbianism,* 334.

26. Throughout the book, Traub italicizes the word lesbian in order to indicate the anachronistic and unstable nature of the term when applied in the early modern context.

27. Henry Abelove, *Deep Gossip* (Minneapolis: University of Minnesota Press, 2003), xi–xii.

28. Michel Foucault, "Nietzsche, Genealogy, History," in *Essential Works of*

Foucault, 1954–1984, vol. 2, *Aesthetics, Method, and Epistemology,* ed. James D. Faubion (New York: The New Press, 1998), 380.

29. Michel Foucault, "The Lives of Infamous Men," in *Essential Works of Foucault, 1954–1984,* vol. 3, *Power,* ed. James D. Faubion (New York: The New Press, 2000), 162–163.

30. For other invocations of historical activity as cruising, see Neil Bartlett, *Who Was That Man? A Present for Mr. Oscar Wilde* (London: Serpent's Tail, 1988) as well as Isaac Julien's 1989 film *Looking for Langston* (Walter Bearer Films), in which he repeatedly figures the search for obscure historical subjects as cruising the graveyard.

31. Michel Foucault, "On the Ways of Writing History," in *Essential Works of Foucault, 1954–1984,* vol. 2, 290.

32. Michel Foucault, "The Thought of the Outside," in *Essential Works of Foucault, 1954–1984,* vol. 2, 162.

33. Maurice Blanchot, "The Gaze of Orpheus," in *The Space of Literature,* trans. Ann Smock (Lincoln: University of Nebraska Press, 1982), 172.

34. "The question of pathology I would as well omit in this context. I prefer simply to return to the observation with which I began this part of our exchange, namely, that for a homosexual, the best moment of love is likely to be when the lover leaves in the taxi. It is when the act is over and the boy is gone that one begins to dream about the warmth of his body, the quality of his smile, the tone of his voice. It is the recollection rather than the anticipation of the act that assumes a primary importance in homosexual relations. This is why the great homosexual writers of our culture (Cocteau, Genet, Burroughs) can write so elegantly about the sexual act itself, because the homosexual imagination is for the most part concerned with reminiscing about the act rather than anticipating it. And, as I said earlier, this is all due to very concrete and practical considerations and says nothing about the intrinsic nature of homosexuality." Interview with Foucault by James O'Higgins, "Sexual Choice, Sexual Act: Foucault and Homosexuality," trans. James O'Higgins, collected in *Politics, Philosophy, Culture: Interviews and Other Writings, 1977–1984,* ed. Lawrence D. Kritzman (New York: Routledge, 1988), 297. My thanks to David Kurnick for suggesting the boy in the taxi as a figure parallel to Eurydice in the underworld.

35. Bartlett, *Who Was That Man?* 216. I take the phrase "how to do the history of homosexuality" from David Halperin's book by that name.

2. Forced Exile

1. Daniel Albright, *Untwisting the Serpent: Modernism in Music, Literature, and Other Arts* (Chicago: University of Chicago Press, 2000), 30.

2. James Joyce, *A Portrait of the Artist as a Young Man* (New York: Penguin, 2003), 268–269.

3. Clyde Taylor, "'Salt Peanuts': Sound and Sense in African/American Oral/ Musical Creativity," *Callaloo* 5 (1982): 1–11, 3.

4. If Taylor seems to minimize the difference between dominant and marginal modernisms, it is perhaps because he makes the criterion of activity so central. For Taylor, extreme situations make people into either active experimenters or into passive victims. In practice, however, it is often the case that extreme situations turn people into both experimenters and victims.

5. See Linda Dowling's account of the affair and its aftermath in *Hellenism and Homosexuality in Victorian England* (Ithaca, NY: Cornell University Press, 1994), esp. pp. 92–103. In her reading of Pater's story "Apollo in Picardy" Dowling offers an account of the extreme swings of Pater's career in a reading of his violent allegory of suspicion and violence: "All the painful burden of Pater's experience at Oxford presses into view here—the intoxicating education, the fiery friendship, the hopes for cultural regeneration and a more liberal way of life, followed by the cold incomprehension, the hatred, the stony exile." Ibid., 140.

6. Walter Pater, *The Renaissance: Studies in Art and Poetry* (Oxford: Oxford University Press, 1998), 150.

7. The book is also addressed to such a number, "the few . . . the elect and peculiar people of the kingdom of sentiment" (10). For a later twentieth-century example of queer texts in search of kindred readers, see Nealon, *Foundlings*.

8. Jacques Khalip, "Pater's Sadness," *Raritan* 20:2 (Fall 2000): 136–158, 138.

9. Maurean Moran, "Pater's 'Great Change': Marius the Epicurean as Historical Conversion Romance," in *Walter Pater: Transparencies of Desire*, ed. Laurel Brake, Lesley Higgins, and Carolyn Williams (Greensboro, NC: ELT, 2002), 183.

10. It is significant that the onset of this new historical era in Heine's story is characterized by the technology of forced confession. The Christian confession is crucial in the genealogy of modern sexual identity that Foucault traces in *The History of Sexuality*.

11. Paul Tucker, "'Reanimate Greek': Pater and Ruskin on Botticelli," in Brake, Higgins, and Williams, *Walter Pater*, 123. The passage from Dante reads:

> And some I knew among them; last of all
> I recognized the shadow of that soul
> who, in his cowardice, made the Great Denial.

> At once I understood for certain: these
> were of that retrograde and faithless crew
> hateful to God and to His enemies. (Canto 3, 55–60)

The Inferno, trans. John Ciardi (New York: Penguin, 1954).

12. We might compare this image of a woman "expecting" to Pater's more positive image of expectation, invoked earlier in the Winckelmann essay—the image of "Memnon waiting for the day" (135). In this stone Egyptian tower, Pater offers an image of pregnancy that is aesthetic rather than biological: the first rays of the sun draw from Memnon a song rather than a child.

13. Trans. Edmund Keeley and Philip Sherrard, in *The Dark Crystal: An Anthology of Modern Greek Poetry* (Athens: Denise Harvery, 1981).

14. Eve Kosofsky Sedgwick and Andrew Parker, eds., *Performance and Performativity* (New York: Routledge, 1995).

15. Herbert Marcuse, *Eros and Civilization* (Boston: Beacon Press, 1966), 161.

16. Homi Bhabha, "The Commitment to Theory," in *The Location of Culture,* 25.

17. Nick Drake, "Time Has Told Me," from *Five Leaves Left* (London: Island Records, 1969).

3. The End of Friendship

1. Willa Cather, *Not under Forty,* in *Stories, Poems, and Other Writings,* ed. Sharon O'Brien (New York: Library of America, 1992), 812.

2. For a related account of Cather's disdain for the public sign, see Judith Butler's reading of the sign "dangerous crossing" in *The Professor's House* in her essay "Dangerous Crossing," in *Bodies that Matter.*

3. Acocella, *Willa Cather.* On the question of Cather's homosexuality, see Sharon O'Brien, *Willa Cather: The Emerging Voice* (New York: Oxford University Press, 1987); Eve Kosofsky Sedgwick, "Across Gender, across Sexuality: Willa Cather and Others," *South Atlantic Quarterly* 88.1 (Winter 1989): 53–72; Judith Butler, " 'Dangerous Names': Willa Cather's Masculine Names," in *Bodies that Matter,* 143–166; Christopher Nealon, *Foundlings;* Marilee Lindemann, *Willa Cather: Queering America* (New York: Columbia University Press, 1999); Jonathan Goldberg, *Willa Cather and Others* (Durham, NC: Duke University Press, 2001); Scott Herring, "Catherian Friendship; or, How Not to Do the History of Homosexuality," *Modern Fiction Studies* 52.1 (2006): 66–91.

4. Adrienne Rich, "Compulsory Heterosexuality and Lesbian Existence" (1980), in *The Lesbian and Gay Studies Reader,* ed. Henry Abelove, Michèle Aina Barale, and David M. Halperin (New York: Routledge, 1993), 239.

5. Lillian Faderman, *Surpassing the Love of Men: Romantic Friendship and Love between Women from the Renaissance to the Present* (New York: William Morrow and Company, 1981), 414.

6. Terry Castle, *The Apparitional Lesbian: Female Homosexuality and Modern Culture* (New York: Columbia University Press, 1993), 95.

7. "I perceive the lesbian experience as being, like motherhood, a profoundly female experience, with particular oppressions, meanings, and potentialities we cannot comprehend as long as we simply bracket it with other sexually stigmatized existences." Rich, "Compulsory Heterosexuality," 239.

8. One may find remarkable intersections between, for instance, Andrew Sullivan's paean to gay friendship in *Love Undetectable: Notes on Friendship, Sex, and Survival* (New York: Vintage, 1999), and Michael Warner and Lauren Berlant's essay "Sex in Public."

9. Michel de Montaigne, "Of Friendship," in *The Complete Works: Essays, Travel Journals, Letters,* trans. Donald M. Frame (New York: Knopf, 2003), 167.

10. Foucault, "Friendship as a Way of Life," in *Essential Works,* vol. 1, *Ethics, Subjectivity, and Truth,* ed. Paul Rabinow (New York: The New Press, 1997), 136.

11. Foucault, "Friendship," 137. He writes, "Yet it's up to us to advance into a homosexual ascesis that would make us work on ourselves and invent—I do not say discover—a manner of being that is still improbable."

12. Jeffrey Weeks, Brian Heaphy, and Catherine Donovan, *Same Sex Intimacies: Families of Choice and Other Life Experiments* (London: Routledge, 2001), 53.

13. For a point of comparison, see Leo Bersani's critique of Judith Butler in *Homos.* Analyzing her reading of alternative forms of kinship in Jennie Livingston's film *Paris Is Burning,* he writes, "Butler rather touchingly sees in the kinship in the various 'houses' to which the drag queens of *Paris is Burning* belong a lesson for all of us who live outside the heterosexual family. Though she has said that she doesn't think of those relations as simply providing a new and better version of the family, her description of houses—as mothering, rearing, caring, teaching, sheltering, enabling—is pretty much a catalogue of traditional family values." Bersani, *Homos,* 51–52.

14. "Beyond Same-Sex Marriage: A New Strategic Vision for All Our Families and Relationships." Full Statement. www.beyondmarriage.org (accessed January 3, 2007).

15. For a critical analysis of LGBT community and its exclusions, see Miranda Joseph, *Against the Romance of Community.* Also compare Cherríe Moraga's reflections on activism and suffering in *Loving in the War Years:* "Quite simply, the oppression of women of color, especially as we have internalized it, holds the greatest threat to our organizing successfully together, intraculturally as well as cross-culturally. I think what is hardest for any oppressed people to understand is that the sources of oppression form not only our

radicalism, but also our pain. Therefore, they are often the places we feel we must protect unexamined at all costs . . . Oppression. Let's be clear about this. Oppression does not make for hearts as big as all outdoors. Oppression makes us big and small. Expressive and silent. Deep and Dead." Cherríe Moraga, *Loving in the War Years: lo que nunca pasó por sus labios* (Cambridge, MA: South End Press, 2000 [1983]), 125.

16. Anna Wilson, "Canonical Relations: Willa Cather, America, and *The Professor's House,*" *Texas Studies in Language and Literature* 47.1 (2005): 61–74, 65.
17. Willa Cather, *The Professor's House* (New York: Vintage, 1990 [1925]), 77.
18. Scott Herring, "Catherian Friendship," 79.
19. Sedgwick, "Willa Cather and Others," in *Tendencies,* 174.
20. Herring, "Catherian Friendship," 70.
21. Herring's essay begins with a reading of Cather's story "Paul's Case," in which he suggests that critics have tried to reinterpret Paul's brief encounter with a college boy before his death as a romance (rather than seeing it as an unnameable form of friendship). I would suggest that even focusing on this friendship in the short story misses the central fact about Paul in the story: his intense loneliness and isolation from all other people. Cather establishes Paul's total isolation in Pittsburgh; once he comes to New York, it might be argued that the only real moments of communion that he experiences are as he looks in the mirror ("he was exactly the kind of boy he had always wanted to be" [482]) and in his final suicidal and inhuman merging with an oncoming train ("Paul dropped back into the immense design of things" [488]). In some sense, the happier ending we imagine for Paul is simply imagining him as making his way back into the human community at all— a fate that in the story seems, on balance, highly unlikely. Cather, "Paul's Case," in *Stories, Poems, and Other Writings.*
22. Quoted in Nealon, *Foundlings,* 23.
23. Walter Benjamin, "On Some Motifs in Baudelaire," in *Illuminations,* ed. Hanna Arendt, trans. Harry Zohn (New York: Schocken Books, 1968), 158.
24. Cather, "148 Charles Street," in *Stories, Poems, and Other Writings,* 846.
25. Jacques Derrida, *The Politics of Friendship,* trans. George Collins (London: Verso, 1997), 296.
26. Maurice Blanchot, *The Unavowable Community,* trans. Pierre Joris (Barrytown, NY: Station Hill Press 1988), 25.
27. Sarah Orne Jewett, *Novels and Stories,* ed. Michael Davitt Bell (New York: Library of America, 1994), 442.
28. Laurie Shannon, "'The Country of Our Friendship': Jewett's Intimist Art," *American Literature* 71.2 (June 1999): 227–262, 229.

29. Willa Cather, preface to *The Country of the Pointed Firs and Other Stories,* selected and arranged with a preface by Willa Cather (Garden City, NY: Doubleday Anchor Books, 1954), 11.
30. Friedrich Nietzsche, *The Gay Science,* ed. Bernard Williams, trans. Josefine Nauckhoff (Cambridge: Cambridge University Press, 2001), 159.

4. Spoiled Identity

1. Friedrich Nietzsche, *The Genealogy of Morals,* trans. Walter Kaufmann (New York: Vintage, 1989), 122.
2. *The Sink of Solitude,* cited in Diane Souhami, *The Trials of Radclyffe Hall* (New York: Doubleday, 1999), 238.
3. Janet Flanner, "Letter," *New Yorker,* October 4, 1930, 84.
4. Quoted in Souhami, *Trials of Radclyffe Hall,* 158.
5. Anonymous reader quoted at the end of Rebecca O'Rourke, *Reflecting on "The Well of Loneliness"* (New York: Routledge, 1989), 127.
6. The reconsideration of Stephen's masculinity in *The Well of Loneliness* began with Esther Newton's groundbreaking article "The Mythic Mannish Lesbian: Radclyffe Hall and the New Woman," *Signs* 9 (1984): 557–575. In recent years, Judith Halberstam's work *Female Masculinity* (Durham: Duke University Press, 1998) and Jay Prosser's transsexual reading of *The Well, Second Skins: The Body Narratives of Transsexuality* (New York: Columbia University Press, 1998), have been crucial to this reassessment. Several critics in the 1980s began to rethink *The Well* in terms of Foucauldian reverse discourse: see especially Newton, "Mythic Mannish Lesbian"; Sonja Ruehl, "Inverts and Experts: Radclyffe Hall and the Lesbian Identity," in *Feminism, Culture, and Politics,* ed. Rosalind Brunt and Caroline Rowan (London: Lawrence and Wishart, 1982), 15–36; and Jonathan Dollimore, "The Dominant and the Deviant: A Violent Dialectic," *Critical Quarterly* 28 (1986): 179–192.
7. Blanche Wiesen Cook, "'Women Alone Stir My Imagination': Lesbianism and the Cultural Tradition," *Signs* 4 (1979): 721.
8. Stimpson, "Zero Degree Deviancy," 364, 369.
9. Cook, "'Women Alone Stir My Imagination,'" 721.
10. Erving Goffman, *Stigma: Notes on the Management of Spoiled Identity* (Englewood Cliffs, NJ: Prentice-Hall, 1963), 107–108.
11. Radclyffe Hall, *The Well of Loneliness* (New York: Anchor, 1990), 378, 387.
12. Stephen herself is a formidable hunter, but she gives up hunting after the death of her father. One day, while riding ahead of the pack of her country neighbors, Stephen imagines that she has turned from hunter to hunted. She dismounts and kneels by the fox—that bedraggled creature with the

"desperate eyes of the relentlessly pursued" (126). Though Stephen's identification with this doomed creature may strike some readers as sheer melodrama, Stephen's intuition turns out to be prescient rather than paranoid. Within two years, Stephen's neighbor Ralph Crossby announces his plan to expose Stephen's aberrant desires: "I'll hound her out of the county before I've done," he swears, "and with luck out of England" (198).

13. The history of female romantic friendships, for instance, was crucial to the construction of lesbian feminism in the 1970s and 1980s. In her writing on this topic, Lillian Faderman describes romantic friendship consistently in terms of "innocence." Innocence in this context seems to refer both to sexual naïveté and to a lack of exposure to the pernicious effects of homophobia.

14. Eve Kosofsky Sedgwick, "Queer Performativity: Henry James's *The Art of the Novel,*" *GLQ* 1.1 (1993): 4.

15. Louis Althusser, *Lenin and Philosophy,* trans. Ben Brewster (New York: Monthly Review Press, 1971), 223.

16. Halberstam, *Female Masculinity,* 98–99.

17. Whether she "faces the guns of Bond Street" (165) or sits in a fashionable restaurant in Paris, Stephen's appearances in public are narrated as a succession of hostile stares and taunts ("Look at that! What is it?" [165]). Stephen's neighbor, Ralph Crossby, annoyed at Stephen for hanging around his wife, comments casually that "That sort of thing wants putting down at birth" (151). Stephen's most intimate relations and friends reinforce such experiences of refusal. Stephen's mother keeps Stephen at a distance from her earliest infancy; having found out about Stephen's affair with Angela Crossby, she seconds the opinion of the world, telling her daughter that she would rather see her "dead at my feet than standing before me with this thing upon you" (200).

18. On Hall's conservatism see Laura Doan, *Fashioning Sapphism: The Origins of a Modern English Lesbian Culture* (New York: Columbia University Press, 2001).

19. "If I were asked to name the chief benefit of the house," Gaston Bachelard writes, "I should say: the house shelters day-dreaming, the house protects the dreamer, the house allows one to dream in peace" (Gaston Bachelard, *The Poetics of Space,* trans. Maria Jolas [Boston: Beacon, 1964], 6). Hall is likewise concerned with the protecting function of the house, but for her, the inwardness of dreaming is not the first priority. Rather, the house provides a vital link between the inward and the outward: it offers a publicness lined with and enabled by acceptable forms of domestic privacy. For Stephen, Morton signifies public acceptance and recognizability guaranteed by the institutions of property, inheritance, and social hierarchy. It also of-

fers an intimate space in which the orderly domestic relations that such publicness presumes can flourish.

20. The distinction that Judith Butler elaborates between melancholia and narcissism aptly describes the gap between expectation and outcome that structures Stephen's birth. Butler considers Freud's formulation that in melancholia the shadow of the object falls on the ego; she then contrasts it with Lacan's understanding of narcissism, in which the shadow of the ego falls on the object. While in narcissism one encounters one's own plenitude in the object, Butler writes, "In melancholia this formulation is reversed: in the place of the loss that the other comes to represent, I find myself to be that loss, impoverished, wanting. In narcissistic love, the other contracts my abundance. In melancholia, I contract the other's absence" (Butler, *Psychic Life of Power,* 187). While the Gordons understand their desire for a son as narcissistic, as a desire for a copy that will reflect their image, Stephen's birth recasts this desire as melancholic. The Gordons hope to transfer their plenitude to a son who is Sir Philip's mirror image; instead, they find themselves inscribed at the site of Stephen's loss: they contract her absence.

21. Teresa de Lauretis, *The Practice of Love: Lesbian Sexuality and Perverse Desire* (Bloomington: Indiana University Press, 1994), 212–213.

22. According to de Lauretis, Stephen can gain the mother's love only by satisfying her narcissistic desire for a daughter who is feminine. But there is no reason why the mother's desire for Stephen should work exclusively along such lines. Several factors in *The Well* work to broaden the spectrum of the mother's desire for Stephen: her prenatal expectations of a boy, Stephen's chivalrous attitude toward her mother, and her close resemblance to her father. Part of what makes Lady Anna's attitude toward Stephen so difficult in the book is that she fluctuates between a disappointed desire for Stephen as daughter and an outraged and ambivalent desire for her as son.

23. Stephen's very longing for masculinity has disturbed feminist critics since the novel's publication. Vera Brittain, who valued Hall's representation of the experience of the inverted, nevertheless criticized her "overemphasis of sex characteristics" in the novel, arguing that she had confused the distinction between "what is 'male' or 'female' or what is merely human in our complex make-up." Brittain's 1928 review in the magazine *Time and Tide* is reprinted in Vera Brittain, *Radclyffe Hall: A Case of Obscenity?* (London: Femina, 1968), 50.

24. Thanks to Rita Felski for thinking through this question with me in relation to her work on tragic women.

25. Elizabeth Grosz, *Space, Time, and Perversion: Essays on the Politics of Bodies* (New York: Routledge, 1995), 153.

26. Castiglia, "Sex Panics," 175.

5. Impossible Objects

1. See Lisa Duggan's essay "The Discipline Problem," in which she speculates about the reasons that history departments have failed to train historians of sexuality: "I don't think this failure is solely or even largely due to conservatism or stark prejudice (though I don't mean to underestimate the continuing importance of these sources of hostility). I would attribute the failure to hire and train historians of sexuality, and lesbian and gay historians specifically, to at least three other significant factors: (1) Sexuality, as a subject matter, is treated as trivial, as more about gossip than politics, more about psychology than history . . . (2) Lesbian and gay history, particularly, is understood as the history of a marginalized "minority" population, as the story of a small percentage of the citizenry and their doings . . . (3) Historians of sexuality fit uneasily into existing job categories" (180). Lisa Duggan, "The Discipline Problem: Queer Theory Meets Lesbian and Gay History," *GLQ* 2.3 (1995): 179–191.

2. The recognition of "oneself" in the past is a complex and charged project, and queer historians have never been able to completely embrace it nor to leave it behind for good. A range of recent critics have attempted to mediate between essentialist and constructionist approaches to the past. See, for example, Halperin, *How to Do the History of Homosexuality.* Carolyn Dinshaw's recent reflections on Foucault's fan letter to John Boswell—perhaps the historian most identified with the project of recovery—also offers a fascinating look at a conjunction between these two approaches. Dinshaw, *Getting Medieval.*

3. Leila Rupp, *A Desired Past: A Short History of Same-Sex Love in America* (Chicago: University of Chicago Press, 2002). On the role of fantasy and pleasure in historiography, see also the introduction to *Premodern Sexualities,* by Louise Fradenburg and Carla Freccero.

4. Sylvia Townsend Warner, *Summer Will Show* (New York: Penguin Books, 1987), 146.

5. Gillian Beer, "Sylvia Townsend Warner: The Centrifugal Kick," in *Women Writers of the 1930s: Gender, Power, Resistance,* ed. Maroula Joannou (Edinburgh: Edinburgh University Press, 1999), 76.

6. For a related account of the affective complexities of Warner's work, see Gay Wachmann, *Lesbian Empire: Radical Crosswriting in the Twenties* (New Brunswick, NJ: Rutgers University Press, 2001), 73.

7. We might compare this reliance on despair as a resource in Warner's book to Marx's theory of revolution: only when economic conditions are sufficiently desperate can we expect social change on the scale of revolution to take place.

8. One crucial exception to the critical responses is Thomas Foster's article, "'Dream Made Flesh': Sexual Difference and Narratives of Revolution in Sylvia Townsend Warner's *Summer Will Show*," which has contributed to my thinking here. Taking on the trivialization of "sexual abnormality" in Lukács' *The Historical Novel,* Foster argues that "the novel . . . implies that neither Marxist nor feminist nor lesbian narratives of emancipation are sufficient to represent the totality of social life" (538). He sees revolution in the novel as a challenge to the ideology of private property and to the division between the public and the private spheres. Foster makes a strong argument that in the novel "the women's story is not merely analogous to that of the revolution but [is] instead structurally implicated in that 'other' story" (550). Foster's account of the inseparability of class and sexual politics in *Summer Will Show* is crucial in understanding Warner's complex account of the relation between revolutionary, world-historical politics and the politics of everyday life. Thomas Foster, "'Dream Made Flesh': Sexual Difference and Narratives of Revolution in Sylvia Townsend Warner's *Summer Will Show*," *Modern Fiction Studies* 41.3–4 (1995): 531–562.

9. Georg Lukács, *The Historical Novel,* trans. Hannah and Stanley Mitchell (Harmondsworth: Penguin, 1962), 65. We might also understand Warner's treatment of 1848 as the "prehistory of the present"—as an explanation of the split between the bourgeoisie and the working class in 1936—as another way in which the novel exemplifies the form as described by Lukács.

10. Claire Harman, introduction to *Summer Will Show* by Sylvia Townsend Warner (1936; New York: Penguin Books/Virago, 1987), viii. Terry Castle cites Robert L. Caserio's article "Celibate Sisters-in-Revolution: Towards Reading Sylvia Townsend Warner" as another example of the tendency to disregard same-sex desire in the novel. However, although Caserio does read the relationship between Minna and Sophia as chaste, he does not ignore it, but rather sees it as central to the novel's politics. See Caserio, "Celibate Sisters," in *Engendering Men: The Question of Male Feminist Criticism,* ed. Joseph A. Boone and Michael Cadden (New York: Routledge, 1990).

11. Janet Montefiore, "Listening to Minna: Realism, Feminism and the Politics of Reading," *Paragraph* 14 (1991): 197–216.

12. Nealon, *Foundlings,* esp. 11–23.

13. Raymond Williams, *Modern Tragedy* (Stanford, CA: Stanford University Press, 1966), 75.

14. Beer, "Sylvia Townsend Warner," 86.

15. See for instance Anne Anlin Cheng's discussion of the difference between racial grief and racial grievance in *The Melancholy of Race.*

16. Benjamin, "Theses on the Philosophy of History," 264.

17. Sylvia Townsend Warner, *After the Death of Don Juan* (London: Virago, 2002), 301.
18. In an unpublished manuscript, Julie Vandivere reads Warner's use of the map in this passage as "a commentary on [Ramón and Diego's] place in history that does not have to do with progression." Her Benjamin-influenced analysis of *The Death of Don Juan* and Virginia Woolf's *The Years* guided my understanding of history and temporality in Warner's work.
19. The second stanza of Marvell's poem also seems apt:

    > Magnanimous Despair alone
    > Could show me so divine a thing,
    > Where feeble Hope could ne'er have flown
    > But vainly flapt its Tinsel Wing.

20. Jacques Derrida, *Specters of Marx: The State of the Debt, the Work of Mourning, and the New International,* trans. Peggy Kamuf (New York: Routledge, 1994), 14.
21. Sylvia Townsend Warner, Diaries, October 12, 1930. *The Diaries of Sylvia Townsend Warner,* ed. and introduction Claire Harman (London: Chatto and Windus, 1994), 69.
22. My thanks to John Connor (personal conversation) for pointing out to me that it was in the drafting of the *Manifesto* that the word "party" (*Partei*) was introduced into political discourse: it replaced the more personal term *Bund* (union or marriage). At the end of *Summer Will Show,* the depersonalizing of politics is set in reverse.

Epilogue

1. Benjamin, "Theses on the Philosophy of History," 257–258.
2. Wendy Brown, "Resisting Left Melancholy," in *Loss: The Politics of Mourning,* ed. David L. Eng and David Kazanjian (Berkeley: University of California Press, 2003), 464.
3. Muñoz, *Disidentifications,* 111.
4. Mattilda, aka Matt Bernstein Sycamore, "Whose Quality of Life?" in *Gay Shame: From Queer Autonomous Space to Direct Action Extravaganza,* www.gayshamesf.org (accessed December 1, 2006).
5. A more shame-filled version of gay shame can be found in the description of the gay shame night or "The Annual Festival of Homosexual Misery" organized by Amy Lamé on the night of gay pride at the London club Duckie. Clearly this version of gay shame does not have the same aims as the Gay Shame collective; the night is about entertainment, not activism. Nonetheless, the promotional material for the 2005 event provides a sense

of the quite different rhetoric of shame that might be deployed in a queer context: "Wear black, look down and help put gay liberation back by 50 years. Hear confessions, explore obsessions and submit to depressions. Featuring Old Fashioned Illusions, Faggot Film Noir, Bad Porn, Public Health Warnings, Pathetic Peepshows, and 10 Spectacular Murders. This event is for Sad Old Queens, Lonely Lesbians, Closet Cases, Bitter Bull Dykes, Men who have sex with Men, and their Friends and their Fans," www.duckie.co.uk (accessed December 1, 2006). The drag duo Kiki and Herb have performed at Duckie; they also offer a version of queerness that is steeped in shame. On Kiki and Herb, see Shane Vogel, "Where Are We Now? Queer World-Making and Cabaret Performance," *GLQ* 6.1 (2000): 29–60.

6. Statement of Gay Shame Conference, www.umich.edu (accessed December 1, 2006).
7. The Gay Shame Conference was marked by several conflicts, though I focus here on the question of activism and academia. For discussions of the question of race and the whiteness of Gay Shame, see "What's Queer about Queer Studies Now?" ed. Eng, Halberstam, and Esteban Muñoz, special issue, *Social Text* 84/85 (October 2005).
8. Published in Matt Bernstein Sycamore, ed., *That's Revolting! Queer Strategies for Resisting Assimilation* (New York: Soft Skull Press, 2004); the piece is also on the Gay Shame San Francisco Web site.
9. www.gayshamesf.org (accessed December 1, 2006).
10. "How to Start a Non-Hierarchical Direct Action Group," www.gayshamesf .org (accessed December 1, 2006).
11. Michael Warner, ed., Introduction to *Fear of a Queer Planet* (Minneapolis: University of Minnesota Press, 1993).
12. Dyke Manifesto, Lesbian Avengers, New York, 1993. Distributed during the weekend of the march on Washington for Lesbian, Gay, and Bi Equal Rights and Liberation, April 1993. Reproduced in *Becoming Visible: An Illustrated History of Lesbian and Gay Life in Twentieth-Century America*, based on an exhibition curated by Fred Wasserman, Molly McGarry, and Mimi Bowling (New York: The New York Public Library, Penguin Studio, 1998, 253).
13. Cvetkovich, *Archive of Feelings*, 3.
14. Elizabeth Freeman, "Time Binds, or Erotohistoriography," in "What's Queer about Queer Studies Now?" ed. Eng, Halberstam, and Esteban Muñoz, special issue, *Social Text* 84/85 (October 2005): 57–68, 58–59.
15. Michael Snediker makes a related argument in his 2006 article, "Queer Optimism." While Freeman suggests a turn to jouissance in queer studies, Snediker suggests that a turn to happiness might be similarly generative.

He writes, "If the insights of the past few decades could newly mobilize shame, shattering, or melancholy as interesting, as opposed to merely seeming instances of fear and trembling; what if we could learn from those insights and critical practices, and imagine happiness as theoretically mobilizable, and conceptually difficult? Which is to ask, what if happiness weren't merely, self-reflexively happy, but interesting?" Michael Snediker, "Queer Optimism," *Postmodern Culture* 16.3 (2006), paragraph 48. Snediker's response to the limits of ideology critique (with its presumed ability to see through simple or deluded experiences of pleasure) owes a debt to Eve Kosofsky Sedgwick's notion of reparative reading outlined in *Touching Feeling*.

16. On being picked last as a queer structure of feeling, see Janis Ian's 1975 song, "At Seventeen": "To those of us who know the pain / Of valentines that never came / And those whose names were never called / When choosing sides for basketball." *Between the Lines* (Columbia Records, 1975).

17. Judith Halberstam, "The Politics of Negativity in Recent Queer Theory," in "Forum: Conference Debates. The Antisocial Thesis in Queer Theory," *PMLA* 121.3 (May 2006): 823–825, 824.

18. Lee Edelman, "Antagonism, Negativity, and the Subject of Queer Theory," in "Forum: Conference Debates. The Antisocial Thesis in Queer Theory" *PMLA* 121.3 (May 2006): 821–823, 822.

19. Part of the conflict between Halberstam and Edelman in this forum is about gender. Halberstam argues that the gay male archive of negativity is narrow and makes an argument on behalf of a queer female negativity, invoking figures such as Valerie Solanas and Jamaica Kincaid. Although Halberstam deals at length with female pugilism (and other forms of female power and aggression) in her 1998 book *Female Masculinity*, it would seem like an oversight in this context not to mention the masculinist framing of this debate.

20. Philip Fisher, *The Vehement Passions* (Princeton, NJ: Princeton University Press, 2002), 5. Fisher specifically contrasts the vehement passions with modern low-energy feelings and moods such as boredom, depression, nostalgia, and anxiety—feelings closer to the queer feelings surveyed here.

Acknowledgments

This book is an attempt to recognize and give space to forms of existence that are seen as outmoded, impossible, or just a drag. The specific impetus for its writing was the upgrade in gay, lesbian, and transgender life in the United States during the last couple of decades. Although I have enjoyed the benefits that have come along with greater tolerance and inclusion, I have been dismayed by the uneven quality of these "advances." *Feeling Backward* records my ambivalence about gay progress, and argues for the significance of some devalued aspects of queer culture. Such a project can come off as nostalgic, retrograde, and conservative, and I am sure that, in some measure, it is all of these things. Still, at a moment so insistently upbeat, I wanted to narrate a critical queer history that did not sidestep bitterness, tears, and heartbreak. My hope was that in making an argument on behalf of bad attachments I might open a space to talk about ways of life—queer or not—that are depressing or hard to credit.

Literary criticism might seem an odd approach to this set of issues, although it is true that literature has been the preoccupation of choice for sad and lonely queers for a long time. My own career of longing is fairly typical, except perhaps for the fact of my exceptional luck in early teachers. I am deeply grateful to Tim Love, Dean Robertson, Christopher Braider, and Barbara Johnson for giving me a sense of literature's reach. They taught me how to live with impossibility, and that has made everything else possible.

I have also been lucky to find the world of queer studies, and with it, a great many generous interlocutors and mentors. I want to thank a few people in particular whose work and conversation guided this project. The recent interest in affect in queer studies has been extremely generative for me; I am grateful to Eve Kosofsky Sedgwick for the example of her work on shame and for turning

189

the field in that direction. David Halperin's powerful response to my work on Radclyffe Hall helped me to understand what this book was about. The phrase "feeling backward" was inspired by Christopher Nealon's concept of "feeling historical" in *Foundlings*. I am grateful to him for writing that book, and for his intensive engagements with this one. Carolyn Dinshaw's *Getting Medieval* was another crucial example: she taught me that I could have the queer past my way. Elizabeth Freeman's work on temporal drag was a key influence, as was Ann Cvetkovich's writing about the vicissitudes of lesbian feeling. D. A. Miller's backwardness sparked this project and he remains my best example—that chapter is still forthcoming. Queer studies is only beginning to absorb the implications of Leo Bersani's critique of the "culture of redemption"; I would be happy to think that this book might contribute to that project.

Many people read this project in various stages. I would like to gratefully acknowledge the contributions of Lauren Berlant, Anne Anlin Cheng, John Connor, Drew Daniel, Laura Doan, Matthew Engelke, Brad Epps, L. A. O. Fradenburg, Elaine Freedgood, Andrew Gaedtke, Jane Garrity, David Halperin, Lili Hsieh, Benjamin Kahan, Eleanor Kaufman, Ben Lee, Catriona MacLeod, Vicki Mahaffey, Douglas Mao, Michael Millner, Brenna Munro, Afsaneh Najmabadi, Derek Nystrom, Swati Rana, Lisi Schoenbach, Ben Singer, Susan Stryker, Aoibheann Sweeney, Kate Thomas, Valerie Traub, Keja Valens, Michael Vazquez, Bryan Wagner, Rebecca Walkowitz, and Robyn Wiegman.

I would like to thank the English Department at the University of Virginia (where this project began) and especially my dissertation committee: Rita Felski, Jonathan Flatley, Susan Fraiman, Elisabeth Ladenson, and Jennifer Wicke. Thanks to Jonathan Flatley for seeing the project beyond lesbian misogyny and also for setting the tone. I am grateful to Judith Halberstam for generously offering to advise my dissertation from afar—it's been my good fortune to have her in my corner ever since. Rita Felski has been an ideal mentor over the past decade; she continues to show me by her example what kind of scholar I would like to be.

I am also grateful to my colleagues at Penn for making the last several years happy and productive. Special thanks to Rita Barnard, Karen Beckman, Nancy Bentley, Max Cavitch, Erin Cross, Thadious Davis, Margreta de Grazia, Jim English, Ann Farnsworth, Amy Kaplan, David Kazanjian, Demie Kurz, Ania Loomba, Yolanda Padilla, Josephine Park, Kathy Peiss, Barbara Savage, and David Wallace. I wish that I could thank Bob Lucid in person.

My work over the past several years has been supported by grants from the University of Virginia, the Jacob K. Javits Foundation, the University Research Foundation at the University of Pennsylvania, the Women's Studies Program at Penn, the Trustees' Council of Penn Women, and the Penn Humanities Forum. I would also like to thank the Woodrow Wilson Foundation: both my Postdoctoral Fellowship in the Humanities and the Career Enhancement Grant for Junior Faculty were crucial to the completion of this project. The Literature Concentration at Harvard provided a wonderful institutional home during my postdoc. I would also like to thank the family of M. Mark and Esther K. Watkins for their generous support of my research at Penn.

Earlier versions of Chapters 2, 4, and 5 appeared as "Forced Exile: Walter Pater's Queer Modernism," in *Bad Modernisms*, ed. Rebecca Walkowitz and Douglas Mao (Durham: Duke University Press, 2006); "Spoiled Identity: Stephen Gordon's Loneliness and the Difficulties of Queer History," in *GLQ: A Journal of Lesbian and Gay Studies*, vol. 7, no. 4 (Fall 2001): 487-519; and "Impossible Objects: Sylvia Townsend Warner's *Summer Will Show* and the Longing for Revolution," in *Sapphic Modernities: Sexuality, Women, and National Culture*, ed. Laura Doan and Jane Garrity (New York: Palgrave Macmillan, 2006). A version of Chapter 1 will appear in *Gay Shame*, ed. David Halperin and Valerie Traub (Chicago: University of Chicago Press, 2009). Thanks to the publishers for permission to use this material in the present work.

I would like to thank Lindsay Waters for his early enthusiasm about this project and for his support along the way, and Phoebe Kosman for her work on the book. Thanks to Caitlin Charos and Stephanie Skier for research assistance and help preparing the manuscript; to Barbara Goodhouse for her careful editing; and to the two anonymous readers for Harvard University Press.

I would like to thank my family, especially my mother for supporting my education. I would also like to thank Laura Amelio, Deborah Cohen, Perry Hewitt, Andree Mondor, and Eleanor Stafford for keeping me in school and (more or less) out of trouble. Meghan Love is the very best. It's been my good fortune over the last several years to know Emaline Kelso and Juliet Kelso—thanks for sharing your lives with me. I am grateful to Mara Mills for love and schooling. This book is dedicated to David Kurnick, best friend and reader. I could not and would not have written it without him.

Index

Abelove, Henry, 42–43
Abjection, 27–29, 38, 103, 112, 114–115,
    122–124, 125, 158
Abraham, Nicolas, 42
Ackland, Valentine, 143–144
Acocella, Joan, 25, 74
ACT UP, 2, 156
Adams, Rachel, 166n3
Adorno, Theodor W., 9–10, 148
Affect, 4, 8, 31–32, 37, 42–43, 92, 104–108,
    110, 111–112, 127; and politics, 10–14,
    26–27, 70–71, 98, 101, 106, 128, 131,
    143–145, 146–163
Affirmative turn, 3–4, 22, 28, 45, 105, 165n1,
    172n3
Agency, 147–152, 155–156, 159–160, 161–163
AIDS, 6, 147, 156, 158, 159
Albright, Daniel, 53
Althusser, Louis, 107
Angel of history, 5, 147–152
Antimodernism, 6, 25, 72, 146
Antisocial, 22–23, 161–162, 171n35
Aristotle, 77, 94
Arrested development, 6–7, 21–22, 146
Ashbery, John, 124
Austin, J. L., 67–68

Bachelard, Gaston, 182n19
Barnes, Djuna, 6, 31
Barney, Natalie Clifford, 35
Barthes, Roland, 1, 32–33, 38–39
Bartlett, Neil, 52, 176n30
Bataille, Georges, 95
Baudelaire, Charles, 135
Beer, Gillian, 131, 138–139
Benjamin, Walter, 5, 12, 13, 86, 90, 135, 140,
    142, 147–152

Berlant, Lauren, 10–11
Bernhard, Sandra, 27–28
Bersani, Leo, 22, 24, 29, 53, 151, 171n35,
    179n13
Beyond Marriage movement, 79–80
Bhabha, Homi, 70
Blanchot, Maurice, 49–51, 94–95
Boskovich, John, 27
Boswell, John, 184n2
Botticelli, 63–67
Bravmann, Scott, 31, 38
Bright, Susie, 16–17, 170n28
Brittain, Vera, 183n23
Brown, Wendy, 12, 149–152
Butch, 26, 115, 118, 121, 170n26
Butch–femme, 101, 105, 158
Butler, Judith, 18, 29, 42, 68, 119–121, 123–
    124, 178n2, 179n13, 183n20

Camp, 7, 105, 170n26
Caritas, 78
Carson, Anne, 34
Caserio, Robert, 138, 140, 171n35, 185n10
Castiglia, Christopher, 127, 167n8
Castle, Terry, 76, 132–133
Cather, Willa, 4, 7, 8, 25, 40, 72–99, 146,
    162; "148 Charles Street," 91–94; "A
    Chance Meeting," 90–91; "Miss Jewett,"
    91; *Not Under Forty*, 72–73, 74–75, 91;
    "Paul's Case," 180n21; Preface to *The
    Country of the Pointed Firs*, 97; *The
    Professor's House*, 74, 81–87
Cavafy, C. P., 67–69
Celluloid Closet, The, 14–17
Chakrabarty, Dipesh, 5
Chauncey, George, Jr., 165–166n2
Cheng, Anne Anlin, 14, 27, 185n15

193